Amusings

by Theo May

iUniverse, Inc.

New York   Bloomington

iUniverse books may be ordered through booksellers or by contacting:

iUniverse
1663 Liberty Drive
Bloomington, IN 47403
www.iuniverse.com
1-800-Authors (1-800-288-4677)

Because of the dynamic nature of the Internet, any Web addresses or links contained in this book may have changed since publication and may no longer be valid. The views expressed in this work are solely those of the author and do not necessarily reflect the views of the publisher, and the publisher hereby disclaims any responsibility for them.

ISBN: 978-1-4401-4606-0 (sc)
ISBN: 978-1-4401-4605-3 (ebook)

Printed in the United States of America

iUniverse rev. date: 6/3/2009

Acknowledgement

My appreciation to Dorothy May, Ted Spitzmiller, Phil Lewis,
and Heidi May for publishing assistance.

I am deeply grateful to my daughter Gretchen May, for
creating and managing my website of stories for many years
(www.theomay.net) and for her help
with design of the covers.

Cover illustration by Morgan Schweitzer

Dedication

To Dorothy, Gretchen, and Heidi

Contents

Interviews

Most people in my generation, I suspect, did not have more than two or three interviews in their entire lives. I had well over twenty interviews (for teaching positions mainly) of which eighteen were failures. I think this might constitute a record of sorts. I became something of an expert in saying the wrong thing: in most cases, I couldn't resist the *bon mot*. The following gives a sampling.

Concord-Carlisle High School

This interview was not going well. For some reason the Interviewer seemed to have taken a dislike to me. He asked me questions, but with the demeanor of one who wanted to trip me up.

For example, when he looked at me with dull challenge in his eyes and said, "I see from your resumé that you write. What sorts of things have you written?", I had a feeling that, had I replied truthfully, "Oh, Marxist-type critiques of present day society in the style of Adorno," he might not have been overjoyed.

And so, as this exercise in futility ground to a close, he asked without interest, "Do you have any other questions?"

I inquired how things were in the Math Department?

"Well, O.K. except for one little thing: the Men and Women aren't speaking to each other."

"That's not a problem", I lightly and immediately rejoined, "I can speak to both sides - I'm androgynous!"

And that most certainly terminated the Interview!

Framingham South High School

This interview seemed to be going well, when the Principal suddenly said to me:

"You might like to know that there is a rule in effect here in

Framingham, that if for any reason a teacher takes a leave of absence for a year, their record of service goes back to zero."

I immediately responded, "Oh, so in such a case would I get to behave as an ignorant first year teacher with no experience?"

That terminated the Interview.

Hamilton-Wenham High School

It was a hot summer for interviews!

I had dressed in my usual habiliments (suit, tie) for my interview at Lincoln Sudbury. There I was greeted by the Math Chairman Larry Davidson - in short-shorts, t-shirt, and sandals.

For my next interview - at Hamilton-Wenham - I vowed not to be physically miserable again. So I wore shorts, t-shirt, and sneakers. There I was ushered into an air conditioned office by the search committee - all of whom were wearing three-piece suits.

Yes, there was an interview of sorts (what I call a phony interview.) But for all practical purposes, The Interview had been terminated.

Note 1: This is known as an a priori nonverbal self-torpedoing.

Note 2: Hamilton has a polo ground; Sudbury does not (the sort of thing it would be well for one to research before going to an interview.)

Houghton Mifflin

This was my interview with a private company. I went despite the fact that I had no experience in publishing.

Yet, even before the interview began, I realized that I would prefer to teach classes of kids rather than sit in a cubicle and deal with page layouts all day. And, that I would much prefer to be the author of a textbook rather than the editor of someone else's book.

The two fellows who interviewed me were both wearing three-piece suits. (My choice of habiliment favored the vest - I owned some 40 of them - and decidedly eschewed the jacket.) They had a very clubby air and seemed to be sniggering together.

As I'd found out to my sorrow in other interviews, there are certain basic questions in any line of work that one should anticipate and prepare the answers for.

The first question they asked me was: "Do you know any books that we publish?"

Now virtually all math teachers know the authors of the books they use in their courses. We speak of using "the Forester" or "the Dolciani". But I would guess that very few such teachers know the publishers of those texts: this is the province of the math chairs who need to order new books.

So I could not be sure of the publisher of any authors I knew. I could take a wild guess, but what if that author were published by a rival company? I decided not to risk this sort of faux pas.

In fact, as they awaited my answer and I desperately wracked my brain, I was able to think of only one book that I definitely knew was published by Houghton Mifflin - and it was not a math text. Would this count, I wondered? Quickly I weighed the pros and cons. But I finally decided that it was better to give some answer rather than no answer, to show knowledge rather than ignorance. So I offered them the name of the book:

"Adolph Hitler's *Mein Kampf*."

Well, that terminated that Interview!

Lexington: Diamond Junior High

The junior high level has never been my first (or even second) choice for a teaching position. But when one desperately needs a job...

I suppose that I could have prepared better for this interview. There are, after all, certain basic questions one might be able to anticipate...

The Principal asked me, "What is the worst thing that has ever happened to you in your teaching?"

First I said, only half-humorously, "Where to begin?!"

I then painted a lurid picture of a classroom situation so horrific that it made "Suddenly Last Summer" look like a Sunday School picnic.

The Assistant Principal then asked me, "What is the best thing that has ever happened to you in your teaching?" I thought long and hard, but I couldn't think of anything.

After these exchanges I detected a certain - ennui - in the demeanors of my interlocutors. I began to pick up subtle signals that seemed to indicate that they wished the interview to conclude sooner rather than later. Finally the Principal yawned and asked, "Do you have any other questions?"

The only question I could think of was, "Do you have a xerox machine available for teachers to use?"

The Principal was ready for this one: "We believe in the good old chalk-and-blackboard approach!"

So was I: "And do you break up the blackboards and hand them out to the students at the end of the period?"

And that most emphatically terminated the Interview!

Melrose High School

Like many interviews I've had, this one was in the middle of the Summer - a time when schools are all but deserted.

I entered the front door of the high school. No one was to be seen, and there were no signs to tell me how to get to the Main Office. I arbitrarily selected a door to my right, which ushered me into the Library.

The only person I saw therein was a sort of grungy derelict wearing a torn dirty sweat shirt. I asked if he knew where the Office was? He motioned to the other side of the Main Lobby.

A secretary welcomed me as I entered the Office. She asked whether I'd had any trouble finding them. I replied, "Well, your directions to the school were clear enough. I guess my only problem was that there are no signs telling one where the Office is. I had to ask some bum in the Library how to find you!"

After a few minutes the door opened to the Principal's Office and the Principal emerged to greet me. And in seeing him, I knew that, for all intents and purposes,

The Interview would be for naught.

Mont Alto

I had been let go from a teaching position at Muskingum College due to, as it was quaintly called a hundred years ago, "moral turpitude". (In this regard I was proud to be in the august company of such notables as Thorstein Veblen and Alexander Scriabin.)

Being in need of another job, I sent out a slew of letters to every college east of Ohio that I thought would have me. About the only hopeful response I received (though see 'Skidmore College' for another) was this one from State College, PA:

"Dear Professor May: You seem like the perfect person to anchor the math department at our Mont Alto branch campus of Penn State."

So I drove to a place called Mont Alto one rainy day in the late Spring. It was nestled in the woods (I liked to say that it was 'in the center of a cultural doughnut') in the neighborhood of Chambersburg. The "campus" consisted of one large brick school-type building, a couple of converted farm houses, and little else. I was to interview with the Director, whose office was in the brick building.

He was an older man who seemed the solitary one there that day (the school year had apparently already ended.) His "office" was in part of a large conference room which was littered with all sorts of school-related paraphernalia.

Our meeting seemed scarcely like an interview at all. He told

5

me what little there was to tell about the school: it was one of twenty-three branch campuses of Penn State University; students came there for the first two years, after which they went to the main campus at State College for the other two; this particular campus was the seat of the state forestry school (whenever there was a forest fire, the school would close while the students went out and fought it); surveying was also a big course of study there (thus the necessity of a good trig course); and so on.

But he didn't ask me any of the questions you might expect in an interview - questions about my teaching and so on. He asked whether I had any questions, but I couldn't think of any (I was remarkably incurious about the place.) In fact, I began to suspect that some wires had gotten crossed and that this man thought I was only someone looking about. Indeed, he was in the impatient mood of one whose time was being wasted.

After awhile he said he needed to do something at home, and would I mind tagging along? So we drove through the rain to his house. It turned out his wife was sick. He opened the bedroom door and I saw a darkened room with a figure huddled in bed. It was a depressing situation.

In fact, everything about that trip to Mont Alto seemed depressing. I could not but be struck by the difference between the school I was leaving (a genuine four-year liberal arts college with an actual campus) and this pathetic excuse for a junior college with no real campus at all. And then, too, there was the non-interview, wherein I was treated like a visitor rather than as a prospective candidate for a job.

I was musing on these things (and my demeanor likely showed it) when suddenly the Director lashed out in angry exasperation:

"Well, do you want the job or not?!"

And suddenly I realized that the position had been mine all along, assuming I assented to taking it. Apparently this trip was supposed to be a *pro forma* one to meet the Director and look around.

The combination of the surprise of the outburst and my depressive ruminations caused me to stutter a bit in response. Indeed, I didn't

6

really want to work there! On the other hand, there were no other job possibilities on the horizon (I had blown an interview at a genuine college a week or two before.) It looked like this was going to have to be It for me.

So I mustered all my resolve to give the man my hand (I even managed a weak smile) while reassuring him, "Of <u>course</u> I want the job!"

P.S. My two years of teaching at Mont Alto turned out to be happy ones. The teaching was sufficiently challenging (there was one course called Technical Mathematics, which ran from Basic Algebra to Calculus in one year; and I taught a course in Logic) and the faculty friendly.

When I did leave after two years to pursue a degree in music, the Director tried to persuade me to stay ("I know you need to get ahead, but still...") You see, by then he liked me.

The Neck

Whenever a teenage girl introduces a young man to her father, there is an implicit assumption that there is a double audition going on. The young man is auditioning for possible son-in-law status; while the father is auditioning (or interviewing) for the position of potential father-in-law.

The following is an account of such an "interview" that I deliberately flunked, for reasons that should become clear.

Midway through high school, our daughter, Gretchen, began dating a fellow whom we called "The Neck." The reason for this nickname was clear from his appearance: he had a thick bull neck. They say "Physiology is Destiny," and in this fellow's case it was most certainly true. For he was a football player; and having such a neck guaranteed that it would not be broken even if a hundred or more players were to pile on top of him.

Of course a personality came along with the neck, and you might say that they were in close harmony, viz: he seemed to be a bit obdurate, unless the topic of "conversation" happened to be sports. (NB: This was the period when our daughter seemed to be dating boys who were burdened by bizarre physical characteristics. She would nickname her next boyfriend "Monkey Boy" due to his excessive hairiness.)(Our other daughter dated a fellow we called "Muscle Boy" - but that's another story.)

You might say that I had already "auditioned" The Neck by hearsay, and found him wanting.

But what about my "interview" with him? We met one cold evening in late January when he came to pick up Gretchen for a date. She was still upstairs getting ready when he arrived. He and I stood awkwardly together in the living room (my wife was upstairs helping Gretchen.) I must give him credit for breaking the conversational ice:

"So, uh, who do ya think is gonna win da Super Bowl, Mistah May?"

I did not hesitate for a second with my response:

"The Celtics, definitely!"

Well! The look he gave me! At first it was incredulous, as if he hadn't heard correctly. But it didn't take long for there to spread over his rough countenance an utter contempt, with a bit of real hatred mixed in. And what those looks said to me was:

"If you think I'm going to spend the next thirty years of my life eating Sunday dinner with you and listening to your inane attempts at sports talk, you're crazy!"

That was the first and last time I saw The Neck. Soon enough Gretchen tired of him. One evening we heard her yelling into the phone using the inimitable Medford accent she would reserve for such occasions:

"You're a LOU-ZAAH!"

Northern Essex Community College

I had begun my teaching "career" at two colleges, and I had

fond memories of light schedules and well-disciplined students. So I approached this interview with great anticipation and care. (This was one of two colleges at which I interviewed after I was unceremoniously terminated at The Rivers School. The other interview was similar to this one in that, after seeing examples of projects my students had done at Rivers, they deemed me in effect "overqualified".)

It was the Summer of 1998 and so I was still walking, albeit with the aid of my cane-chair. I was deliberately vague about my disability, hoping they might think it a mere case of the gout.

I was ushered into the interview room by a full committee: this included the Math Chair, who was a frail older woman.

Someone asked me what sorts of things I enjoyed teaching. I told them that I had taught two sections of Introduction to Calculus this past year. That I had integrated (Pun intended!) the graphing calculator into the course content through the use of a lab manual in addition to the regular (if inexpensive) textbook. And that the year had culminated in group projects wherein each group attempted to design a roller coaster with the greatest thrill (defined in terms of slope, etc.) I passed around some of the better efforts I'd received.

"Is this the sort of thing you had in mind?" I asked with the smug self-confidence of one who is secure in the knowledge that that was indeed the sort of thing they most certainly had in mind.

The Math Chair replied, "Actually, we were more interested in finding someone who could teach Subtraction of Whole Numbers."

Shocked, I recovered enough to stammer, "Five minus three, or three minus five?"

But she persisted, "Seriously, how would you go about teaching this?"

I said, "I intend no irony in what I am about to say. If faced with such a task, the first person I would consult would be my wife: She is a superb second grade teacher who has helped countless students love doing math."

That pretty much terminated the interview.

The committee murmured its thanks and I arose to go. One of my legs had fallen asleep during the interview. As I stood, the leg collapsed beneath me. I lurched for something to break my fall - and found myself desperately grasping the shoulder of the Frail Older Female Math Chair.

North Shore Community College

Some of the happiest teaching of my career happened when I was part-time at Bradford and Salem State Colleges simultaneously in the 1980's (the two together made for a full-time load in teaching, but only a fraction of the pay.) At some points, the math department of each school took it upon itself to recommend me for a full-time position. (I frankly don't know which school I would have chosen had both these happened: the two schools were so different, and yet I enjoyed being at each one.) But both administrations turned down the request on the grounds that I didn't have a doctorate. (Ironic, in that virtually no one in either department had such a degree!)

And so, by dint of grim necessity (paying the mortgage on a newly-purchased house), I was forced to take a full-time teaching position at a public high school which was offered to me in mid-year. The school was Peabody Veterans Memorial High School.

It was during one summer (perhaps around 1991) when I was at Peabody (of course, I was always yearning for greener pastures when I was there) that I spotted an ad in the Boston Globe for a full-time math position at North Shore Community College in Lynn. I saw this as one of my last chances to land a full time college job. So I wrote a letter of application.

When the math chair called me to arrange an interview, he told me that he wanted me to present a lesson to the math department. He gave me four major topics to choose from. I remember choosing the derivation of the Quadratic Formula as my topic.

For some reason I cannot now fathom, I made the decision to derive the special case where the coefficient of the quadratic term is 1. I have no notion as to why I decided to do this, but I remember thinking that I was being enormously clever.

It was as if I were asked to give a lecture on the book Tom Sawyer and I decided to talk about Becky Thatcher.

(Now, over 15 years later, I realize what I probably should have done: I should have begun with simple concrete problems and worked gradually toward solving the most complex ones. Only then would I have effected the derivation with the abstract algebraic symbols – and of course with the quadratic coefficient any number 'a'.)

Anyway, I showed up for the interview in the habiliment I used for teaching: one of my 40 vests and a tie, but no suit jacket. My mother would not have approved. (By the way, I had a piece of chalk in the pocket of each of those vests!)

For some reason (perhaps because I was dressed a bit less formally), I adapted a casual, jocular air – this despite the fact that my interviewers were all uniformly serious.

During the interview I did something that betrayed bad manners: I interrupted the department chair while he was speaking to make some kind of inane remark of my own. Neither he nor the rest of the department seemed pleased by this gaucherie.

When it came time for me to teach the lesson, they offered me a piece of chalk. "Voila!" I exclaimed and drew one from my vest pocket with the flamboyant gesture of a magician. I thought this was very cute, but no one laughed or even smiled.

What does one do when one believes oneself to be utterly charming, but it becomes obvious that no one else thinks so?

I guess in that case one decides to play it serious. So I began a serious, careful, and reasoned derivation of the Quadratic Formula. Or at least an abbreviated, condensed, truncated (emasculated?) version of that venerable Formula.

Of course, my explanation of what I was about to do was greeted with exclamations of surprise and disbelief. I saw only frowns and grimaces. But I was allowed to complete my demonstration, much as a condemned man is allowed to smoke a cigarette before he is hanged.

And that is how I blew an interview that, with sterling recommendations from two four-year colleges, I had every reason to think was a formality.

Notre Dame Academy

I hesitated about applying for this job at a girls' Catholic high school. For I wasn't Catholic, nor did I have any particular attraction to this religion (in part because it used the organ less than any Protestant denomination.) I had also heard about the low pay in Catholic schools; I was (and still am) a fervent believer in coeducation; and, I am a confirmed atheist.

Nevertheless, I was in a somewhat desperate need of a job. Beggars cannot be choosers, as the saying goes.

I had been told that I would be interviewing with the Principal of the school, one Sister Margaret Ann. As I drove up to Tyngsboro, I pictured in my mind the usual Mother Superior: an older woman inhabiting a severely starched black-and-white habit, with rimless glasses and all the rest of the accoutrements of such a personage.

So imagine my shock and surprise when the door to the principal's office flew open and out flounced an attractive young woman in a flower-print dress!

Flustered as I was, I was yet able to greet her:

"Sister Ann Margaret, I presume?"

And so, while we went on to have a very pleasant chat about how I could teach catechism in homeroom and all the rest, for all practical purposes,

The Interview had been terminated!

Rivers

I had prepared well for this interview, for I was anxious to escape the dastardly confines of Peabody (see most of the vignettes under "Disciplines" to get a flavor of the place.)

I also made a resolution to be on my best behavior during my two interviews here.

Thus, when I was asked why I wanted to teach at a private school, I resisted the honest answer, "Because, despite the lousy pay, private schools have better disciplined students in smaller classes; and I'd only have to work 143 days instead of 180!"

Instead, I gave another honest answer, but one much more palatable: "Because I am tired of hearing my fellow teachers talk about retirement when what I want to talk about is making the math curriculum more exciting and relevant for the students."

And so it went, scores of questions like this. Until, at a crucial moment, I grew weary of giving the scripted response.

At some point they asked, "How would your students describe you?"

Yeah, I know I should have regurgitated some of the old saws, such as "Caring" or "Knowledgeable" or "Kind" or any of the other virtues beginning with capital letters. But I didn't mention any of those phony things. Instead, I replied:

"I think they'd call me Eccentric."

No one gave any evidence that I had committed a faux pas (yes, they kept a Stiff Upper Lip.) Indeed, the rest of the day went well. I only found out later that, with that one word, I had set off a firestorm and very nearly terminated the interview!

Over the next week or two, my various references told me that they were called frantically by various members of the interview committee, asking whether I really was "eccentric". Of course, I seemed to be in a no-win situation here. For if my friends replied yes, then I had the undesirable trait and so was screwed; whereas if they said No, then I would be unmasked as a liar and therefore screwed as well.

Fortunately for me, my friends were very smart, and so they went between the horns of this dilemma. Namely, they first acknowledged that, indeed, I was eccentric. But then they went on to prove that those faculty members termed "eccentric" are precisely the most interesting and creative ones.

So I got the job at The Rivers School despite my worst intentions!

Skidmore College

When I was forced to leave Muskingum College, I set out to find another four-year college that would have me. But the only interview I got at such a school was at Skidmore College in Saratoga Springs, New York.

I had recommendations from administrators and colleagues at Muskingum which told of my sterling record as a teacher and colleague. Unspoken - the elephant in the room - was my relationship with the female student there. (The official reason for my dismissal was that I didn't have a doctorate.) This silence was a good thing, since Skidmore was an all-female college at the time.

But the great-teacher accolades were nonsense too. No one had ever observed me at Muskingum, and so they didn't know what a terrible teacher I was (although I think a few adverse reports from students had filtered back.) I was teaching at least one subject (in Foundations) that was over my head because I'd never had a course in it. Then, too, at the time, I "taught" as I had been "taught" by most of my college professors: by adapting a haughty mien and lecturing over the students' heads.

In short (to sum it all up succinctly), I was an arrogant ignoramus who had the potential to be a serial seducer. This was the individual the female math chairman was unwittingly interviewing that day.

But the interview went well. None of the above *seeped out* as I chatted with her. I was able to present myself as erudite and charming, one who would make a worthy addition to any math department.

Then I frankly asked her how the interviews seemed to be going, and what my status might be amongst the applicants. She replied that she was interviewing four people; I was the third. "And so far you are my top choice."

That certainly buoyed my ego! Really, how good could that fourth person be? Not very good, most likely. I felt like I essentially had the job already!

I was introduced to two (male) members of the math department, whose job it was to show me around the campus and answer any questions I might have. The only place I recall visiting was the faculty room: this was a beautifully appointed room with a fireplace, leather Morris chairs, and so forth. But the thing I most remember was the fact that there was a decanter of sherry available for the faculty to imbibe.

Well, I was feeling at home already! With the words, "I could really get used to this!", I dispensed myself a glass of sherry from the cut-glass decanter into an exquisite little crystal glass, took it over to a leather Morris chair the color of ox blood, and placed the glass on a little mahogany side table. I sat myself down and kicked up my feet onto a hassock which matched the chair. Then I lit up a long green *Garcia y Vega* cigar.

The two math professors stared at me. I saw one give the suggestion of a raised eyebrow.

When I called about the status of the job a couple of weeks later, the female math chairman told me that they had hired someone else. No details of the decision-making process were provided. But I can just imagine.

P.S. As was the case for many of my interview fiascoes, not landing this job proved to be a blessing in disguise. By default I wound up at the Mont Alto campus of Penn State. There I flourished, precisely because that school lacked the pretense of an elite private college.

Mont Alto had at least one other advantage over Skidmore: it was within driving distance of a certain girl living near Philadelphia who most likely would not have become my wife had I resided in the more remote town of Saratoga Springs.

The Boston Home

This was the one interview I had which, secretly at least, I did not want to be successful. And I very nearly got my wish!

As my condition due to multiple sclerosis got worse, it became harder and harder for my wife, Dorothy, to deal with my physical needs. Her own health was suffering because of the strain of lifting me and so forth. We had agreed that I would stay at home "as long as possible." But what is "possible" shrinks over time until a critical point is reached and you know it is no longer really "possible."

At the same time, Dorothy and I were very close to one another and dreaded being apart. That is the problem with being happily married. (Of course, the happiest marriage can feel the strains in this sort of situation.)

In short, my head told me that I really needed to move; while my heart wanted desperately to stay where I was.

Once it began to appear that something would have to happen sooner rather than later, I tried to visualize as positively as I could my life in a nursing facility. I even romanticized my possible transplantation as follows: Back in the 1960's, the Canadian pianist Glenn Gould wrote columns for "High Fidelity" magazine in which he raised the idea of "Desert Island Discs" - that is, those recordings that one might choose to have with one while marooned on a desert isle. (Gould himself was so reclusive that he essentially lived on such a place.) I would impishly pose this question (of course with CD's supplanting vinyl records) to my various visitors and note their responses. (After awhile I would expand the question to include books, art, etc.) Finally, I would reveal the reason for the question.

Anyway, Dorothy finally applied to The Boston Home, a superb place dedicated to caring for people with MS, in January of 2005. And then we heard virtually nothing for months. Since we had understood that the waiting time to get in was around two years, this did not fill us with optimism. Finally, though, we received a call and set up an appointment for a woman to do a home interview on May 6.

I was determined to show myself to her as belonging to the type most sought after by The Boston Home. But what sort of person would that be? I had no idea. So I thought it best to show her <u>both</u> sides of each character trait. (And of course resting in my subconscious was the knowledge that, while one of those traits might act in my favor, the other might just as well act against me. Thus I could have it both ways - my head and my heart - and trust to fate (i.e. this woman) as to the final decision.)

Q: "Can you still transfer yourself?"

(Let me see: would they want someone to be able to do this or not? On the one hand, it would seem to be a desirable thing to have this sort of independence, thus giving the staff a break from having to get me up each day. On the other hand, people who transfer tend to fall on occasion, and it is hard to get them up off the floor.)

A: "You know, it's funny you should ask this at this moment of my disorder (or is it a disease?) For, up until very recently, I have been transferring just fine, thank you! But - and this is a big "but" - I haven't transferred since I was in the hospital a few short months ago. So I don't know whether I can relearn this valuable skill or not, but I am perfectly willing to try if that's what you think best; otherwise, I think I could relinquish it with few regrets."

Q: "Can you still feed yourself?"

(I know that they ask these sorts of things to try and trip us up. This is how they filter out the 'undesirables.' But what is "desirable" in this case? On the one hand, again, perhaps they want some independent residents to save the staff from having to feed everyone. On the other hand, maybe this is a facility that specializes in more helpless cases and would deem me "still too highly developed" to belong there. So I shall have to show myself as just barely helpless, as one on the cusp of helplessness, in that no-man's land between self-sufficiency and helplessness...)

A: "How to answer this question succinctly? First of all, I can only use one hand - but that one hand is pretty good. But not <u>too</u> good! Basically, I can pick up something (preferably food) with a fork or a spoon and lift it successfully into my mouth around 80 percent - no, 20 per - no, <u>exactly</u> 50 percent of the time. The food does have a tendency to fall off the fork - but not <u>too</u> often. In short, I am able to feed myself just enough to maintain basic nutrition, thus keeping myself balanced precariously on the knife edge between being well-fed and malnourished."

There was only one time when I did not "behave" myself. When the woman asked whether I have any brothers or sisters, I replied, "I have a brother, but he's an only child." My wife gave an embarrassed laugh. Our visitor was writing and didn't laugh, and I wondered whether I had blown it right there. But finally I assumed that she'd heard "I have a brother", but not the rest. Or else she heard it all but didn't care. Or did care, but hid it well. Whatever.

(And who is to say that humor would be a bad thing at The Boston Home? No doubt they may be in need of a few laughs, a few healthy guffaws!)(Or maybe not. Perhaps it hurts MS patients to laugh!)

Anyway, things were going fine, when she suddenly posed a question that caught me utterly by surprise. Remember that we had heard that the waiting time to get into The Boston Home was two or more years. But now she asked:

Q: "Would you be ready to enter The Boston Home in three to four months?"

This question was so unanticipated, so shocking, that I lost my train of hyper-equivocation. I was stunned, and could only mumble: "I - I don't know if I would be or not - it seems awfully soon, though it would give us the summer together..." (Of course, even in this panicked flailing I was <u>still</u> equivocating. Could I ever take a definite position on <u>anything</u>?)(Maybe or maybe not.)

This, as it turned out, was not the answer the lady wanted to hear. Afterwards Dorothy told me that the woman gave a visible start at my answer.

For her part, Dorothy stated frankly that she herself, due to increasing physical injury caring for my needs, was very ready for me to enter The Boston Home whenever an opening came about. (Dorothy is not one to hesitate or equivocate!)

The lady soon left and Dorothy told me the gist of the above. "Oh well," she said, "It probably doesn't matter." There was a sad little resigned smile on her face. But I couldn't tell whether it was the smile of "Now you can stay longer at home with me," or "Now we'll have to put you in a real nursing home!"

And thus, despite all the elaborately constructed equivocations, did I blow the most important interview of my life.

Or did I?

How often have we all said something that later we would wish to take back? In particular, which of those many interviews I botched could I have rescued by the retroactive retraction of an overly-hasty bon mot, a misplaced phrase? (Probably none, for the simple reason that virtually none of my interviewers wanted me to begin with!)

But I was determined to rescue this interview!

Once I knew Dorothy's feelings for certain, I called and left a message on the woman's phone. Finally, I made a direct, unequivocal statement: "Sometimes even people who have lived together for 35 years don't always know one another's thoughts on even the most important subjects. And so, now that I know how my wife feels about this, I will say that, yes, I would be ready to come in three or four months."

(But did they want a man who automatically acceded to what his wife thought was best? Well, yes - if the wife is wise. But what if she wasn't?)(And could this woman tell whether Dorothy was wise or not?)

Unfortunately, it was late on a Friday afternoon, so the woman would not be getting my message until Monday (I realized that I was calling her office phone.) What mischief could be wrought in that time period? Perhaps she was speeding towards another, worthier candidate even as I was attempting to call her!

I heard nothing on Monday, which just fed my paranoia. On Tuesday she called me. She was friendly, but she didn't say anything one way or another as to my status. And then the phone was silent for three or so weeks.

I was watching/listening to a DVD of Strauss's Salome (wherein John the Baptist unsuccessfully "interviews" the title character to urge her toward piety) one Thursday afternoon late in that month of May, when the phone rang: it was our female visitor, and she asked me point blank: "Would you be able to come into The Boston Home this coming Monday?" This time I had learned my lesson: I said "Yes", forthrightly and unequivocally (even as my heart all but stopped beating.) A minute later I asked where I was in the cue. She replied, "You are first in line."

And that was that. I actually entered the Home on Wednesday June 1, 2005. There would not be another opening there for a male for a full year.

By the way: I have now lived here at The Boston Home for well over a year, and I still don't know for sure which answers (if any) got me in here. Ironically, it could have been due to a political connection unrelated to me directly. Or I may have been seized upon as a good match for a roommate, wherein my personality traits and interests mattered far more than my fractured responses to a few questions.

What I do know is, that my misplaced witticism was not a faux pas at all. For, amidst all the rest of the humor here, there is a "jokes night" each evening.

Theta Chi

I did my undergraduate work at Lehigh University from 1961 to 1965. In that era, Lehigh was still an all-men's school. (My mistake in going there: women were my favorite sex.)

Now at Lehigh in the 1950's (I was seeking a bid in 1962, but sociologically we were still part of that earlier era) the social life of upperclassmen was rooted in the fraternities. Lehigh had no fewer than 31 of these self-centered havens for troglodytes (do my resentments show?)

But I wanted to be a troglodyte too! I wanted to belong to an exclusive club and look down my nose at those who didn't! I wanted to pay huge dues to finance silly parties! I wanted a bunch of half-wits (whom I'd be calling my "brothers") to distract me from studying when I didn't even know how to study when it was quiet! I wanted to be sent out to do stupid inane things as a pledge, so that I could send out other pledges to do the same sorts of inane things the next year! Yes I did!

Well, not necessarily. The truth is, I remember myself being decidedly ambivalent about all that: I was attracted and repulsed. (I was particularly repulsed by the fact that most of the fraternities had national charters that excluded Blacks and Jews.)

But Theta Chi seemed to be an exception. It had a reputation for being the "intellectual fraternity", an oxymoron. It did accept Blacks and Jews. The biggest attraction for me: most musicians of any caliber (what is the caliber of an oboist?) belonged to Theta Chi. Indeed, many of my compatriots in the Glee Club were members there.

So this seemed like the place for me. And, given my connections, one would think that I was a shoo-in.

I received a dinner date. I went. I ate. I conquered - I thought.

I don't remember the dinner portion of the evening. No doubt there was food and conversation. At the time I think that I ate a bit too ravenously and spoke a bit too haltingly - neither of which would have suited the refined atmosphere of that fraternity.

After dinner there was singing with guitars around the fire in the living room. This I do remember. All the songs were ones that I knew well - because we always sang them at parties following the concerts with women's colleges. So I sang out with gusto and assurance, breathing new life into the vapid ditties of the Kingston Trio and others. I think I even wailed forth with a couple of solo verses - all the while clapping my hands to show I had good rhythm.

A friend of mine from high school had been there with me (I pitied him because he could neither talk nor sing.) After we left, he told me that I was virtually assured of a bid for membership: "You were the life of the party!" So I was understandably disturbed when a second dinner date did not come my way.

My friend had the ready reason for my rejection: "You were too good!" he exclaimed. By that I assumed he meant that I would constitute a threat to my fellow brothers with my superior social and vocal skills.

Yes, that was the explanation that soothed my wounded vanity and allowed me to accept the prospect of a dismal social life for the next three years: I was TOO GOOD for even the best fraternity!

But of course even a cursory examination of this "reason" would conclude that it is absurd. Fraternities, as is well known, attempt to pledge the best recruits they can. No fraternity would reject someone because they were "too good" - on the contrary.

The sad probable truth is, that I was judged NOT GOOD ENOUGH.

In short, I was too emotionally, mentally, and, yes, physically callow for that fraternity. Or any other, for I received exactly zero bids to join a fraternity.

So I went to live in drab Taylor Hall for my last three years. The University proudly touted this gray, moldy edifice as "the first poured concrete building in the United States" (one depressing look would verify this.) It was something out of a Bronte novel. My attraction (if this is not too strong a word) to this dorm was precisely its quasi-ruined, bucolic state, with a nice quadrangle out front. This latter was framed by trees and by the U-shape of the building; it was champs du guerre for many a lusty game of frisbee.

Taylor, I soon found, drew to it the eccentrics of Lehigh: nerds, misfits, misanthropes, introverts, anarchists, pickpockets, cutthroats, and other such assorted lowlives. The dorm itself mirrored its residents: it was itself eccentric. In an era of blandly uniform room design (as was true of the other upper class dorm), this place had rooms of at least relative character: doubles, two- and three-person suites - and of course (the main attraction of the solipsistic set) a plethora of singles. Many of the rooms had eccentric shapes as well, thanks to the four 45-degree turns of the building.

It was only in my senior year that I realized that Taylor Hall had one distinct advantage over even the fraternities. This was during

Houseparty weekends, when any Lehigh man worth his salt had a date. Now in that era, those parties were heavily chaperoned by middle-aged women, who attached themselves to virtually every living unit and made regular inspections of bedrooms and the like. (I recall one tale of a matron catching a couple *in flagrante*. The hapless miscreants could only attempt this pathetic excuse: "We were only making out in the nude!")

There was one place, however, to which chaperones were not assigned. Taylor Hall had no parties during Houseparty weekends, for the simple drear reason that its residents had nothing to celebrate. Everyone knew that those occupants were too misanthropic to have dates, too nerdy to feel they needed to blow off steam after a hard term of studying. Indeed, the dorm emptied and was virtually dark those weekends as its residents fled the drunkenness and debauchery on campus.

But I didn't leave those weekends. And on the lovely spring weekend of my senior year I actually had a date. After visiting a few of the fraternity parties up on the hill (I did not envy the freshmen pledges who would have to clean up those messes on Sunday) I brought my date back to my dorm room (a single), where no chaperone would be interrupting our frivolities.

And so then, finally, at the very end of my college career, I realized I was genuinely glad that I did not get into Theta Chi!

Trinity Lutheran Church

I had been living in Chambersburg, Pennsylvania for a year when I heard about this opening for an organist. I was a bit hesitant about applying, since I had not been playing much for the past two years. But I finally decided to audition, for the experience if nothing else.

Now that (1969) was the year before I was married. I was slim (skinny?), had long windswept (greasy?) hair, and a raffish mustache. I was told I vaguely resembled Egyptian actor Omar Sharif, the lead in "Dr. Zhivago" of four years before; and I encouraged the resemblance by wearing a Russian black fur hat in the winter. In short, I thought myself dashing. Probably I most resembled a lothario in a silent film melodrama!

I entered the church nave and the music director, a friendly young woman, came up to greet me. She asked me to play something.

I wanted to give her a taste of the breadth and depth of my repertoire. So I played the Bach A Minor Prelude (by memory) as an example of the Baroque; a salient part of the Franck Choral No. 3 from the Romantic repertoire; and a movement from the Second Sonata by modern composer Paul Hindemith. I played well all the hymns she placed in front of me, even improvising an interlude for one on the spot. And I showed myself to be a sympathetic and versatile accompanist in vocal pieces, as well as someone apt in sight-reading choral parts. In short, I acquitted myself admirably in every domain (if I do say so myself!)

I had scarcely finished playing when the music director came striding down the aisle, grasped my hand warmly, and declared me to be the new organist for Trinity Lutheran Church.

Of course I was elated to have gotten such a job on the spot (I've found that usually I had to wait days or weeks - if not forever - to hear about my fate after interviews.) So I was frankly curious as to what I had done to tip the scales (so to speak) so decisively in my favor. Had it been one of the solo pieces? The hymnody? My accompanying?

She laughed. "None of those really mattered. Oh yes - of course it was good to hear that you could actually play the organ. But the simple fact is, <u>I knew you were the one I wanted the moment you walked through the door!</u>"

Needless to say, I would never again duplicate this - sudden success - in subsequent interviews!

Walpole High School

I got up out of a sick bed to undertake the one-hour drive to this interview. As a result, I probably appeared even more pale and neurasthenic than usual!

My public school teaching experience at this point in my "career" was scant - mainly substitute teaching in a couple of schools.

At Walpole High School I was admitted into the Principal's office. And the very first thing he said to me was:

"I see that you've worked at Lincoln Sudbury Regional High School."

"That's a very liberal school; they let kids get away with murder there."

"If you think that this is that kind of school, maybe we'd just better forget the whole thing right now!"

I visibly took my right hand, pinched my left arm, and said,

"Have I made a mistake and wound up at Walpole State Prison?"

And that terminated a decidedly short Interview!

Wilbraham Academy

I interviewed at this boys private school for a position of Organist and Glee Club conductor.

But the more the interview "progressed", the more I got the sense that the purpose of this institution was to instill prissiness and priggishness into its charges.

For example, when for some reason the question of smoking came up, my interlocutor declared sniffily, "We don't believe that young gentlemen should smoke in public."

I replied, "Well then, it will certainly cause them to doubt my character when they observe me strolling down the street smoking a cigar!"

That terminated the interview!

Winchester High School

I was looking for a new teaching job after the money for my position at Oak Hill Middle School in Newton had dried up, when I noticed no less than three math positions at Winchester High School advertised in "The Boston Globe".

By this time I had been in a wheelchair for nearly three years, and I was pessimistic about getting another job. The reasoning behind this feeling was pretty well founded. In the wake of being fired from The Rivers School three years before, I was, at first, up front about my illness in all the applications I sent out; consequently, the phone did not ring. So finally I decided not to mention it, and then I began to get interviews. But once they saw my fitful walking (see "Northern Essex"), I think they shied away from me. If my dear friend Murph Shapiro hadn't hired me at Oak Hill, I doubt that I would have gotten a job back then.

Now, three years later, it was worse. But I thought that I had at least a shot at getting a job at Winchester High, not only because of the multiple jobs, but also because I knew Sue Morse, the principal, pretty well (from church) and I knew she liked me.

It took about seven minutes to get from my house to the high school, and I remember thinking how convenient that would be. When I arrived, I found the commute <u>into</u> the building to be less than easeful: the high school was a sort of island built up on a platform. So anywhere one chose to enter, there was a steep incline of brick. It was to me like a sort of moat. I only managed to get up in my manual chair by traversing this incline obliquely.

Inside I met the Math Chair, Eileen, in a large open area stacked with returned textbooks. She was friendly, even bouncy, and we hit it off right away. She asked what I liked to teach, and I told her of my Math Topics course at Rivers and the fifteen projects I had devised. She seemed excited by that, as such a course was already being taught there (though, since it is not in the mainstream math curriculum, no one wanted to teach it.) When she asked what else, I mentioned my Introduction to Calculus classes, wherein I integrated (pun intended!) the graphing calculator. This excited her too ("I don't see why we can't rotate the calculus around and let new people teach it!")

In short, the two courses that I had had the most success with in my whole career were perfect matches for their department there.

Eileen and I were bonding. I dared to joke about her name. ("Is one of your legs shorter than the other?") And I strongly inferred that I would be one of those hired. ("Where would be the room in which I'd be teaching?") We kidded one another as we walked down to meet with the principal (which I knew would be a mere formality.)

Then abruptly she told me that the principal had gone on medical leave the day before to be treated for acute leukemia. Suddenly the mood had turned somber: I was distressed for my friend, and uncertain as to what to expect. Eileen told me I would be meeting with the Acting Principal.

That gentleman was cold and abstracted. I'm sure he had a lot on his mind. Suffice it to say that the meeting with him was not a formality. The one exchange I recall was when the subject of part-time came up: When I remarked, "I think that two classes would be the most I'd like to teach, given my stamina," he growled in retort, "You'd teach three if we decide that's what we need!"

I went home with doubts but hoping for the best. After all, there were three positions open. And I had hit it off so well with the department Chair.

After a week of not hearing anything, I called the school and asked for the Math Chair Eileen. The secretary replied, "Oh, she's gone to Martha's Vineyard for the summer." For The Summer?! Didn't she have three positions in her department to fill? The secretary knew nothing about the status of the jobs.

During the next couple of weeks I called the school a few more times asking to speak to the Acting Principal. But he was either "out" or "too busy" to take my call. I never even received a letter informing me I hadn't been hired. Apparently from the standpoint of Winchester I had become, (to use George Meany's immortal phrase about Nixon), "a non-poison."

P.S. As with so many other instances in my teaching career, this implicit rejection was a blessing in disguise (although of course it was well disguised at the time.) For it made me available for the job at Newton South High School - a place enormously sympathetic to my plight. I got that job (crunch time!) the day after Labor Day. The interview (see "Newton South") was essentially the opposite of the one described above.

Oh yes - at Newton South I taught two courses. As four courses is a full load there, this means I was half-time. So on a base salary of $60,000, I was making $30,000. Whereas at Winchester, where five courses is a full load, I would have only made $24,000 for teaching two courses. So I made 25% more by teaching in Newton.

Winthrop High School

I had lost my teaching position at Lincoln-Sudbury nearly a year before and I was desperately in need of another job. Now, gone was the mindless aplomb, the devil-may-care hubris described at the end of that Journal entry 30 March 1983. Now I was running scared! This one at Winthrop High, to fill in the rest of the year for a pregnancy leave, was to open in March 1984.

This school, otherwise undistinguished (though there was an excellent camaraderie amongst the faculty) attracted me because it was a literal stone's throw from the ocean. (Of course I would never see that ocean, being occupied as I was with my classes. But my students would see much of it - especially on lovely spring days when they should have been in my class!)

Now I had learned my lessons from all the failed interviews of the past. I prepared for all possible (and some impossible) questions that I could be asked - including the inevitable one on discipline.

My interview was with the principal in his office. I had met all kinds and sorts of principals in my extensive career of job searches, including those who resembled thugs and bums (see selected vignettes above for confirmation.) This gentleman - for such he was (I regret not remembering his name) - was utterly different. He was nattily dressed in a sporty three-piece suit. He sat back comfortably and casually in his swivel chair. In his hand was a pigskin pipe; and on his face was a big welcoming smile. He exuded the confident air of a secretary of state (at least those secretaries of state who are confident!)

He asked me about seven or eight questions (one of them had to do with discipline, of course. And, no, I did not use the word "seduce"!) I answered each one thoughtfully and eloquently. He signaled that not only was the interview over but I was to be hired when he said, "Well, you have answered to my satisfaction the question that interested me the most."

I asked him which question that had been, even as I mentally raced over the various queries and my responses.

"It was 'Can you teach Trigonometry?'"

My "thoughtful and eloquent" answer had been: "Yes".

PS: I almost lost the Winthrop job before I began it. A secretary gave me a sheaf of papers to sign. One of them was a loyalty oath wherein I had to swear I wouldn't try to overthrow the government. I asked her: "Do I have to sign this?" She was taken aback: "I don't know - no one has ever refused to sign it before!" I said, "Well, why don't we just pretend I never saw this and forget about it!" And I replaced it down in the pile.

But at home the next day I received a call from the superintendent (whom I'd met when I interviewed: he looked like James Arness of "Gunsmoke" fame.) He asked me why I hadn't signed the oath. I said that I thought it an ill-conceived instrument. "Look, there are three kinds of people who would sign such a thing: those who lack the mind to imagine a situation wherein it would be one's patriotic duty to overthrow an unjust and tyrannical government; those too cowed to refuse to sign; and hard-core Communists who are willing to lie in order to get a foot in the door."

He replied, "Well, it'd be a shame if you couldn't come to Winthrop and teach!"

I got the point. I signed - "UNDER PROTEST".

PPS: There was another community that (in 1976) demanded I

sign a loyalty oath in order to work there: Lexington, Massachusetts. I thought that was fittingly ironic! (When I asked what would happen if I didn't sign, the secretary replied that I was welcome to teach there - I just wouldn't be paid!)

Fiction: Interviews

He decided, after all, to dress up. Not elaborately, but carefully and correctly, complete with tie and jacket. It would have been nice to have gone casually (but neatly) -- he knew he'd feel most at ease that way, most himself. But uncertainty as to what was expected, what would weigh the balance in his favor -- or against it -- made him decide to take no chances. "Better slightly overdressed than underdressed!" was the motto he had heard somewhere -- probably from his mother. After much hesitation he chose the thick scotch plaid -- he winced at the thought of wool encircling his neck in the middle of the hot summer; but with its delicate lines of red and gold the tie completed and complemented admirably the blandness of the navy blue suit and shirt.

The interview went well, he thought afterwards -- much better, in fact, than he had dared hope or expect. He had fielded their questions with calm, deft assurance, inserting just enough humor to show them that, as an employee, he would be pleasant but not frivolous. Yes -- he had even asked a few questions himself, subtly calculated to show a penetrating interest in the school system, and of course to indicate not only a willingness to accede to their authority, but to give them a chance to exercise their knowledge for him. In his response to questions concerning his own field, he had replied with the use of just enough terminology to show an all-embracing familiarity.

When the inevitable question of discipline reared its ugly head, he was prepared to state, "Yes, of course discipline is important, essential in fact, but necessary in the service of learning; of course if a teacher is able to <u>seduce</u> his students into wanting, even needing, to address and solve a problem, then discipline usually takes care of itself". A brilliant and clever answer; and he even believed it. He did not even eschew showing a pragmatic side -- "I suppose I should ask the inevitable mundane question as to the salary level". At the end they all shook hands with him and expressed their pleasure at having met and spoken with him.

In the car on the way home (he drove slowly, drinking in the exhilaration of having "sold himself admirably"), he afforded himself the luxury of feeling the choice was now up to him. He finally decided, after indulging in a few bagatelles of criticism of certain aspects of the job, to accept it when it was offered.

As soon as he left and the door was shut behind him, the three members of the Search Committee began to discuss critically the candidate they had just interviewed.

The Principal (who happened to be a woman) remarked that he seemed "a nice, personable young man". The Math Chairman (who happened to be a man) nodded uneasily, while the Personnel Director (another man) disclaimed, "Yes, I suppose -- but they all are, aren't they? I mean, if personableness were all we were after..." The Principal hastened to say that, of course, she hadn't meant that this was all she was looking for -- "he did seem to know a lot about his Field, for example..."

Math Chairman: "Yeah -- he knew the jargon, but that can be picked up in a day, from a course catalog -- we hire someone, only to find out later he doesn't know anything after all -- just jargon!"

Personnel Director: "Well -- and take his responses on discipline..." Principal: "Yes -- I think he was bull-shitting -- pardon my English -- but, let's face it: discipline is discipline -- and..."

Math Chairman: "...not seduction?" All laughed bitterly.

Principal: "He can use words like that, and all those young girls he'll be teaching -- seducing -- !"

Math Head: "Well, he did seem to have a sense of humor -- we could use that in the Department!"

Personnel Director: "He didn't make me laugh! Some people try to be funny and it just falls flat -- ever notice? Now, where's the humor in Math, I ask you? If a fellow knows what he's doing with those equations, he won't need humor -- it's always a crutch!"

Principal: "Yes, I believe that, too -- they try to cozy up to the students with their stupid little jokes -- it's the pupils that stand to lose, even if they think they've gained a friend!"

Math Head: "We certainly need to build up the Department with solid academic types. This guy, the sick jokes aside, seems to have a pretty impressive background, though -- taught everything under the sun!"

Personnel Director: "That's it -- Jack of all Trades, Master of None!"

Principal: "Well -- it'd certainly help of we could observe him teach!"

Personnel Director: "If we can't tell everything we need to know about someone from an interview, then forget it! Now this guy -- seemed like a bit of a con man-- you know, he came on strong but not too strong -- there is such a thing as a Professional Interviewer, ya know -- people who take courses in the thing!"

Math Head: "He seemed to know all the answers. And all the right questions too, I might add! It did seem suspicious, just a bit..."

Personnel Director: "More than suspicious, I'd say!"

Math Head: "He <u>was</u> pretty slick!"

Principal: "Yes, he was -- personable, presentable -- just a little too much so for my taste".

Personnel Director: "Frankly, he was perfect -- showing he'd fit right in and get along with everyone! We don't need people like that -- it's not human anyhow -- yes, he interviewed <u>too</u> well for my money!"

Principal: "Well, I myself felt a bit inferior, if you will -- I mean, I know my own faults, but he doesn't seem to have any. I don't know as I'd like to have someone like that around -- it's an unspoken accusation in my book!"

Math Head: "Yes, he'd fit right in with the Department -- but that's the problem -- we have our problems, our little squabbles -- every Department does -- I can't see a person like that, being everyone's friend -- it doesn't happen in Real Life."

Personnel Director: "Decidedly not. He asked for our opinions, but you could tell he thought he knew it all. And as far as I'm concerned, that cute little question about the <u>mundane</u> salary -- I mean, who does he think he's kidding? Money is money, you don't beat around the bush about it -- it's too important! Anybody who can't speak straight about it doesn't deserve to work for it -- that's my opinion!"

Principal: "Well -- he seemed well-dressed enough -- but that's presentability again, I guess..."

Math Head: "But that's the whole point -- math teachers don't dress like that, somehow -- I mean, navy! My god, how long would that guy last with a piece of white chalk?!"

Personnel Director: "Yeah, he was dressed fine -- correctly. That's it in a nutshell right there! He wasn't overdressed, or underdressed; he was dressed just right -- <u>too</u> right. Which is to say, wrong! Well, I mean, that seems to decide it, doesn't it? He interviewed <u>too</u> well, he was dressed <u>too</u> right, he spoke <u>too</u> well -- what else can I say -- I rest my case!"

A week later the candidate received a xeroxed rejection form letter in the mail.

Disciplines

The following vignettes, humorous to me now, were anything but that at those times when I prayed for the bell to ring.

Bust Balls

The Department Chairman at this high school was a streetwise tough who'd grown up in a working class suburb of Boston. Thus, his ideas for classroom management were rudimentary, to say the least. For example, once when I was experimenting with a class in the formulation of mathematical principles (we were having a parliamentary debate), the Chairman poked his head in my room, took me aside, and said, "You gotta be a cocksucker - they can't do nothin' creative!"

Yes, he preferred psycho-sexual imagery, this Chairman who reserved the Honors pre-Calculus class for himself while relegating the "problem" classes to the likes of me.

One afternoon near the end of the school year, I was about to enter a classroom to teach when the Chairman called to me from down the hall:

"Don't forget - next year you have to bust some balls!"

I don't know which took me aback more - the suddenness of the admonition; the public place in which it happened; or its brutal frankness. Whatever - I entered the classroom in a daze. One student at least noticed and asked me what was wrong. Fed up, I decided to throw caution to the winds:

"I just saw my Department Chairman in the hall, and he told me that next year I was going to have to bust a part of my students' anatomies."

"Their asses?" inquired a fellow helpfully.

"No, not that", I replied.

"Their balls?" asked a sweet demure girl.

"Yeah, their balls", I assented.

"But that's not you, Mr. May!" she said with feeling.

Cheez-It

It was a typical afternoon in my pre-Algebra class. Which is to say, they were failing to take seriously my exhortations as to how, with a little more effort, they could pass from the "pre" stage of Algebra to its actual Essence. No, they chose to fiddle while Rome burned; or, rather, they set Rome ablaze and then they fiddled. And so, since things were flying at me up front whenever I turned my back, I decided to remove two of those conditions contributing to my discomfort (and their merriment), namely: that front, and my back.

So I set them to work on some problems, and I stood facing them over to their side. After all, I reasoned (which shows to what lowly state noble Reason had sunk in my mathematics class!), no one can launch a missile obliquely, and certainly would not dare to do so while I am watching their every move. So I watched all their profiles all the time. Not even daring to blink, I watched and watched and watched...

And then, abruptly, a Cheez-It bounced off my forehead.

Well, they thought that was the funniest thing ever! As for me, well, once I had gotten past a certain loss of dignity (that only took a second or two), I found myself in something like - admiration - that something like that could be carried off - something so imperceptible and yet so accurate!

So I smiled, shrugged, and shook my head to indicate the range of my emotions: my own incredulity about the act; my admission that, despite the best-laid plans, I'd been Had; and just a hint of an admonishment.

Finger

There was a student in the worst of my pre-Algebra classes (which is to say, the Bottom of the Barrel) whom I shall call "Louie" (I have thankfully purged his real name from my memory-bank.) Louie was a truly troubled lad, totally devoid of any moral scruples.

One day when I was trying to teach this class some math, I noticed Louie (who was sitting right in front of me) calmly rubbing the bridge of his nose with his middle finger.

"Please stop doing that!" I directed him.

Louie was irate, a model of One Wronged:

"Doin' what?? I wasn't doing nothin'! How dare you accuse me of somethin' I wasn't doin'?! I'm sittin' here in the front mindin' my own business! You're just out to pick on me and it's not fair!"

Beginning to doubt my own judgment, I was on the verge of offering Louie an apology, when he suddenly exclaimed:

"Oh, did you think I was doing this?"

And he proceeded to thrust up his middle finger and vibrate it in angry obscenity before my face for several seconds.

At that point I did a rather unusual thing: I told Louie to go see his Housemaster.

Fireball

Is there anything worse than a classroom situation wherein a "crime" has been committed and, when asked who the perpetrator was, the class is silent? We shall see.

I was helping a student in the back of a pre-Algebra (of course) classroom, when a cry went up of "FIRE!" I looked up and there, in the center of the room, was a large ball of paper in flames.

"Who did that?!" I yelled in true anger.

"I DID!" was the jubilantly shouted reply by every student in the room.

How did I respond? I no longer recall. Obviously, I should have punished them all - and would have, if I had not set such a bad example by displaying on the wall a print of Magritte's painting of a Tuba in Flames on a Beach!

Game Boy

It was around my second year at Peabody that these hand-held electronic games came out. They became a rage at our high school. But students usually put them away at the start of class.

Not this fellow. I spotted him playing with it in the back of the room.

I wondered what to do.

Do I attempt to cajole him by flattery ("You're much too bright to be using that thing!")? But I realized that he would simply counter that he wasn't as bright as I thought he was. (His opinion would be buoyed by my obvious lack of sincerity.)

Do I use my father's oft-stated admonishment to me ("Don't be a sap - wise up!")? Well, no: sadly, I figured it wouldn't work any better for this fellow than it had for me.

So I proceeded to give him a veiled warning wherein I alluded darkly to "the possibility of confiscation if present trends continue."

But he didn't stop (he was hooked.) Finally I strode resolutely to the back and lifted the infernal machine from his dainty hands. "You may have this after the period is over," I declared as, despite his protests of "Gestapo tactics", I placed it in a drawer of my desk up front.

I was scrawling some new algebraic hieroglyphs on the board when I heard something rustle at my desk. I turned just in time to see my friend hustling away my rank book.

"What are you doing?" I demanded.

"You took something from me, I take something from you. Quid pro quo."

Within five minutes he was sitting in the principal's office, weeping.

Hangin' Out

Every teacher knows the feeling of being tested. But some are tested more than others.

I was walking down the hall at Peabody ("Puberty") High one day when one of my (male) students greeted me thus:

"How's it hangin', Mr. May?"

How should a teacher respond to such a thing?

In my experience, there were two kinds of teacher-testing: the benign and the malignant. The latter types tended to be malicious and mean-spirited. They were meant to embarrass, humiliate, or even physically harm the teacher. I had some instances of those at Peabody.

The benign type of testing, on the other hand, is actually friendly in intent. In this case the student likes the teacher, and is simply probing to see how much of a common level he can find with him. There may be some embarrassment, but it is of the comedic sort.

I decided that the student's greeting to me fell in the benign category. But as I said: How to respond?

One extreme response would be to cut the student with silence and a glare, thus signaling that he had unacceptably crossed a line and offended the teacher's dignity. Or the teacher could state something like:

"Sorry - I don't dignify those sorts of inquiries with a response."

But this seems narrow-minded, harsh, unfair to a student who most likely is just being, if not totally innocent, at least happy-go-lucky and friendly. Better would be to respond literally, as to a greeting, thus:

"I'm fine. And how are you?"

Thus has the teacher deflected the lascivious implications of the greeting and, at the same time, maintained cordial relations with the student. It is a decent response; but, unfortunately, not a very interesting one. We feel cheated, precisely because we expect something that engages the spirit of the original greeting.

The problem, of course, is those two little words - the pronoun, and the verb-form which charges it so absolutely. The challenge is to make use of those words, but in a way that does not encourage the student to escalate to further libidinousness.

After much thought (far too much, I'm afraid, to engage in during the split-second one is mulling a response in the hall), I came up with this construct:

"Fine! And how are things hangin' with you?"

This seems good: it removes the expression from oneself with one single word, and simply tosses it back to the student. At the same time, with the word "things" it subtly changes to plural, thus managing to avoid the more charged singular. Note also the carefully chosen word "with", and compare it to "for" or even - gasp! – "from". This is, in fact, a masterful response.

What? You want to throw caution to the winds? Well, there's always this one:

"It's danglin' dandy! How's yours hangin'?"

Now that's really one swingin' teacher!

Mother Teresa

Cheating probably occurs in any competitive environment in which the outcome of a contest rewards the highest achievers. So the person who cheats does so out of basic human instincts for survival. I strongly feel that it is the competitive milieu itself that causes certain people to cheat - that a true education would pit a person in competition with their own curiosity and nothing else. For these reasons, I have always felt a strong sympathy for cheaters. Which didn't stop me from punishing them when I caught them: yes, I am schizophrenic!

When cheating occurs in school during a test, the cheater is usually thought to be the one who 'steals' the information from another's paper. Rarely do we regard with equal contempt the student who conveys information to the other. After all, that sort of student is not only knowledgeable but altruistic as well. Yet there are times when the cheater could not cheat at all without help from his abettor in crime. Should not the abettor be punished too?

I had an Algebra class in which one student, a pudgy little fellow, seemed to know significantly more than his classmates. I was only curious as to why one so facile never handed in his paper until the last moment. One day, during a test, he asked to go to the boys' room, and I noticed that he casually left his paper face up on a neighboring desk, where other students could consult it at their leisure.

When he returned, I accused him of being an accessory in crime. I told him that he had two choices for punishment: either to receive a zero on his test; or to be the first proud recipient of The Mother Teresa Award. Of course he was curious as to the latter sort of chastisement. I replied that this award "is given to anyone who attempts to ameliorate the plight of the Poor Unfortunate Ones." I told him that this would oblige him to emulate that sainted lady in one other respect: he would have to wear a white kerchief with a blue stripe on his head during class for the space of one week.

Of course you may guess the punishment he chose (yes, he looked cute in his kerchief!) And thereafter he handed in his test promptly when he'd finished it.

Moving Up

The academic year 1975-76 dawned and I had no teaching job. I had squandered the year before in the Labor Party when I should have gotten myself certified to teach. So now I was forced by dint of economic necessity (Dorothy was ready to have our first child) to take relatively menial work.

So I put in my name to substitute in the Arlington Public Schools. The phone did not ring very often, but when it did it was usually for something irrelevant to my field, such as Machine Shop. In those instances I was not expected to teach, but rather to reside over a virtual study hall.

However, I did get called once to actually teach mathematics: that was in a ninth grade Algebra I class, a subject and level I felt absolutely confident to teach.

What I didn't feel confident about was maintaining discipline in a classroom. After all, my only teaching experience had been at the college level, where the students were mainly docile. And I'd already had one bizarre experience at a middle school there in Arlington (See "World Series"). So I knew I would have to be on my guard.

Now, with over thirty years of hindsight, I know what I should have done: I should have walked amongst the students as I took attendance. Then, from the back, I could have asked, "Who can show us something they learned while doing their homework last night?" and we would have been off on a series of student presentations.

But of course I didn't do that. Instead, I stood up in front and demonstrated, as teachers have done from time immemorial.

Still, the class seemed fine when I first faced it – serious and well-mannered. I recall asking whether there were any questions on the homework, and then working some examples for them on the blackboard. Of course this involved turning my back on the class for extended periods.

At one point, I thought I heard the slightest, the most subtle scraping sound on the floor. When I turned to face the class, I did not notice anything untoward – everyone seemed to be diligently taking notes. When it happened again, I thought I saw the barest hint of a smile on some boys in the front row. I knew I needed to be watchful; but was I beginning to imagine things? I sought to rationalize it:

"What is that scraping, I implore,
That scrape-scrape-scraping on the floor?"
"'Tis the creaking of the door;

'Tis the room and nothing more."

I turned back to write on the board. When I heard the scraping sound again and turned around, the front row seemed to be a mite closer to me. Now I knew I was imagining things:

"As I did stand my watch upon the hill,
I look'd toward Birnam, and anon, methought,
The Wood began to move."

Shaking my head to rid myself of those phantasms, I turned back to face the board once more. Someone had asked a detailed question, and that demanded a detailed answer. So I was writing for quite a spell. I heard the scraping noises again, but I ignored them as a figment of my fevered imagination.

Suddenly I felt something nudging against my thigh. Turning for a last time, I beheld the entire front row of boys, their faces now wreathed in open grins, and their desks, as far forward as they could go, wont to push through me and the very board itself. I was pinned - utterly penned in.

What could I do? I grinned, threw up my hands, and mockingly exclaimed, "I see that this little teaching sojourn has turned into a pressing engagement!"

And, by doing that, I had effectively turned the tables: now it was the students who felt punned out.

Pony

In the same Algebra class as Robin (see "Robin") was a sardonic fellow named Joel (again, not his real name - not that I'd have any compunction about publishing it had I remembered it!) Joel would wear a hat on which was written:

See Dick drink
See Dick drive
Don't be a Dick

So Joel had a taste for the risqué masquerading as social conscience.

One drowsy afternoon I was writing problems on the board for the students to work on in groups. There was a low, satisfying hum of activity in the class. Through that hum I heard Joel's voice from the front row:

"Say Mr. May, did you hear about that college kid who had to go to the doctor because of anal bleeding?"

I decided to deal with this one creatively. So I replied:

"You know, Joel, for some people mathematics is so exciting it almost has the effect of an aphrodisiac on them. Maybe if you work hard enough on these problems they might begin to have that effect on you!"

No luck here. Joel continued his sordid tale as if I hadn't spoken:

"So they decided to set up a secret camera in his dorm room."

I tried once more: "Joel, telling stories like this can grow hair on your palms. Then what'll people think?!"

Joel: "They found out that his roommate would drug him..."

At this point I decided to pointedly ignore Joel. After all, what thing can be worse for the incurable raconteur than a spurning audience? So I turned my back to him and gave a good imitation of indifference.

Why "imitation"? Because in truth I was by this point all ears. I had been swept up into the story of the poor student with the anal bleeding, and was eager to hear the outcome. Yet of course it would not do for me the teacher to be interested in such a low tale. So I had to feign indifference, even while my whole being quivered to hear the punch line. Which Joel offered directly:

"... and then, when he was knocked out, the roommate would ride the baloney pony."

Well, I thought I was going to lose it right there! All I could do was say to myself, "Stay calm! Keep writing as if nothing had happened! Whatever you do, don't laugh! Think about Death or something!"

The class continued; students worked math problems. I never did admonish, nevertheless punish, Joel; for I hadn't heard what he said - right?

Rob

The single most interesting student I had at Peabody High was named Rob Savoie.

I had Rob in my homeroom for three years. There, for fifteen minutes each morning before school, we would chat about whatever interested us (and that included a sizeable number of topics.) Rob carried a notebook around in which he would record, among other things, his own poems and original theorems he had devised. He was the only student I ever had who would ask such questions as, "What would it mean for an angle to have a negative number of degrees?"

Rob was also in my math classes for two years. The first year it was a medium-level geometry class. Such a class had the potential to cause disciplinary problems under normal circumstances. But this one was held in a room without windows. And so, periodically, as I was going around checking homework, someone would sneak up front and shut off the lights. This sort of thing, as you might imagine, precipitated much yelling and banging on desks and other sorts of merriment best effected under the cover of darkness. And yet, through the din, as I felt my way to the front, I could hear Rob's plaintive voice in the front row beseeching: "<u>I want to learn, Mr. May</u>!"

That year Rob won the first vest. That was a prize I gave out, in reference to the favorite part of my habiliment (I owned some 40 vests myself), to any student who achieved a perfect '100' average without benefit of a curve. There was a formal 'investiture' ceremony in class in which the vest (Rob's was a tan corduroy, as I recall) was placed on the honoree. The most interesting thing about it was that this oft-raucous class was actually quiet - that they seemed in reverence of Rob and his achievement.

The second year I had Rob for a higher level Algebra II class, and this was as different from the other as night and day (literally: there were windows in this room.) All the students were achievers, and so there were no disciplinary problems in that class - only mathematical ones.

Rob had the Department Chair, "Broderick", for Honors Precalculus his last year. I think that Broderick was jealous of Rob's attachment to me, for one day he told Rob that he wanted him to derive Hero's Formula for the class the next day. I don't think Broderick knew how arduous that task was (the proof was ten pages long.) Anyway, Rob actually prepared the derivation and was well into it in class when Broderick growled, "That's enough!" That year I was experimenting with my "Build-A-Book" geometry classes, and Rob was my greatest cheerleader.

And then Rob graduated. He went to Hampshire College - a school admirably suited to his off-beat learning style and passionate mode of inquiry.

One day during the year after Rob left, I was "teaching" (that is, attempting as usual to cut through their hostility and derision) a typical pre-algebra class. Suddenly, as if in answer to a prayer, Rob appeared at the door. It was the first time I had seen him since he had gone off to college. I noticed that he had already assumed some of the counter-cultural aspects of his school: long curly locks, and in general a decidedly bohemian air. We greeted one another warmly.

Somehow the class and I saw Rob as a worthy diversion from the failed business at hand. For, a couple of minutes later, Rob was sitting on the desk up front facing the class, he having agreed to a no-holds-barred question session.

Q (Important things first!): "Do you smoke pot?"
Rob: "Well, I'm vice president of the Cannabis Club at school! I have an official membership card (takes card from wallet) - see?"

Q (in awe): "Does that mean you can smoke pot there?"
Rob: "Yes. We can smoke in the office and other designated places."

(This established Rob's "credentials": from then on he could do and say no wrong.)

Q (Fishing for embarrassing information): "Is Mr. May gay?"
Rob: "I thought he was at first. But then I went to his house for dinner and saw that he had a wife and two daughters."

Q: "That could be a cover."
Rob (laughing): "That seems like a rather elaborate cover to me!"

Q: "You had Mr. May as a teacher?"
Rob: "Yes - twice. And for homeroom too."

Q (More fishing): "How did you like him as a teacher?"
Rob: "Mr. May was the single greatest teacher I've had anywhere!"

And so it went. Rob held forth until the end of the period. And then he left. I would like to say that the encounter with Rob changed this class's attitude toward me - that would be a suitable ending for a feel-good story. Alas, I'm afraid that, after the initial shocks wore off, things reverted back to normal: my attempts to instill even a fraction of Rob's curiosity in them, and their strange refusal to accept the possibility that they could become thinkers.

Robin

Robin was a slight, olive-skinned girl in one of my level 3 Algebra classes. She was basically a good kid, but she always had a mischievous gleam in her eye.

She had told me that she wanted to become a pharmacist, and that she was taking an Anatomy and Physiology course. "Well, that's great, Robin," I replied. "I hope you learn a lot - though not too much, if you catch my meaning!"

One day I was in my classroom waiting for the Algebra class to come in. Robin was the first to arrive. I asked her how her Anatomy class was going. "Fine," she replied. "Here's something we learned today, Mr. May: Do you know what that hole at the end of your thing is called?"

"Robin..." I began to admonish her.

But she continued unabashed: "The MEATUS."

"Robin," I could only retort in resigned humorous exasperation, "Were you born Outrageous, did you achieve Outrageousness, or have Outrageousness thrust upon you? Or was it perhaps all three?"

Funny - I can only recall a handful of names of students from my Peabody years, but Robin's is one of them.

Serpent

I got the teaching job at Winthrop in March: I was to take over from a teacher who was going on maternity leave.

So I went in during her last couple of days to observe the classes I would be teaching as well as confer with her about the students.

She was showing me her rank book, when she wrote (in ink) an 'S' by a couple of students' names. I asked her what it stood for (perhaps "superb"?) She replied: "'SNAKE': they're devious little sneaky weasels!"

She then wrote (also in ink) "PS" in front of some other names. I was at a loss as to what that could mean "'Pre-Snake"?), but she soon told me: "'POND SCUM': because they're little more than masses of quivering protoplasm lying there and doing nothing!"

Needless to say, once these classes became my own, I ignored those quaint little designations, preferring to encounter my students on our own terms. But I don't recall any students who were particularly slithery or scummy!

Stupid

The Math Chairman was a macho man who liked to swagger and to bluster and, in general, to throw his considerable weight around. In fact, I would refer to him as "Broderick", after the veteran actor who played the top cop on the "Highway Patrol" TV series in the 50's.

It was not uncommon for Broderick to walk by my room, intuit a commotion, and, sashaying in, confront a student he didn't even know with real or imagined crimes. Sometimes he would "merely" belittle the student in front of his fellows; at other times he would take the student (always male) out into the hall, place him against the wall, and then, with legs outspread and arms crossed over his chest, his face within a couple of inches of the student's, challenge him with "You got a problem, son?"

(Did Broderick, I wonder, have unresolved issues from his childhood?)

And so it was that, on one of the many days I was having trouble with a certain pre-Algebra class (see "Cheez-It" for a sample), Broderick came storming in and confronted a student, one Louie, with his (Broderick's) usual swaggering stance and verbal challenge. Today he asked, "Are you stupid, son?"

Immediately, Louie shot back a response. It flew out of his mouth in one rapid burst:

"MAYBEYUSTUPIT"

Broderick was taken aback. He had thought he had heard something heretical but he didn't know for sure. So, with just a hint of uncertainty in his voice, he asked, "What did you say?"

"ISEDYOUSAYINIMSTUDITMAYBEYUSTUPIT"

Broderick's swarthy skin blanched. This was the first time I ever saw him too paralyzed to act, and frightened in his own impotence. Finally he had to withdraw with a pathetic "You'd better watch yourself, son!"

And, although in general I found Louie to be a sneaky vicious little weasel (see "Finger"), I was definitely on his side that day!

Tribunal

While I was at Rivers, one of my advisees was ordered to appear before the Discipline Committee for having committed some sort of faux pas.

I had hardly ever encountered discipline committees in the many schools at which I've taught. In fact, the only other school

I even recall having one was the Mont Alto branch of Penn State. There I was on the Discipline Committee. (I remember but one case that we heard: it concerned a student who had apparently gotten drunk and driven his car up the sidewalk to his dorm. He had to appear before us with a person who would speak for his defense. Of course they had no real defense, as the student had been caught red-handed; so they basically threw themselves on the mercy of the "court". I remember thinking what a monumental waste of time this was for a lot of people - that the case could have been handled with quick dispatch by a single dean.)

In fact, I began to assume that the purpose of discipline committees was to intimidate the defendant through sheer force of numbers, through the ponderousness of the body confronting the miscreant. (I thought they could have an even greater effect if they were sitting on a dais arrogantly looking down on the poor defendant.) I also thought their purpose was to diffuse the verdict, so that no one person could be accused of a personal vendetta.

Anyway, my advisee at Rivers was ordered to appear before the Discipline Committee at 7:15 A.M. (I thought that perhaps they also chose to intimidate my client through this summons at an early hour. The real reason, however, was probably more practical: it was the only time when everyone on the Committee was free.) The intimidation factor was further enhanced by the Committee Chair, Tom Walsh, who had a deep booming voice.

My advisee was to meet first with the Head of the Upper School, Martha Shephardson. I gathered that the purpose of this particular meeting was for her to "soften up" the defendant before he appeared in front of the Committee. She would get him to confess his crime and then browbeat him a bit on the subject; then the Committee would only have to breathe hellfire and damnation on him to complete the session.

The problems for me were two-fold: first, that no one had bothered (or shown the courtesy) to tell me what my advisee had (allegedly) done. The second was that no one had ever told me what my role was in that proceeding - that is, why I was there in the first place. Was I there to (symbolically) hold his hand? Or to function as a sort of defense council? (If it was the latter, then the situation was - from my standpoint at least - kafkaesque, since I wasn't told what the charges were.)

So I sat there with quiet dignity, as befits those who don't know what the hell is going on. And of course my mind raced over all the probable crimes that this young fellow might have committed.

Certainly it was not murder or rape or even assault, otherwise this youth would probably be in the custody of the police. Indecent exposure? A titillating possibility to consider! What else?

Martha and I were in a room alone with the supposed miscreant. She was confronting him with his crime while I looked on. (I wondered anew: was I there to act as a witness? I could be a truthful one if he were to claim manhandling; or a false one should she slap him around a bit.)

But now she stated her accusation plainly: he had called another boy a name - a "hurtful, awful" name. Aha! That narrowed it down a bit! Good old argumentum ad hominem! (I tucked this expression into the back of my mind for possible use as defense council, knowing full well that Committee Chair Walsh was the school's Latin teacher.)

I cast my mind over the multitude of names I'd been called in my younger years. Were we talking about such prosaic possibilities as "dufus", "dweeb", "geek", "dolt", "goon", or "idiot"? But I doubted these were serious enough to warrant a hearing before the Discipline Committee.

So was it one of the more sexually suggestive names such as "douchbag", "numbnuts", "jerkoff", "dildo", or "dickhead"?

Perhaps it involved sexual identity, such as "sissy", "queer", "fairy", "homo", "queen", or "faggot?"

Or did he enter the delightful realm of ethnic slurs? Just recalling the ones my father used makes a sizeable list, of which "dego", "hunkie", "sheeny", "polock", "shine", "spic", and (he did not even spare his own ethnic group) "heinie" constitute just a few. (Lenny

Bruce would do routines wherein he repeated those sorts of words so much that his audience could not help laughing - nervously.)

Or was it something more exotic, like "narcissist"?

I was mulling over this realm of possibilities when I heard Martha say to the boy, "I mean, what were you thinking when you called that fellow a 'fudgepacker'?"

Well, I practically fell off my chair! I had never heard that expression before. And my reaction was similar to the one I had had when the minister of a church at which I was playing offered a prayer for "those caught up in the grips of masturbation." In short, it conjured up a certain image in my mind. I had to turn away and try as best I could to keep my body from shaking.

Did I realize how "hurtful and awful" that name was? Of course I did. But somehow the combining of two ordinary everyday words into one super-charged one was too funny.

I managed to compose myself enough to turn and face them again. And I was even able to simulate a look of disapproval.

What was the punishment meted out? Probably a stern warning and a period of probation. As for myself, I never exchanged a word with anyone that morning. I guess I was merely there to be advised that my advisee was a real shmuck.

Ups & Downs

I wanted to tell another horror story from my teaching at Peabody High.

One day toward the end of the period when an Algebra II class was starting work on the homework, two big fellows suddenly stood up. I knew that they were both football players, though I'd never been to a game. Both of those guys, like true jocks, were suitably attired in sweat pants.

They stood silently facing one another. One of them (who I knew to be fairly bright) seemed to be acting the part of the doofus: dumb, panting, even drooling. I gathered that he was impersonating the faithful dog; or perhaps a goofy guy who just wanted to be the other guy's friend.

I know that I should have asked them what they were doing, standing up like that in the middle of class when they should have been working. But – shall I confess? – I found myself caught up in the doofus act. I was the victim of a natural human curiosity: what could this mean?

I soon found out. The "straight" fellow pointed up in the air. Obediently, the goofy guy looked up. Curious, I raised my eyes as well. But all I saw was the ceiling.

When I looked down again, I was horrified to see the goofy guy's pants around his ankles. Apparently the other fellow had yanked them down in a flash while the goofball was dutifully looking up. He had completely fooled the poor doofus! (Indeed, the pathetic fellow stood there looking down, scratching his head as if to say, "Now I wonder how <u>that</u> happened?")

But of course in another moment the truth hit me: <u>I</u> was the one who had been fooled; <u>I</u> myself was the fall guy. <u>I</u> was the doofus.

(I was just grateful that the "goofy" guy was still wearing a pair of boxers!)

I don't recall the outcome of that little incident - I think the bell rang at the climax. But it is a good example of the sorts of things that happened when I taught in a room that wasn't my own: the kids had nothing to look at apart from me except one another. And, as the above shows, sometimes what they saw was artfully staged!

Watching My Back

I once had a pre-algebra class at Peabody High that was so bad, so malignant, that it made all the other pre-algebra classes I'd taught seem like paragons of virtue by comparison.

This class had some students from the Vocational School. These kids would take their technical courses down there in the morning, and then come up to the high school for their academic courses in the afternoon.

It was easy to see how they might feel like second-class citizens at the high school. And they acted out their frustration and rage in my class.

One day I thought I saw a way for them to be useful and productive. The telephone in my classroom wasn't working. The Voc students told me that they had had instruction in phone repair, and that they could fix it for me. So I trustingly handed over the phone to them.

They took it all apart, and then just left it that way. (Of course they claimed they couldn't fix it after all.)

After that things only got worse. The climax came when a couple of them began shooting thick U-shaped pieces of insulated wire at me when my back was turned. I actually began to fear for my physical health. But the two students only shot at me when I wasn't watching; so I could never catch them in the act.

In desperation, I began casting about for someone to help me.

That year I shared cafeteria study with another math teacher named Earle Nason. The kids there actually did study, so Earle and I had a lot of time to talk. Earle did most of the talking, while I egged him on.

He had lived all his life in the seaport town of Gloucester. (At this time he was fifty, divorced and living in a motel room.) He would spin endless tales of adventures he'd had in his hometown, which included bar brawls with sailors. The interesting thing about his stories was that many of them did not end in his favor - far from it; some had no resolution at all. (What Earle needed was an amanuensis to write his stories down for him. I would kid him about making another "Winesburg, Ohio".)

Did we talk about mathematics? Never! When he wasn't telling tales of youthful adventures, Earle was flaunting his own prodigious sexual appetite. He bragged that he had three times the normal amount of testosterone, and that he and his girlfriend would have sex four times per week (The poor woman! I thought.) He showed me a little notebook he would carry around: it contained a record of every sexual encounter he'd had since he was fourteen. There were a number of itemized columns which he'd check off. I saw thousands upon thousands of neat little checks in the book.

(I didn't bother showing him the notebook I carried around with me - I was using it to write my opera libretto.)

I learned a lot of other miscellaneous things about Earle. For example, he had organized a summer softball team wherein all the other members were in their 20's. The team was called "The Dukes of Earle". He deliberately wore short-sleeved shirts to show off his bulging muscles. (Needless to say, he had no discipline problems in his classes.)

It seemed like Earle Nason might be just the person I needed.

I decided to tell Earle of my plight in the pre-algebra class. I would have been too embarrassed to tell virtually any other teacher; but I surmised - correctly - that, opposites though we were, Earle and I had developed a rapport. Besides, I knew he'd relish a tale about violence and feel challenged to do something about it.

It turned out that Earle had a free period at the time my class met - or so at least I assumed. So we agreed that he would come in and sit in the back behind the offending students, reasoning that his mere presence would act as a deterrent.

We were wrong. Brazenly, defiantly, a student shot at me as soon as my back was turned. Earle immediately collared the offender and led him out of the room. The student received a five-day suspension. Soon the other student was similarly caught and punished. Our 'method' was working!

But then, only a couple of days later, I was approached by my department chair, 'Broderick', who told me that he didn't want Earle doing that any more. I asked why, but he wouldn't tell me. I wondered whether Earle had had a class that period after all and had just left them alone to help me (yes, he would do such a thing)? Or was it the macho 'Broderick' and his belief that every teacher should be able to solve their own problems by themselves?

Whatever. I don't recall any more dangerous incidents in that class. So perhaps the suspensions - and one dose of Earle Nason - worked!

Winking at Success

During the three years that I taught at The Rivers School, there were a handful of African-American students there. By far the most interesting of these was named Evan Burroughs.

I'm afraid that Evan fit the stereotypes for his race. He was an excellent jazz musician (I once heard a superb piece he had written for the Jazz Band); and he was the star of the school basketball team (he made over 1000 points while at Rivers.) He was also an indifferent student academically. Oh yes, he made a few stabs at studying; but his heart just wasn't in it.

Evan was in my geometry class during my first year at Rivers. That was when I started having trouble walking -- and my classes were in far-flung buildings (the school eventually moved my room.) Even standing up and writing on the board was difficult, so that my whole way of teaching was being called into question.

At the same time I was under some misguided assumptions about what kind of behavior to expect from private school students. I assumed that all of them would be docile and obedient out of the fear that bad behavior would get them thrown out into the public schools. I found out soon enough how wrong I was.

One bit of subterfuge that Evan and at least one other student would use was to ask to go to the bathroom, and then not return for the rest of the period. A combination of my concern with my own physical problems and a fuzziness about the rules there (though you would think that not returning to class would constitute a violation of a universal rule for schools!) resulted in my missing those infractions. So I'm afraid that Evan received neither a good geometry education nor a respect for my disciplinary skills.

I had Evan in my Topics class two years later, and everything was different. By that time, I knew my students and I knew what the rules were. I had also taught the same course the previous year: it was my one success story, as I had used the material to develop a student-centered classroom free unhindered by my limited physical skills.

So when Evan tried his little trick of asking to use the restroom and then not returning, I immediately turned him in for detention. He was soon cured of that peccadillo!

But he was dramatically resourceful. It was not infrequent that Evan would be the first one to my class when the period was starting. He would come up to me and throw his arms around me and bury his head against my chest in a big long silent bear hug. The first few times this happened, I would say to myself in wondrous disbelief: "He loves me after all!" But then a doubt began to steal over me. And sure enough -- it turned out, incredible as it may seem, that Evan had not done the homework due that day.

I was the basketball timer for the men's team in my third year at Rivers, and so I got to see Evan's skills on the court close up. He really was as awesome as people said he was even though he stood well under 6 feet tall.

One afternoon I got to the Fieldhouse early in order to set up my timing apparatus. The team was busy running through some drills shooting baskets and the like. One time as he ran by me, Evan casually dropped a sheaf of papers on my table. I picked it up and looked at it: it was the latest project for our Topics class. I had to marvel at the dramatic flair, the aplomb of the man in carrying off this graceful and humorous gesture -- something which was only diminished a bit by the fact that the project was several days overdue.

It was near the end of the men's championship basketball game that I saw Evan's true nature.

Rivers was down by one point and had possession of the ball. There were nine seconds left to play in the match.

The Fieldhouse was in pandemonium. People were screaming and stamping their feet. Players were melting down. Evan was inbounding the ball, and it happened to be right in front of my table.

Just before he threw out the ball Evan turned around, looked directly and deliberately at me -- and winked.

Do you see? Everyone else was playing their own role as spectator, player, timer or coach. But, uniquely, Evan was above all of that: he was playing a meta-role wherein he saw himself as part of an absurdist drama in which he had the central part.

More than any other student, Evan could be both endearing and exasperating at the same time. He is also the only student from Rivers whose name I still recall.

(8 July 2008)

World Series

The account below is an exception to most of the discipline tales, in that the setting was not Peabody ("Puberty") High School.

In the Fall of 1975 I was desperately in need of a teaching position. But college jobs, hitherto my bailiwick, were now closed to me due to their requirement of a doctorate. And I had not yet gone back to obtain my certification to teach in the public schools. (I do not recall looking at private schools.)

So I put my name in as a substitute teacher in the Arlington (the town in which we lived) MA Public Schools.

Now it is crucial to this story to recall that, at the time this tale takes place, the Red Sox were playing the Cincinnati Reds in the World Series. So nearly everyone was glued to their TV set. Dorothy and I were among the few exceptions, for we had just moved to Boston a couple of years before and so we had not yet been bitten by the Red Sox bug.

I was called as a substitute in a middle school science class.

Science was a subject I was not qualified to teach, while middle school was not a level at which I had teaching experience. Mix these two together, add the catalyst of an open classroom design - and you have a potentially explosive substance!

The substance did so explode. With my laid-back (which is to say nonexistent) discipline "methods" in force, the kids were running randomly rampant (or was it "amorally amok"?) about the room. As one energetic youngster ran by me, I heard him fleetingly ask, "So what did you think of the game last night?"

Distracted as I was, I only half heard him. So I said:

"WHAT GAME?"

Every student in the room froze in position. They became utterly (or is it "unutterly"?) silent, as my interlocutor continued:

"You know - the Baseball Game!"

I don't know what happened, but I had one of those moments of - fiendish inspiration. For I asked:

"WHAT'S BASEBALL?"

At that point, all those frozen students began to move again, but this time slowly and silently to take their seats.

And, as my questioner began to explain: "Well, you see, there are four bag-like things called 'bases', and then a wooden stick called a 'bat' which you use to hit a special ball called a 'baseball'...", the other students engaged themselves in a low-key debate over what country I might be from.

And that sufficed for that science class on that particular day!

Humoresques

An Accident

I was driving our new Taurus home late one night many years ago from the Rosebud Café (my favorite bar in Somerville where I went each evening to smoke and drink wine and write.) It had been raining a bit. As I drove up College Avenue near Tufts, a beat-up old Datsun pulled out in front of me very slowly from a side street. I plowed into the rear section of that car, totally decimating the fender with a humungous dent. When I inspected my own damage, I saw that my bumper had absorbed the impact; the only damage was that the left light fixture had popped out unbroken. The other fellow got out of his car.

Below is a transcription (as accurate as I can recall it) of our conversation in the wake of the accident. He, like me, was (so he told me) a teacher of some sort. As a result, the reader will notice a certain - *restraint* - in the exchanges which would probably have been missing had two members of the working class been involved (I call it *hyper-civilized*.) I have embellished the conversation with some added lines; but the essential tone is the same as it was that night.

Him: "Well, if you will pay me right now for my damages, then we can be on our ways to our respective homes and hearths."

Me: "I am curious as to why I should pay you."

Him: "Because you were the one who hit me. I believe it is common knowledge that the hitter is at fault and is thus obliged to pay the so-called hittee."

Me: "Well, there may be other criteria for determining who is at fault besides who hit whom."

Him: "Such as?" (Nice grammar, by the way!)

Me: "Thank you. Such as, that I was driving on a main

thoroughfare, whereas you were entering from a side street. Ergo, I had what is quaintly known as The Right Of Way."

Him: "Actually, that would be true if another fact did not possibly trump your card."

Me: "And what would that metaphorical fact be?"

Him: "Is it possible that you were driving too fast for the conditions?"

Me (seriously pondering): "I think that I was driving entirely appropriately for the conditions. I never speed here on College Avenue because there are often students crossing. Then, too, whenever it is raining, I try to cut my speed back by an additional ten miles per hour or so."

Him: "So you don't think it possible that you bent your own rules a little bit and were speeding just a *mite* too much?"

Me: "I sincerely don't think so. Besides, all speeds are relative."

Him (yawning): "Is this to be a lecture on Einstein?"

Me: "No, don't worry! But it seems to me that you might have pulled out a *smitch* too slowly from that side street there."

Him: "Perhaps only because you were traveling too quickly: as you have said, all speeds are relative (do you like how I turn your own argument back on you?)"

Me: "No (although objectively I admire your wit!) Yes, that seems to be a tossup. However, you also cannot forget that there is a further thing to consider here *vis a vis* your behavior."

Him: "Oh dear, not something else! This is becoming a veritable labyrinth of *quid pro quos*!"

Me: "Sorry, but yes. I hate to point this out to you when your arguments seem to be going so well, but didn't you have what is known as a Stop Sign over there?"

Him: "I don't know - I suppose I might have. Or not - what's the difference (as if I didn't know)?"

Me: "The difference is Fundamental and Profound, as you ought to know. The Stop Sign is one of the most Basic Bedrocks in the Sizable Canon called Rules Of The Road, and..."

Him (interrupting): "Goodness gracious, you're not going to get *pedantic* on me, are you? I always found that so boring in school!"

Me (blushes): "Sorry - I forgot myself there for a moment. I'll try not to let it happen again."

Him (relieved): "Thank you. I hope you're not that way in your classroom."

Me: "Of <u>course</u> I am! But, pedantics aside, you must admit that this Stop Sign-business throws a bit of a monkey wrench into the machinery of your argument..."

Him: "Ouch - now <u>you're</u> tossing in the metaphors! But I have a defense which <u>must</u> be acceptable to you."

Me: "Which is..."

Him: "...your own! You said that speeds are relative? Well, so are *distances*! It is true that I must come to a complete stop and yield to you if I have a Stop Sign. But yield to you when you are <u>where</u>? The Driver's Manual doesn't say; but the implication is: when you are sufficiently close. But how close is *sufficiently* close? For example, is a mile away 'sufficiently close'? Of course not! If you are a mile away, it would fairly be judged that I did not pull out 'in front of you' - since you are nowhere to be seen. So you can see my dilemma: How close is <u>too</u> close? I must estimate not only your speed but your distance as well, and do a quick speed-to-distance ratio calculation. That's not easy."

Me: "Obviously not - it seems to have failed you rather spectacularly in this case."

Him: "I still think it's all a matter of relatives..."

Me:" ...you mean like my father?"

Him: "Ouch - if that's a *segue,* it's a terribly crude one."

Me: "Well, it allows me to bolster my case with an example.

It was my father who erred in a way similar to how you have erred (sorry - *allegedly* erred) tonight: he turned our 1950 Kaiser in front of an oncoming car (and on a wet road much like this.) I know this scenario too well since I was in the passenger seat."

Him: "Did they hit your door? Perhaps the accident caused some brain-damage, which explains your confused mental state here."

Me (laughs): "No - our car was hit in the rear fender, same as yours. But with much less dramatic effect: obviously a Kaiser could withstand such a blow much better than a tin-box such as yours."

Him: "I will ignore your aspersions on my vehicle and ask: don't you defend your father - and hence me - in this case?"

Me: "No - I knew from the beginning that my father was in the wrong: he had turned in front of the other car with a maddeningly slow nonchalance - something of the sort you seem to have exhibited here tonight."

Him: "My goodness - comparing me with your father! Should I be flattered?"

Me: "Hardly. He blustered about taking the other driver to court, and he talked of having me testify for him. I was terrified, because, even at the age of eight, I understood that I would either have to commit perjury, or betray my father's trust in me. Can you even begin to understand such a dilemma?"

Him: "No wonder you're confused. So which did you do - tell a lie, or play the Oedipal role?"

Me: "Neither: thankfully, there was never any trial."

Him (sighs): "Too bad. But you are still trying to fight your father, and I am the latest scapegoat..."

Me: "Don't flatter yourself: believe me, my problems with my father are in a whole league of their own. Besides, that's not the only accident like this one that I've been involved in..."

Him (looking at his watch): "Gee, I'd love to hear your entire autobiography, but the evening is wearing on and my warm dry bed beckons."

Me: "Don't worry, this won't take long - and it is of sociological interest."

Him (frightened): "Egads, the worst!"

Me (ignoring his protest): "I was driving home from South Carolina in my Corvair..."

Him: "Speaking of tin-boxes!"

Me (defensive): "It was a cute little sporty runabout, loads of fun to drive! And was it my fault that it was judged to be Unsafe At Any Speed?"

Him: "No, it was Ralph Nader's fault - he's always been a spoiler."

Me: "For once we agree on something. But on to my story: it was a cold day in January and, strangely, it was drizzling just like this. I was on Route 1, and someone pulled out of a side road in front of me very slowly, just as you did here."

Him: "And was he or she as erudite as I am?"

Me: "If you meant to say 'troglodyte', the answer is no. There were four older black men in the car out for a Sunday drive. I hydroplaned on the wet road. You know how it feels in a movie when you see a crash about to happen, but you the viewer are left untouched? Well, I felt that way. And then my car slammed into them, my face hit the steering wheel, and a huge gash opened in my lip. There was blood all over the place!"

Him: "Tsk tsk, not wearing a seat belt eh?"

Me: "Actually, I was. But in those days (it was 1966) there were no shoulder harnesses."

Him: "Thank goodness you were wearing one tonight! I would hate there to be any more damage to that pretty face."

Me: "Yes, well back then this even prettier (since younger) face had to be stitched up. But I was most worried about getting the insurance settled with the offenders. And then a strange thing happened: an older man took me under his wing."

Him: "Egads - the plot thickens!"

Me: "No, it wasn't that. He apparently was eager to show me how the white folk down there in South Carolina dealt with the black folk in a so-called *civilized* way. It was most instructive."

Him: "I hope no one was lynched."

Me: "No, fortunately. He didn't even use the N-word (though I heard it a lot in town that morning) - it was much more subtle than that."

Him: "I'd always assumed that the South was as subtle as a sledgehammer."

Me: "So did I. But this was as subtle as the 'b' in 'subtle'. The man took me out to the black driver's house in the pine barrens. It was in reality a one-room cabin up on stilts. The inside was whitewashed and only had a few pieces of furniture - a bed, a dresser, a chair. But what I recall most vividly was a pungent smell, the likes of which I've never experienced before or since."

Him: "From burning pine wood?"

Me: "Perhaps. Anyway, my Great White Knight spoke quietly to the black fellow about, I assume, finding his insurance papers - there were never any shouts or threats. All the while I watched the black man and his wife: they were quiet and deferential and respectful. A little too respectful - I would use the words *frozen in fear* to describe their demeanor. In fact, I would say that this was the most effective exercise in *intimidation* I've ever seen, so subtle and quiet was it. And all that happened was that two white men had walked into the home of a black man and his wife."

Him: "So your sympathies were most emphatically with the black couple?"

Me: "Yes - I felt deeply for them."

Him: "Well, then, between your sympathies and the History of the Civil Rights Movement, can't you cut me a little slack here tonight?"

Me: "My sympathies and the Civil Rights Movement didn't

stop me from wanting my cohort to succeed at getting that insurance information!"

Him: "Always the pragmatist eh?"

Me: "Most emphatically. So are you convinced of your guilt yet?"

Him: "Of course not!"

Me: "So you think we are in a stalemate here?"

Him: "It appears so."

Me: "Maybe we need a fair, impartial arbiter..."

Him: "Sounds good. Whom might you have in mind as this arbiter?"

Me: "Well, why don't we just call the Police."

Him (suddenly agitated): "No! No! Let's not be hasty here!"

Me (as my interlocutor gets into his car to flee): "Then, like the Monty Pythons, are we going to have to call this a Draw?"

Him (yells out the window as he pulls away): "No! My insurance company will be contacting your insurance company!"

Me (forlornly, calling after him): "But we haven't exchanged any information!"

Ball Boy Tells All

I wanted to talk about my life as a ball boy. Oh -- if you think that this is going to be the Catcher in the Rye where a kid is trying to find meaning in his life or any of that crap, you can stop right here. This is the story of a ball boy, pure and simple.

I suppose you're the kind that wants a name for the narrator. So call me Joey if you like, though you can bet that's not my real name. I work for a major league ball team. You can ask me until you're blue in the face, and I won't say the name of that team neither.

I'm 11 years old, and my dad tells me I can have this job next year too if my voice hasn't changed by then. You see, they want kids doing this to really look and sound like kids. I suppose I look like a typical 11 year old; I even have freckles (they seem to like that kind of stuff.)

The reason I got this job is, my dad is good friends with the Vice President for Baseball Operations. They went to school together or something.

Each ball park has its own ball boy. Unfortunately, this means that I don't go to the away games. That's okay though: there are 81 games at home in a season, and for our team a lot of these are day games. This means that I get out of school early on those days in April, May, June and September -- sometimes by 11 a.m., which is fine with me. School is pretty boring anyway.

I just want to make clear what I'm talking about when I use the term ball boy. I'm not talking about those tennis ball boys, who crouch on either side and scoot across and pick up balls when they hit the net. That's strictly little-kid stuff. You have no control over any of the tennis balls, so what's the use?

I'm also not talking about those kids who stand down the first- and third-base lines during a baseball game and snag ground balls when they're hit foul. Some of them are even girls! They feel really good about themselves because, after they scoop up a ball, they get this big stupid smile on their faces as they bobble over to some kid in the front row and present them with the ball, as if it's the crown jewels, and the kid loves them for it like it's Christmas or something. That kinda stuff makes me feel like throwing up. I mean, what kinda job is that? I wouldn't do that even if you paid me a heck of a lot more than I'm making now.

No, I'm the kid who brings exactly five new balls out to the home-plate umpire whenever he runs out of balls in his pouch.

People talk about going to college and learning stuff that they can use to get a job when they get out. Well, I learned to be a ball boy, and it weren't by going to no college neither. When I was about three my dad told me I could be a ball boy when I got bigger but I'd have to practice at it.

So I started training with my dad as my coach when I was still very little. And the first thing he taught me was how to move. "Son," he would say, "Ya can't just run out there! Running means speed -- that you want to get some place as quickly as possible. But that ain't baseball! Baseball is a *leisurely* sport, as you can see from all the players standing around out on the field. So you have to learn how to *scamper*. Scampering says that you're not in a big hurry." When I asked him how fast that was, he said, "Somewhere between a saunter and a trot. Let your whole body slouch and take quick small steps. Whatever you do, avoid big strides!"

So I practiced scampering while he watched. Later he would have me do it casually just to check up on me. He'd say stuff like, "Why don't you scamper out to the street and bring me back the newspaper" -- stuff like that.

Once I learned all that, he would pace off 30 feet. And then I would scamper that distance with five cherry tomatoes in my hands, hand them to my father, and then scamper the 30 feet back. Later, when I got to be five or six, I would do it with golf balls. In this way, I worked up to the real thing. I was scampering with five baseballs by the time I was eight or nine.

I also practiced with sacks of potatoes. You see, the baseballs are delivered to the ballpark in sacks of 60 or so balls. When I run out of baseballs I go over to the stack of sacks, take one, carry it over to my workplace, cut it open, and dump it into my Ball Bin. That's why, when I was still a little kid, my father would have me carry sacks of potatoes around on my shoulder. My mother accused him of child abuse, but my father answered, "Look, would you let me handle the kid? I know what I'm doing!" Just between you and me, it was a little hard carrying those sacks. But it trained me to do the job, so who am I to complain?

But the hardest part was not the physical workouts but the math -- you know, mental stuff. For one thing, my father had me practice counting up to five from the day I was born, or something. That was bad enough. But when I was about four, he began giving me problems like: "An umpire has five balls in his sack. Two of the balls are fouled out of play. How many balls does he have left?"

That's subtraction, which is higher math for a four-year-old! Lucky for me, my father was a natural born teacher (at least that's what my mom said.) So he said he was starting me with concrete, though we were only using the five cherry tomatoes (I even got to eat the two tomatoes I was taking away.) When I mastered that, he had me using one of my hands. (He would say, "Son, that's why we have five fingers on each hand!" My father knows a lot of cool stuff like that.) Finally I began to do those kinds of problems in my head -- and I was still only four years old. Boy but that was tough!

The reason I have to bring new balls out to the umpire is that the old ones keep disappearing. Home runs are smacked out or balls are fouled off into the stands. When that kind of stuff happens, I have to be very attentive and count how many balls have been used up. Because when the umpire throws out the fifth ball, I know it's time for me to bring him more. Sometimes one batter will foul off 10 or 12 pitches. There's one umpire who would say to me when I brought him out fresh balls for the third time, "We're hemorrhaging balls, kid!"

Balls also get dirty on occasion.

When a ball is pitched in the dirt, you'd think the end of the world had come! The umpire has to look at it and examine it through a microscope to see whether it had bucolic plague or something. Because everybody knows what can be done with a dirty ball. If a pitcher normally has four or five pitches at his disposal, he can increase that to about 37 or something with a smudged ball.

So that ball has to be removed from the game immediately. The umpire throws it over to me, I catch it and put it into the Bad Ball Bin. Eventually those used balls are given to poor kids who play baseball with broomstick handles on crummy lots full of trash.

Occasionally, a pitcher will sidle over to me all nervous and look around to make sure no one is listening. He talks low and mysterious-like out of the corner of his mouth -- just like in the movies (he even puts the back of his hand there.) He says, "How would you like to earn a few extra perks, kid?" When they ask me that question. I know exactly what they're talking about. They want me to "fix" a ball for them.

I know what each of the pitchers like. One guy likes me to cut a couple of the stitches for him (I do that with a box cutter.) Another one likes me to put a nice crimp in the rawhide (I do that with my grandad's hedge trimmer.) Once I cut through the cover of a ball by mistake. That would have been a tremendously stupendous ball to pitch! Unfortunately, the ump saw it and threw the ball away. But he just assumed it was a defective ball from Haiti, or wherever they're made.

But my favorite is the spit ball. And I mean this for real. I don't just get the ball wet, I actually spit on it. And not just a little spit neither -- I drop a good thick gob on the ball! I rub some of it in, but I make sure there's still some spit showing so the pitcher knows I'm giving him the real McCoy. One pitcher, who I won't mention, once threw a no-hitter with my spit balls.

Naturally I make sure I'm not chewing tobacco on the days I make spit balls.

Of course I have to be able to sneak all this stuff past the umpire, but actually that's not too hard. For one thing, those guys are more worried about the batter getting mad at them because they called a ball a strike. So I know I can bring out a fixed ball when the biggest batter is up. The umps also worry about whether their arm is strong enough to reach the pitcher when they throw out a fresh ball. In other words, their biggest fear is that people will think they're wimps (which they are.) So I found that, while they're worrying about looking bad, I can slip an occasional fixed ball right by them and they never notice.

When the pitcher gets one of my fixed balls, he thanks me by glancing slyly over in my direction and giving me a broad wink. He also pats himself on the bottom, as if his wallet were there, to reassure me that he would indeed "pay" me.

You may wonder what the pitcher meant when he said, "Wanna earn some perks, kid?" Well, a couple of the pitchers adopted me as the sort of mascot. When we have a good series against another team (thanks in no small part to my fixed balls), it's natural to want to go out and celebrate. They take me to the back room of some kinda private club, the kind for rich people who like to hang out with each other in places with dark wood and cloth napkins and that sorta stuff. They give me steaks and beer just like I was a grown-up or something. Once I had three beers and I almost got sick but didn't. I was pretty drunk though! My old man said to me, "You can drink as long as you don't drive!" He can be pretty funny sometimes, my dad.

But the best perks come after I do the injections. I started doing those when a couple of players (actually three) came up to me in secret and asked if I would like to do something "very hush-hush for huge perks." They said that they needed injections, but that no one else could do them but me because I was, as they put it, 'beyond suspicion' (whatever that means.) They told me that I would find the needles in my locker when they needed it done.

Well, that really made me nervous! I mean, I never handled no needles before -- I thought only doctors did that kinda stuff. And then the idea that I would have to stick it into somebody made me feel like fainting. I would break into a cold sweat just thinking about it.

So the players let me practice by sticking it into their arms without injecting anything. The first time I did it, I just wanted to get rid of the needle as soon as I could, so I threw it like a dart but it bounced off the arm onto the floor. That made them mad -- they were saying it was valuable stuff and all that. So I learned to sort of toss it at the arm without letting go.

But that wasn't the gross part. I found out that I was going to have to inject it into their butts. I said I would try it but when the time came, the sight of that big white butt almost made me want to puke, I swear to god! The only thing that finally made me able to do it was that the player would only pull his pants down a little way so that I didn't really see much of his butt. But it was still pretty gross.

But the perks made it worthwhile, I can tell you that! We would go to one of the player's houses and smoke. (He'd say, "Hey kid, let's do a joint at my joint." Very funny!) I'd smoked cigarettes a couple of times when a friend of mine stole some from his parents. But that had just made me feel a little woozy. And as I said before, getting drunk just made me feel sick and groggy.

With the joint, though, it was totally different. I got this incredible high where I felt terrific and at peace with the world and not caring a fig about nothing. It was awesome! After that first time, you can bet I was willing to give injections, the more the merrier, and in the whole white butt to boot!

But I had to promise like I was swearing on a million Bibles that I wouldn't tell no one -- not even my father -- about any of this stuff. They said to me, "It's really hush-hush, kid -- we know you wouldn't want to get nobody in trouble, would you. And you certainly wouldn't want those perks to end." No sir, I certainly wouldn't!

Well, that's pretty much it, the life of what I'd call a typical ball boy. I'm sure you'll agree that it ain't a bad job to have when you're 11 years old!

<u>Voice through a microphone</u>: "Well, I think that'll be enough for today. Thank you sir -- your testimony before the House Subcommittee on the Use and Abuse of Minors in Major League Baseball has been most enlightening, even if you have apparently decided to effectively take the Fifth Amendment against self-incrimination by keeping players and teams and even your own identity a secret. But tomorrow is, as they say, another day, isn't it, Mr. er..."

"Joey. Just call me Joey okay? Joey."

(5 July 2008)

Baseball

As a boy, I enjoyed playing sports *informally*. But with one exception, I never sought to join a school-sanctioned team. After all, playing interscholastic sports took time after school -- precious time

I needed to practice the organ (the church was a nice walk from the high school down to the other end of Fairview Avenue.)

But I decided to go out for baseball in my junior year of high school. Now why did I do such a thing? Did I enjoy playing the game? Of course. Did I want to get off on the bond of a common noble endeavor with my teammates? To be sure.

But the major reason was the uniform. I yearned to wear that thick flannel in the hot sun! I craved to be seen in those baggy knickers and those long stockings! I fervently wished to course the outfield grass with those black spiked shoes! Here was a costume which only lacked a powdered wig and some lace to complete the look of an 18th century country gentleman.

The trouble was, I had one perennial problem as a youngster: as I was pale and neurasthenic, I was always more coordinated, more adept at a sport than my physique suggested. This caused me to be chosen last (if at all) for teams -- which then would usually be pleasantly surprised at my true skills.

My appearance notwithstanding, I did get on the junior varsity baseball team. (I now wonder whether anyone was rejected? I don't think so: in a perversion of the Groucho Marx quote, any sports organization which would take me would take anyone.) There was only one problem: there were 16 players on the team, but only 15 uniforms available.

I was told that I was the one who would have to go without a uniform.

At that point, I probably should have quit. In retrospect I suppose this was Coach Woody Litweiler's backhanded way of getting me to leave. Yet, as far as I can recall, neither thought occurred to me until this moment of writing 45 years later. For some strange reason ("strange" because of why I went out to begin with) I stuck with it.

It wasn't easy. Fifteen of our players came to the plate arrayed as baseball players. I was the only one to step up dressed in chinos and a sports shirt. Needless to say, I felt I stood out. Fortunately, a bit into the season Don Cereface, a friend on the varsity, heard of my plight and loaned me a uniform from a summer league he had played in. And so I wore a baseball uniform after all.

Even the fact that its colors were blue and gold, whereas our team uniforms were maroon and gray, didn't really matter too much.

One reason it didn't really matter was because Coach Litweiler almost never played me. I was put up to pinch hit exactly four times that season.

I have said that teams who chose me last were usually pleasantly surprised by my prowess. But it is difficult to demonstrate one's prowess if one is almost never played.

Well, how did I do? Four at-bats don't provide a very good sampling. As John Updike said, "Baseball is a game of the long season, of relentless and gradual averaging-out." I did not have this advantage; my season was brutally short.

Of the four at-bats, three resulted in outs -- whether strikeouts or ground-outs or fly-outs, I do not recall. But the fourth! The ball went between the shortstop's legs. Was it an error on his part? I prefer not to think so, for to score it that way would result in an abysmally low batting average. So I made the assumption that my ball was so viciously hit that no shortstop could have handled it.

That would give me a hit, and I would thus end the season with a .250 average. That's not bad for a third-string player!

Oh yes -- there was one time when I showed my true prowess. During a batting practice, I hit everything thrown to me over the fence. My fellow players were exclaiming in disbelief.

Unfortunately for me, Coach Litweiler was at a meeting that afternoon, and thus missed my handiwork.

And how was I as a fielder? Well, it seems I was serious enough about that role, that I had my father buy me a new glove. And that glove -- and my reputation -- received the ultimate test the one time I was playing center field. It was the ninth inning; there were two outs and two men on base; and our team was ahead by two runs.

The batter hit a huge towering fly ball to deep left-center field.

I took off like a shot and ran as fast as I could after the ball. It was a similar sort of situation that Mickey Mantle faced in that 1956 World Series game, when he had to run down a long Gil Hodges line drive to deep left center: by catching that ball he saved Don Larson's perfect game. And so likewise did I just reach this ball. I put up my glove and the ball landed gracefully in it.

And then it immediately bounced out. For my glove, being new, wasn't broken in.

Since there were two outs, everyone was running on the pitch. And the hit was so long and deep that, by the time I could retrieve the ball and throw it in, the batter was able to score as well. So we lost the game by a run.

Mercifully, the baseball season -- and my school-sanctioned sports career -- ended shortly after that game. But I did go on to become a pretty decent organist!

The Belt Story

(NB: The author has found that this story works excellently as a performance piece, wherein every nuance (the teeth of that zipper!) is drawn out *ad nauseum*. The following represents an attempt to capture the gist of this in print form.)

One summer at Silver Bay on Lake George, where we vacationed each year, I had to stay an extra day for some reason after my family left. I was assigned the back room of Spruce Mountain Lodge to sleep in that night. This was a quirky corner room with windows hinged at the top, and one pull-cord light in the middle of the ceiling. That ceiling was sloped, which gave the room a cozy, hut-like feeling. One entered the room by stepping up two steps. It was next to the back door, making it easy to get to after late night sojourns.

The room had two beds. The other bed was to be occupied by my adolescent nephew, Todd.

After dinner that night, Todd and I discussed our plans for the evening. He knew about my regimen, since I did the same thing every night: at around 9:30 P.M. I would walk down the road to

The Hearth, a local tavern, where I would drink burgundy wine and smoke and write. I told Todd that I would not be getting in until around 1:00 A.M. "Well," he replied, "I'll be long in bed and asleep by then - there isn't much for me to do here at night."

I knew what he was talking about. A precocious fellow, he had little use for what passed for nocturnal adolescent emissions up there:

A: "So wadda you wanna do?"

B: "I dunno. Wadda you wanna do?"

A: "I dunno. Do you wanna get some beer?"

B: "I dunno. Do you?"

A: "I dunno."

B: "So wadda you wanna do?"

A: "I dunno."

Todd was more apt to "wanna" chat about a Shakespeare play or exuberantly sing all the parts of a Gilbert & Sullivan operetta. But I knew he wouldn't find any takers.

I noticed it was a dark moonless night as I walked back from The Hearth. Someone had turned off the outside lights at the Lodge, so I had to use my flashlight to locate the back door. I entered the building noiselessly and found my way to the steps at the threshold of our room.

And then the formidableness of what I needed to do hit me. For it seemed that I was going to have to enter that room and then undress and get into bed - all without waking Todd.

How difficult, I wondered, would that be?

It is well known that most adolescents sleep long and deeply. Once they doze off, it is virtually impossible to awaken them. I had known an adolescent who refused to wake up even while a whole series of fireworks exploded in his room. There was also the case of one who was not awakened by a huge meteorite crashing through the roof of her bedroom. But perhaps the most extreme example was the famous Wabash Cannonball express train which, on a track proximate to a house, derailed and went smashing through the house, basically destroying it. By some miracle, an adolescent sleeping in the house was left unharmed - and was still sleeping soundly after the train had passed!

Less well known, however, and far rarer, is the opposite syndrome - that of the *ultra-sensitive* adolescent. This sort of individual wakes up at the slightest hint of stimuli. A mere sliver of light will bring them to wide-eyed confusion; a pin dropped onto a rug (never mind a floor!) will have them sitting bolt upright.

My instincts told me immediately that my nephew was the ultra-sensitive kind of adolescent.

Thus by definition I could never be too quiet. I decided to pose not waking up Todd as a *challenge* to myself. In fact, I made it a point of personal *honour*, and swore an *oath* thus: 'I regard Todd's sleep as sacrosanct, and I will do <u>whatever it takes</u> to keep him in that sacrosanct state!'

The room was pitch-black; all I knew was that our beds were at right angles to one another, the heads being together. It goes without saying that I could not use my flashlight (that crucial sliver of light!) I felt the foot of Todd's bed, and managed to make my way over to my own. And, standing there beside my bed, I proceeded to begin undressing.

I was wearing a pair of jeans shorts which were held up by one of those military-type web belts. Such belts have brass buckles with a moveable piece of brass to cinch the belt at a desired length. There was also a strip of brass as a decorative feature at the end of the belt.

I loosened the cinch and drew the web belt slowly through the buckle. This was noiseless until I got to the brass tip: I knew this would make a scraping sound (the perfect thing to awaken a sleeping sensitive adolescent!) against the buckle. So I placed my free hand over the whole buckle and then drew the belt through slowly, so that all that was heard was a brief *swish*, the faintest *suggestion* of metal against metal.

But *prends garde*: once the belt is out of the buckle, the brass of the cincher would clank against the brass of the buckle - something that couldn't have made the military brass very happy! (I wondered about the advisability of fashioning a belt that would alert enemy scouts every night at bedtime.) So, hand over buckle, I held the cincher immovable.

The snap, I realized, presented a problem all its own. True, its undoing was of the briefest sort, but that isolated metallic POP! could prove to be *my* undoing in popping up the adolescent sleeping next to me. So I covered the snap with my hands even as I pulled the pants apart, so that all that was heard was a muffled "plumpf". ('Boy, that was a snap!' I punned to myself.)

And then, with a sickened heart, I realized that I had a whole zipper to undo -- a <u>metallic</u> zipper. (Why, I wondered, did my pants have to be so damn <u>well-made</u>, with sturdy brass buckles, snaps, and zippers? How I yearned, just that one time, for cheap plastic fasteners - the sort that wear out quickly but which at least do so *soundlessly*!)

I briefly considered pulling the zipper down with the lightening finality of a decisive ***ZIP!***, as one might yank a band aid off a hairy arm. But then, luckily, I recalled the effect such an action has at climactic moments in various works of literature (cf: "Peyton Place.")

I realized it would have to be done <u>tooth by agonizing tooth</u>, each brass zipoid in turn carefully and noiselessly *coaxed* from its brass socket. This little exercise in *tooth extraction* lasted for some minutes, but was finally accomplished.

I was now able to remove the shorts, which I did while still carefully holding the buckle cincher. Then, quickly and soundlessly, I removed my shirt and briefs and slipped the night shirt on. I trained my ear in Todd's direction but I heard nothing. Therein I concluded that the first phase of my getting ready for bed had been accomplished successfully.

I now had to lie down on the bed.

Like all the other beds there at Silver Bay, my bed had deep-coil springs -- the kind that squeal like a stuck pig when you sit down on them. I realized that I was going to have to sit down slowly -- <u>very</u> slowly -- if the springs were not to squeak. I estimated, in fact, that I would have to extend this simple-if-excruciatingly slow process to five full minutes. Can you imagine the leg muscles needed to be able to sit down with this amount of *gradualness*? Fortunately I had such leg muscles, thanks to the seven sets of tennis I had played that summer!

But then, just because the bottom is down snuggled amidst those springs, do you think that's the end of the story? Do you imagine that I, sitting there on my self-congratulatory backside, was going to spend the night in that position?

And so, finally, I had to lay my torso down while simultaneously bringing my legs up onto the bed. This too had to be done with muscle-aching slowness. The precise order of operations was as follows: 1) Bring legs up and simultaneously rotate body so that I was perfectly balanced on my coccyx for a few entertaining moments; 2) lay torso down (legs rising higher up in the air) with the same excruciating slowness (those springs!) until head is resting on pillow. (I hoped - prayed? - that I wasn't too high on the bed - that my head wouldn't come down onto Todd's face (that proximity of pillows!)); and finally 3) gradually lower my legs whilst simultaneously extending them out straight onto the bed (those stomach muscles!)

By such a tortured series of steps did I become, finally, supine.

The first thing I did after everything was complete was to listen. Did I hear Todd yawning in wakefulness? I did not.

I had succeeded: I was in my nightshirt lying on my bed, and Todd hadn't awakened. I had met the challenge I had set for myself - my honour was intact. For the first time in a half hour or so my whole body relaxed. I lay back on my pillow and listened for the gentle breathing of my sleeping nephew whose head was proximate to mine.

I didn't hear it. There was no sound of breathing at all.

A panic seized me. Somewhere I had heard of an obscure fatal disorder called A.C.S. or "Adolescent Choke Syndrome", which, I assumed, was similar to the Sudden Infant Death Syndrome. Was Todd a victim of this? If so, it would be ironic indeed after all the care I had taken to not disturb him! I lay there paralyzed in a fit of terror, scarcely breathing myself in my efforts to hear <u>his</u> breathing...

The back door slammed. Someone came clomping up the steps into our room. The cord was yanked and 5000 watts of light flooded the room.

"Oh Hi Uncle Ted. Sorry for waking you - I didn't think you'd be back yet!"

Belvoir

One male in a hothouse of young females

I played the piano for ballet classes at a girls' fine arts camp for two summers back in the late 1960's.

A young woman I had just met and hit it off with, named Dottie Allen, had gotten a job teaching voice in that camp, and had recommended me for the ballet job as 'someone I'd like to spend the summer with'.

The name of the camp was Belvoir Terrace; it was (still is) in Lenox, MA, and it was owned by Edna and Sam Schwartz. Sam and Edna had bought the estate originally belonging to Morris K. Jessup, the man who had financed Perry's expedition to the North Pole in 1909. This included a sprawling castle of a house, a barn and gatehouse, and beautiful, spacious grounds.

Sam had made his money in the meat business, a fact you intuited when you shook hands with him (he only had a thumb on his right hand).

When she was a young girl, Edna Schwartz had had a fascination with the color purple. So this hue was diffused through everything at the camp. The uniforms were purple; Edna's dresses were all purple; streaks of purple ran through the faux marble table tops in the dining hall; and even Sam's golf cart was purple.

Belvoir was a gynocracy – that is, an institution run by females. At the top were Edna and her daughter Nancy Goldberg. (Sam was merely an eccentric fixture.) Then came the androgynous program director Bev Belson (always carrying a whistle on a lanyard) and her assistant, "Rusty". Then the 16 or so female instructors: each of these had a bunk consisting of a few girls. Finally there were the 100 campers themselves.

There was also, seemingly by an accident of mutation, a handful of males: a painter, a writer, a flautist, a guitarist, a jazz instructor, and the ballet accompanist (me.)

As the reader can see, there was an interesting ratio (around 20 to 1) of females to males. Men could be easily distracted there; this man was. Dottie had gotten me that job so that she could spend the summer with me; but she had chosen the worst possible place - one rife with smoldering, adolescent, female passions.

I had never been in a ballet studio before, nevertheless played for a class. The one at Belvoir, a converted carriage house, was quaint (one entered through a large stone arch). The ballet instructor was a taut little Argentinean spitfire named Nora. Madame (as she was also called) cultivated all the mannerisms and eccentricities of her Latin heritage: these included elaborate kisses on both cheeks, and a few quaint terms she used in class, such as "Push colita!" (which meant "Tuck in your tush!")

There was a decent grand piano in the studio. And there, for the first time in my life, the vast repertoire of piano music I had learned could be put to a definite use - and I would get paid in the bargain. I had only to learn which sort of music was appropriate for each bar exercise.

I found the ballet studio to be an incubator for fostering narcissism.

Any artistic endeavor which involves the body invites narcissistic tendencies. A pianist will be particularly concerned about his wrists and fingers. A singer will be even more self-absorbed, since a part of her body is itself the vibratory mechanism.

But dancers! As their entire bodies are involved in their artistic performance, they are naturally concerned with their whole body – not only its health and well being and its ability to execute the desired maneuvers, but the very looks and appearance of that body itself.

And so what one sees in a ballet studio are balance bars - and mirrors on every wall. A studio may have only a handful of dancers in it, but these are multiplied by reflections and reflections-of-reflections, until the space seems absolutely choked with dancers.

Given this sort of reflective environment, there is the temptation for a dancer to gaze at herself – and then gaze at herself anew. I have seen the gamut run by dancers in this respect, from those who, more or less indifferent to their looks, constantly sought to hone their technique, to those who were drunk with their own reflections.

I think (pace, McLuhan) that the ballet studio, with its plethora (partly reflected) of young ballerinas, was a cool medium. That is, those glances and gazes in the mirror tended to be haughty and self-critical. (But woe if the gaze wandered: it might very well turn to ice at the moment that it revealed another ballerina who seemed slimmer or more beautiful or more agile!)

But what happened when a single male was dropped into this mix? What was cool became hot; what had been some harmless narcissism became a simmering caldron of intrigue.

I knew a few of these girls outside of the ballet studio. In the course of getting to know them, I suppose I might have kidded around with them a bit. (Okay, let me be blunt and say I flirted with them. I only hesitated to use this word because, as I was 24 while they were 14 or so, I could already hear the Ladies of the League of Decency sharpening their knives. I would therefore like to assure them that this was innocent, harmless fun. [Cue sound of grinding wheels starting up.])

Once we were in the studio, all this – communication – was reduced to the compact form of glances at one another in the mirrors. Girls who were used to looking at themselves now enjoyed the pleasure of being regarded by what is known as The Male Gaze. I learned the art of the quick ardent glance, the locking of eyes for an instant, the fleeting form of a wink. Thanks to mirrors on all sides, I could send flickering glances to several girls in quick succession. It was a veritable kaleidoscope of suggestion!

But I went further: this sort of communication extended to the very music I chose to play for the various bar exercises. I had established with each girl a favorite piece which could trigger a memory of our relationship: a Chopin Nocturne for one (useful for pliés); a Brahms Waltz for another (good for balancé); and so on. (Yes, I drew heavily from the Romantic repertoire [my specialty] for these associations!) And of course there was the fallback piece which allowed me to communicate with all of the girls simultaneously: Mendelssohn's 'Wedding March' (which happened to be perfect for grand battements.)

With all those distractions, I was utterly ignoring Dottie. Finally, tired of waiting, she asked me out on our first date: it was to see the movie, "Rosemary's Baby". But she could not compete with the intrigue in the ballet studio; and that was pretty much the story for my first year at Belvoir.

My playing at least was good enough that I was invited back for the following summer. Dottie and I saw one another a few times over the winter; and, free of the distractions at Belvoir, our relationship blossomed.

But when we returned to Belvoir the next summer, I once again felt drawn as if by a powerful magnetic force back into the web of the young females there. Besides the ballet, there was an additional attraction that second year: a bright older camper who was a great conversationalist. She and I would chat for hours about religion and politics and a whole host of other subjects.

I want to write about the last night of camp; for that is where the most interesting things happened - and when some incidents occurred in relation to that particular camper.

On that last night the geraniums were removed from the huge flower pot in the center of the circular drive behind the house, and a fire was built in the pot. Everyone stood around this blaze in a huge circle and linked arms and sang various sorts of sentimental ditties. Of course there was a lot of crying and swearing of eternal friendships and all the other things you would expect in such a situation.

What interested me was the ways in which those final evenings would begin to resemble A Midsummer Night's Dream. People who had behaved like perfectly rational beings during the rest of the summer would do crazy irrational things on that last night. I myself was in a distinctly puckish mood that evening: I was feeling wild and reckless.

I was wanting to see my comely conversationalist. But the darkness of the perimeter had swallowed her up. I knew that her room was somewhere on the second floor of the house. So I went right into the house through the back door there. The stairs were to my left.

No one was watching. A thrill ran through my body as I began the slow ascent of the curved wooden staircase leading up to the girls' living quarters.

Now I know what the reader is probably thinking: that I was that worst kind of vile male scum known as the stalker. But this is clearly not the correct term; for it implies that I knew where the girl was at all times and that I was putting myself proximate to her despite her desire not to see me. But, first of all, she never expressed any such desire; and secondly, I had no idea where the hell she was. I was in fact looking for her; so rather than stalking, you might say I was prowling.

Ah, but to what end (asks the jury very insistently)? Am I hearing another unpleasant word being whispered – that of predator? Then I must protest again because of what that word implies. Ladies and gentlemen of the jury, as incredible as it may seem to you, as hard as it may be for you to believe, the absolute truth is that <u>I only wanted to talk with the girl</u>! (Yes, conversation was my aphrodisiac at that time.)

Whatever my appellation, I slowly ascended the staircase to the lair of young girls, much as Cary Grant did in "Notorious" to rescue Ingrid Bergman. (I know, this is not an apt analogy, since I wasn't trying to rescue anyone. I think I'm thinking more of the electrical charge occasioned by climbing up into a forbidden and dangerous realm.) Of course, Cary half-ran up with a distinct sense of purpose. Whereas I crept up with a very foggy purpose in mind.

I finally reached the top of the staircase, and I began my stealthy sneak down the hall. I glanced into the first room (no one saw me, luckily: I could just imagine the hue and cry! Or would they feel safety in numbers and give me the Falstaff treatment?). – Some girls were packing and chatting.

And suddenly, the full idiocy of what I was about hit me. What was I doing up there in a forbidden area, blatantly tempting fate? I stepped back into the shadows in an alcove off the hall. However, this was not a place I could hide: someone coming by would certainly spot me. I was almost wont to curse my stupidity for putting myself in this position. (I say 'almost' because in truth I was still caught up in the thrill of my adventure.)

Suddenly I heard Nancy Goldberg's voice: she was on her way up the stairs; in a few more seconds she would see me there, hiding like a common criminal. (But gentlemen: I protest the use of the word 'common' here!) What could I do?

Well, I could act as though I had been sleepwalking, and that I had just awakened, horrified at where I was. (But that would hardly be convincing, considering it was still relatively early in the evening.)

I could pretend that I had been kidnapped and dragged up there against my will. I could scream holy hell, thus turning myself from perpetrator to victim in one deft maneuver. (But then I would have to identify my captors; after all, everyone knew everyone else in that small community.)

Or: I could make it look as though I had come up there under mistaken assumptions. Perhaps I might have thought that there was an "open house" in the girls' living quarters on the last night. Using this charade, I would have to appear utterly innocent and devoid of all subterfuge.

Nancy was proceeding apace - I had no time to formulate any

other excuses. (Sometimes we have to go with the excuses we have, rather than the ones we wish we had.) So I put my hands in my pockets, affected a casual devil-may-care air, and, stepping out of the shadows, sauntered right by Nancy while whistling "My Funny Valentine". She saw me and was, of course, aghast. "What are you doing up here?!" Me: "I thought we could visit up here on the last night." Her: "Men are <u>never</u> allowed up here!" "I found that out!" I replied laughingly as I started down the stairs.

Somehow I met up later with the girl I was seeking. We wandered over to the churchyard next door, and clambered up onto the tops of the two stone pillars on opposite sides of the entrance. And there, chatting merrily across ten feet of separation, we were found by Nancy Goldberg in her purple camp station wagon at 2 A.M. (She would later tell people that she had caught us in a 'compromising' situation.)

I knew that that was it for me at Belvoir – I had burned my bridges behind me.

The following summer, just as Belvoir with its manifold intrigues was beginning again, Dorothy (her true name) and I were on our honeymoon up at my family's cottage near the Delaware River.

Bibliomania

Selective violations of the Eighth Commandment

The word bibliophile refers to a lover of books. This term has all sorts of warm-fuzzy associations, such as curling up by a fire to read a leather bound volume on a cold rainy Sunday afternoon. It is reminiscent of all things cozy and sweet. But it has virtually nothing to do with what I am going to talk about here.

By contrast, the word bibliomaniac implies a darker, pathological relationship with books. The term contains notions of compulsive, even obsessive behavior. In its extreme form, it can include the actual theft of books one desires.

I was a bibliomaniac a few times in my life.

It is true that, as a child, I loved books in an innocent, wholesome way. I was given many lovely volumes which I devoured hungrily. So I was a bibliophile; the mania came later.

1. When was I first introduced to bibliomania? I think at college as an undergraduate. There was a fellow in our dorm who prided himself on being able to steal anything from the University Bookstore. I recall that, out of skepticism, my roommate and I challenged the fellow to get us each a copy of Apostol's Calculus [i.e., a hefty tome]: he had them in our hands within the hour.

He would do this by the most elementary of methods: he simply placed what he wanted to steal on the counter beyond the register; thus the attendant would assume the items were already paid for and so not ring them up. His most blatant theft was a huge, pink, stuffed dog.

I must admit, I was a bit in awe of this fellow, who had the nerve to pull off such stunts. (Certainly I never would have dared do such a thing!) Yet, should I add that I felt a bit of disgust as well?

I never dreamt that I myself would become pretty disgusting within the next several years.

2. At the University of Illinois, there was a fellow music composition student who had a nice little library of political writings. But when I looked at one of the books (it happened to be Adorno's <u>Prisms</u>), I noticed that it was the property of a public library near Chicago. As my friend was supposedly a socialist, I confronted him: "How can you violate the most perfect socialist institution in this society - one founded on utter egalitarianism and supported by the government?" He gave me this cynical answer: "It's simple May: I asked myself, 'Who would find this book more useful - me, or all the other residents of Evanston Illinois? The answer was obvious!'" He added, "'To each according to his need' - remember?" I concluded sadly that my friend was not a socialist at all, but rather an elitist. (The fact that Adorno was a socialist writer only heightened the irony.)

So yes, I was still disgusted by such behavior then. But I'm afraid that a seed was planted in my head at the same time.

3. In my third year at Illinois, I got the job as page for the Music

Library at $1.70 per hour. This involved picking up books, scores, and records fresh from the publishers and bringing them back to Smith Hall. As such I had official access to all the holdings of the third largest university library in the country. I was never stopped or even questioned as I was leaving a building with books. It was like having letters of transit signed by General De Gaulle himself! Can you imagine the sheer number of temptations in such a situation for the budding bibliomaniac? Putting such a person in the position that I held would be like hiring a dipsomaniac to manage a chain of liquor stores.

Fortunately for the libraries of the University of Illinois, I was not yet at this stage of my - development - when I worked there. Yet, I found myself hugely tempted!

(Question: How can you tell when a bibliomaniac has been in a library? Answer: By ail the water-damaged books - from the excessive drooling.)

(Another question: How could library officials devise a job application which would screen out bibliomaniacs? Naturally the questions would have to be subtle enough so that the potential miscreant is lulled into betraying himself. Here are two samples:

Sample Question 1: Complete the sentence: 'I like books...'

    a) not at all

    b) a little

    c) quite a bit

    d) more than my life.

Sample Question 2: Do you have library books at home?

    a) No.

    b) Yes. They are all due in the next three weeks.

    c) Yes. But they are all overdue.

    d) Yes. But none of them has a due date.)

4. So when exactly did I abandon all scruples and pass over to the dark side? When, one day, I found myself holding a book which

didn't belong to me [yet], and being suddenly overwhelmed by a desire for it. Not the desire to read it per se (though that might be part of it), but rather the need to possess it utterly and in perpetuity.

I hesitate to confess my first offense, since it is so transparently evil in so many ways. First, I lifted (I shall use these sorts of euphemisms often in this treatise, since words like "stole" and "theft" are so – harsh) the book from a lending library; second, the library was part of a Christian association; and third, the book so pilfered was - gasp! - a Bible.

Now before you start scourging and mocking me, would you allow me a few words of defense?

First of all, no library employee was present at the time I effected this - transfer (the library was unstaffed in the afternoons.) What can I say about an organization so trusting? I would contend that this library was virtually inviting people to steal from it; I simply took them up on the invitation.

Second of all, as this was a Christian conference center, there were, between the members and the association itself, a plethora of Bibles already there. (The place was lousy with Bibles, fer chrissake!) So, in that sort of situation, I was actually relieving them of an unwanted surplus.

And then, third of all, I took the plainest, most down-to-earth Bible. True, it was the Oxford edition of the King James, with good sturdy finely-etched black type; and it had the Apocrypha in the middle between Old and New Testaments. But there were other, no doubt more valuable Bibles on the shelves. For example, there was an obscure 19th century edition with 'an exact and faithful translation' of the original texts. So I turned to Luke and made a comparison of this with the King James version. I leave it to the reader to guess why I made the choice I did:

KING JAMES: "She wrapped him in swaddling cloths and laid him in a manger."

NEWER EDITION: "She wrapped him in bandages and laid him in a stall."

5. Once I had broken the bibliomaniacal ice, other situations would follow. From my local library I would lift a copy of short stories by Hermann Broch (quasi-obscure German contemporary of Thomas Mann) called (another irony?) The Guiltless. I was attracted to its dust cover, which showed two people, hand in hand, running through a wild landscape. And of course it just happened to fill a gap: I had, in hard cover, the other two Broch novels available in translation.

(Didn't I feel guilt about taking from a library? Of course. But I was able to rationalize it thus: as I was a citizen of that town, I in effect owned a small fraction of each book. So all I was really doing in appropriating books was augmenting my ownership portion a bit.)

From another library I would appropriate a (abridged, regrettably) deluxe edition of "Don Quixote" illustrated by Salvador Dali. I was attracted to the handful of paintings (there was also a plethora of sketches), which were (as one would expect from this artist) garish and outlandish and, well, utterly over the top.

(And how, you ask, did I manage to smuggle those things through the electronic detection devises? Actually, I did those things before the advent of said devices. In fact, they were installed precisely to put a stop to people like myself (he said, bragging.) Of course, a few proverbial horses had left the barn by then!

(But shall I confess? I also harbored resentment against the library authorities for installing those things. Yes, I was indignant that they would think me - untrustworthy.)

(Still, I recall at least one attempt on my part to beat those detectors. I had found a lovely little book called "Goethe in Italy" in the library of a community college at which I was teaching part time. The frontispiece had the most engaging drawing of the young Goethe sporting a broad brimmed hat and sprawling languidly before an exotic landscape. I wanted that book very much! (Indeed, I never saw another copy anywhere.) So I spent an inordinate amount of time frantically attempting to pry (pull, yank, wrest) the magnetic strip from the spine of the book. But to no avail: whoever had inserted that strip knew well the wiles of bibliophiles! (I know, I should have written 'bibliomaniacs', but I couldn't resist the rhyme.)

(I imagine that one could beat the detectors (though, never being present with accomplices {accessories?}, I never tried this) by simply walking through said device while holding the desired book over and outside it. (Would my arms be long enough? Dry runs needed to be undertaken to resolve this issue!) Of course, the attention of the library staff should be diverted as one is pulling this off. (See Appendix 1 for a masterpiece in this genre.)

6. When I was a teacher, books would sort of leech into my own library as follows: I would bring books home to use as references for my courses. (Sometimes the definition of 'reference' was stretched mighty thin. For example, how could I justify bringing home a volume like Courant & Robbins's "What is Mathematics?" for which there was no course? Simple: the book 'enhanced my general mathematical erudition', thus 'making me a better teacher'.) And at the end of the year when the course was over? I might bring them back to school, but sometimes I wouldn't; after all, they might prove to be useful again! And often they were.

But what does one do when one is going to a new school system? Well, I might return them - but maybe I wouldn't. For, after all, by using them so extensively, haven't I in a sense earned the right to keep them? (Besides, isn't there a statute of limitations which states something about coming into ownership of property you've "maintained" for a certain number of years?) By such rationales did books drift into my library.

7. A few years later I was teaching music at a high school whose music department had an excellent library. Besides the usual musical songbooks, it contained genuine scores as well as writings by composers themselves. And so, for example, beside a full score of Wagner's "Tristan und Isolde", might be found Debussy's polemical tract, "Monsieur Croche, the Dilettante Hater", and Berlioz's "Memoirs". And many of these were cute, little, out-of-print, hardcover monographs.

One day I noticed that no one had claimed the desk next to the music library. So I immediately moved all my stuff over. And there I would sit, like a nobleman in his baronial manor, surrounded by books I loved and coveted. I would dip into one or another of them on occasion in order to relax after a grueling class. Indeed, it was, for all practical purposes, my library, since none of my colleagues seemed to have much interest in it. And yet I had no desire to transfer it to my own house, especially as it enhanced my life at school so much. So you might say that it functioned as a sort of branch library for me.

I began to feel genuinely protective of that little music library. When I noticed that a colleague had borrowed something from it (a rarity, but still) and then didn't return it in a reasonable amount of time, I would hound them for it. (Yes, I even threatened fines!) Indeed, I guarded its integrity as a mother dog would guard her young.

Then one day I was told that my contract wouldn't be renewed for the following year. Outwardly, I maintained my devil-may-care attitude (a seasoned faculty member even said I had 'class'.) But inwardly I was furious. I wanted to get back at the institution that had wronged me.

So, integrity of the collection be damned! I plundered that wonderful little library and made many of those scores and treatises by Debussy et al my own. And then, not content with that, I rifled through the main library of that less-than-august institution, and thereby appropriated such niceties as some hardcover editions of books by Marshall McLuhan to complete my own holdings by that author.

(Was I not guilt ridden by these thefts? Please - the word "theft" is so - blunt! I preferred to think that I helped myself to a small severance package.)

8. Several years after that debacle, I got a job as chair of the math department in a private school. This position included the administration of a significant budget, which I could use to purchase anything of use to the department.

"Anything?"

It did not take me long to realize what sorts of things I wanted to buy. In fact, I grasped immediately that this would allow me to continue practicing my bibliomaniacal ways, but this time, through perfectly legitimate means.

What sorts of books did the math department "need"? By definition (and by some wild coincidence), the very books that I lusted after and craved! (Should I have bought books I didn't like [he asked defensively]?) So every Saturday morning I found myself at the Boston University Bookstore or the MIT COOP, both of which had sizeable math sections. (In particular, I found some nice books on mathematical modeling [or is it 'modelling'? I have books that use both spellings.])

So, for the first time in my career, I was able to create the library of my dreams. As I bought the books, I introduced them to my colleagues at department meetings. That library, I decided, would become my legacy to the department once I retired.

And when I was canned from that job (but not, I hasten to reassure the reader, for suspicious or fraudulent use of the math budget!)? Well then I was able to augment my own home mathematics library with all sorts of wonders I never could have afforded myself. (Did I pillage the library? That is too mild a word, for it implies that I was selective. No - rather, I transferred it whole-hog; for, in a sense, wasn't it "my" library already?)

But once I had completed that exercise in wholesale hijacking, something changed in me. Perhaps I had reached a saturation point concerning such booknapping. Or perhaps my old disgust with such a silly and stupid enterprise had returned. Whatever the reasons, I never appropriated another book that wasn't my own.

9. An interview with the Morals Police (MP)

MP: "So - is this blatant series of admissions in reality a kind of confession?"

Me: "You may think of it that way if you like. I myself prefer to view it as a sort of primer for the budding bibliomaniac."

MP: "And is this brash manifesto to end for you as it did for Alec Guinness in "The Lavender Hill Mob" - with its protagonist being led away in handcuffs?"

Me: "Hardly. No search warrants have been issued for my house. No officials have come calling. I seem to have gotten away with all of the above scot free."

MP: "In the midst of all the braggadocio and the bravado, is there no - remorse?"

Me: "Well, yes, it seems that there is a price to be paid for all those shenanigans, and that price is, at the very least, a bad conscience."

MP: "Haven't you joked that you sleep soundly at night precisely because you have no conscience?"

Me (smiles): "I assure you, I do have a conscience."

MP: "Ha! It's easy to have a guilty conscience after the fact, but what use is that? One person feels lousy, and $(n-1)$ people are robbed of their books; so everyone is a little more miserable. Why couldn't you have had your self-indulgent attack of conscience before you stole the damn books, thereby saving everyone a lot of heartache?!"

Me: "True. But another reason (besides the conscience) that I have come to realize that lifting books isn't worth it, is that the book so heisted is somehow not the same in one's own collection as it was originally. It loses that attractiveness, that allure it had when it was forbidden fruit. My favorite books are ones that I purchased."

MP: "Oh great. You might just as well have left those books where they were. Or made amends later..."

Me: "Amends? Well, I recently donated my entire mathematics library (the vast majority of which I purchased by legitimate means) to the math department of a school which treated me well when I taught there. How is that for a start?"

MP: "Too little too late!"

Me: "By the way - I never stole (ugh - there, I've said it!) anything other than books. No stereos. No cars. No social security numbers. Not even a pack of gum from the corner store. Nope - I was a bibliomaniac, pure and simple, and that's it. Nothing else particularly interested me - at least not that much."

MP: "What do you want - applause?"

10. Oh yes - there is one more peril that I need to caution the budding bibliomaniac about: the perforated library identification tool. This pernicious bother will cut the library's name into a page by means of scores of tiny holes. Gone are the simple days of the ink-stamped ID, which could be covered over with Wite-Out, neutralized with that old standby Ink Eradicator, or even erased using a sufficiently abrasive tool. I have thought long and hard about how to counter that unfair one-upmanship on the part of the library.

One rather far-fetched notion I had was to study the process of making paper from wood, thence to fashion a sort of paper "putty" which would allow one to "spackle over" that multitude of tiny holes. Such a method might actually work; but it would require much time and effort.

Recently, though, I have hit upon a much simpler solution to this perforation problem: Go to a stationary store and purchase an ink pad and a stamp. The stamp should simply read, in big block letters: DISCARDED.

Appendix 1: A Masterpiece in Diversion

Although this has to do with general kleptomania rather than the particular bibliomania, I include it here for its entertainment value.

When my wife, Dorothy, was in middle school, her minister father had a church in Newark, NJ. Dorothy's older brother fell in with what then were called "hoods": toughs with leather jackets and ducks-ass haircuts and taps on their shoes.

A gang of five of these juvenile delinquents (including the brother) set their sights on knocking off the local Five-and-Dime.

Were they intent on shoplifting? Hardly - that was small potatoes. Their goal was to rifle the cash register itself.

Two of the hoods were sent into the store to begin with. One wandered to the very back, looking furtive and suspicious and, well, hoodsy. Naturally the store owner gravitated back there as well to keep an eye on him.

The cash register was in the middle of the store, and the second hood took his place right beside it. Wasn't the owner worried that this urban menace would attempt to steal from said register? No. He knew that if the lad depressed even one key, the register would emit a resounding and cheerful "DING!", thus alerting him to the nefarious attempt.

At that precise moment, the other three hoods entered the store, marching together in lockstep with their taps:

Click! Click! Click! Click! DING! Click! Click!

They divided up the take on the parlor floor of the parsonage.

Appendix 2: The Master of all Bibliomanics

My peccadilloes were child's play compared to those of a fellow who had attended the University of Illinois before my time there.

He began stealing from the Music Library over an extended period of time, as follows: first he pried off the grate from a large air duct on the second floor. Into this cavernous open shaft he then threw various books and scores he had coveted (and, indeed, what better way to assuage the sin of covetousness than to steal the things one desires and make them one's own?) He would then retrieve those goodies from the bottom of the air shaft in the basement at his leisure.

I think it was universally agreed that this person held the record for the sheer volume of his thefts, which numbered in the hundreds. Indeed, it seems clear that he had an enormous, a voracious - indeed, an unquenchable - appetite for books and musical scores.

And not just any old books and scores! One example should suffice to show how discerning he could be as a connoisseur of fine things. Stravinsky had hand written his score to The Rite of Spring in four different colours of ink. The U of I Music Library had purchased a beautifully bound hardcover facsimile of this for at least $100 in the 1950's; and this was one of the multitudinous things he had tossed willy-nilly down into the air shaft.

(But as well, due to the sheer volume of things stolen here, is it not conceivable that this fellow became less selective and began tossing any and every banality he could lay his hands on? That, in fact, his mad goal might have became to eventually steal everything in the Library? After all, if something so absurdly impossible becomes possible, why not try to do it?)

In the face of such - thorough behavior, the word "theft" seems paltry and anemic indeed. No, we must seek more robust words: we could say that he was looting, sacking, or even ravaging the library.

But I'm afraid that the exploits of this young man went beyond mere bibliomania. For, in his role as poseur, he brought misery upon another person. This outrage indirectly concerned George Hunter.

George Hunter was Professor of Harpsichord at Illinois. (I myself studied with him.) A student of the great Ralph Kirkpatrick, he was a dapper gentleman of impeccable taste and bearing. And: he was the soul of discretion.

One day the bibliomaniac (I shall refer to him as 'Biblio' here) was practicing the harpsichord by himself in Hunter's studio (yes, he was one of those high-strung effete individuals who studied that instrument) when there was a knock at the door. It was an undergraduate who had never met the Master. "Professor Hunter?" asked the student. "At your service," replied Biblio with a slight bow. The student asked whether he could audition for him. Biblio stepped aside and motioned elaborately toward the instrument: "The magnificent Dowd awaits your gentle touch!"

But the student had barely begun to play when Biblio smashed his fist down on that "magnificent" instrument (thereby probably upsetting its delicacy enough to put it out of tune) and began to rant and rave at the student. He said that the student hadn't even the slightest hint of musicianship; that he was 'a heavy-fisted lout'; and that, if he

(Biblio) wanted to massacre Couperin, he would sooner take an ax to the score. He finished by demanding to know what the student's father did. The poor student, hardly able to speak, stammered that he was a pipe-fitter. "That seems like a good profession for you!" replied Biblio with a sage nod of the head. Then he screamed, "Get out!" and the student was treated to Biblio's foot on his backside as he lurched out the door.

Well - the various outrageous exploits of this arch-miscreant were eventually found out, and he became persona non grata in the University of Illinois Music Department.

I wish I had known him!

The Boat

Below is the gist of the exchange which occurred on my very first day of school (kindergarten) in 1948 and which I claim taught we more about myself than most of the rest of the experiences I'd have throughout my schooling.

There was a pile of toy boats in the center of the room. These were each hand-made of wood and individually painted. Each was different from the others and a beautiful work of art.

The teacher had us sit on the floor around the pile of boats, and then she asked that we each choose one. There was one that in shape and/or color particularly attracted me.

But it attracted at least one other person. Donald Gray was the biggest student in that first class of mine (I was a four-year-old in a kindergarten class of mostly five-year-olds.) He would remain bigger than me throughout school. And he did things the big kids did, such as play football in high school. Our mottos in the yearbook showed the divide between us in the starkest terms. Mine was: "What fools these mortals be!" His was: "His limbs were cast in manly mold." Do you see? He <u>worked</u> at Being Big, and it informed his very thought-processes.

Anyway, here is the essence of my one exchange (I recall no others over the next thirteen years) with Donald Gray:

97

Me: "Can I have that boat?"

Him: "No - I want it!"

Me: "Okay."

That's it. It isn't very much, is it. True - it does tell (or imply) a lot in a brutally short space of time. But still, we yearn for more, we wish to read between the lines. This will take more - *sophisticated* - actors. I will make them anonymous beings:

A: "Can I have that boat there?"

B: "No."

A (startled): "What?"

B: "No. I want that boat."

A: "But I asked for it first."

B: "Actually, you didn't ask for it at all. Strictly speaking, you merely inquired as to the possibility of the boat being given to you. I answered that it was not possible, precisely because I wanted it."

A: "'The possibility'?"

B: "It's your use of the word 'can'. Do you hear how a lot of our classmates ask to use the bathroom? They say to the teacher, 'Can I go to the bathroom?' Her response to that should be: 'I don't know - see your urologist!' Of course they really mean to ask '<u>May</u> I go to the bathroom?'"

A: "Well then, may I have that boat?"

B: "You are asking for our permission to have the boat? And then one of us turns you down and you're surprised?"

A (confused): "I don't quite see..."

B: "If you want something, say so - don't beat around the bush!"

A: "But I was taught that that is the way people ask for something in so-called polite society - that there is a hidden understanding that it is a request and should be honored as such."

B: "Not here. This ain't 'polite society' - it's down-and-dirty society. You need to be direct here."

A: "Very well: Please give that boat to me."

B (laughing): "You will be polite at all costs, won't you, even when you're giving an order. And I find it interesting that you subordinate yourself into the objective case."

A: "I think people tend to put themselves in the objective case, even when it's incorrect grammar. Think of 'It's me'."

B: "Yes. A lot of people say that."

A: "A lot? It's universal."

B: "<u>Virtually</u> universal. As a matter of fact, I say 'It is I' whenever I get the chance, just to see the surprised looks on peoples' faces."

A: "Well, you're one of the very few. There's a supposedly true story about Harvard President Charles Eliot which illustrates its pervasiveness. One evening he went up to see a student on a matter of urgent business. The student was studying hard and had his door locked. Eliot knocked and when the student asked irately who it was, he replied, 'It's me - President Eliot'. The student then launched into a string of invectives. You see, he did not believe this was the President because such an august personage would never make such an elementary error in grammar."

B: "Why do you suppose people do this?"

A: "Ignorance?"

B: "Certainly not in President Eliot's case."

A: "Then it must be due to a reluctance to use the subjective case, a loathing to put oneself forward quite so blatantly. It's too threatening..."

B: "My boy, most people aren't burdened by the possibility

of being personally threatening just because they use the subjective case! No - I would ascribe it rather to ease of execution. Quite simply, 'It is I' has no closed consonants; and consonants are what move things along. So the explosive of the lips following the vowel in 'It's me' is the perfect antidote - one which millions of people sub-consciously intuit. (I find that I can reverse the order of consonant and vowel and use "'Tis I" quite serviceably. But that's me - er, I!)"

A: "I still think there's truth in my notion..."

B: "Poor chap - you are really trapped in your own little prison of personal reticence! I'd hate to hear how you'd make a request for something of real significance. For example, how would you ask a girl to go to bed with you?"

A (blushes): "That's a highly personal question."

B: "It's just a rhetorical exercise. How would you do it?"

A: "Why don't you give some samples that I can choose from."

B (laughing): "You really are something! But I'll try to oblige and run through the repertoire of choices. Are we assuming that words are to be used?"

A: "What's the alternative?"

B: "Pure raw naked physical force."

A: "Such as?"

B: "Oh, such as tearing her clothes off."

A (disgusted): "No, that's horrid!"

B: "Oh, I don't know - sometimes the element of surprise is just the ticket..."

A: "And other times?"

B: "They cry rape. Obviously, you need to be able to make quick judgments about what's appropriate".

A: "I can't imagine ever using physical force..."

B: "It's the elephant in the room whenever two or more people are negotiating for anything. Didn't you feel its palpable presence when we first started talking about the boat?"

A: "Now that you mention it, yes. But I instinctively run the other way when there's any suggestion of force - unless of course there's someone bigger on my side. No, I need something more - *verbal*."

B: "Well then, how about a frank expression of desire: 'I want to make love to you.'"

A: "That is a bit too frank. Can you make it a little more vague, more - *hypothetical*?"

B: "You mean something like this: I would like to make love to you."

A: "Yes. And can you do something about the uni-directional aspect of it? After all, I want the result to be mutual..."

B: "I see. How about this bi-directional gem: I would like to make love with you."

A: "It's getting better. But now I have that same old problem with the *aggressiveness* of the subject case..."

B: "First thing you know you'll be having me having her asking you to make love to her! How about, Make love with me!"

A: "Ouch - an order."

B: "Well, then I'll have to turn the original statement inside out (assuming it's topologically feasible) and recast it as a question: 'Would you like to make love with me?' That puts you in a modest little corner of this polite request where you can await her coy reply."

A (thoughtful): "If indeed I have to be there at all..".

B (starts): "What? You want to disappear completely?"

A: "Well, maybe. Yes."

B: "But that means you would have to ask something like, Would you like to make love?"

A: "I think I'd have to."

B: "The utterly vulnerable self..."

A: "After all, what if she refuses?"

B: "Well, with me it'd be the start of a discussion..."

A: "I couldn't stand that."

B: "You wouldn't take the chance?"

A: "It's just too risky."

B: "Well then, I have just recalled a statement which seems like it was invented just for you. It's written on the back of every check in every diner in America."

A: "What could it be?"

B: "It has been a pleasure to serve you."

A: "You're right - it's masterful."

B: "It's a statement by a non-subject,..."

A: "...a totally servile entity..."

B: "...and it's you!"

A: "It's me."

The teacher, Mrs. Davidson, comes over.

Mrs. D: "My goodness, are you all still talking? You each need to select a boat! Teddy, can you make a choice?"

Teddy: "Yes. (Thinks for a moment, then points to The Boat and says with absolute conviction): I want that one!"

Mrs. D: "Well, Teddy, I can certainly give that boat to you, but only if you ask for it nicely."

Teddy: "What did I do wrong?"

Mrs. D: "You gave me a demand, and that's not how we ask for things here. Can you make a polite request?"

Teddy: "May I please have that boat?"

Mrs. D: "Good, it's yours. And you Donny?"

Donny (laughing): "I'll take any one, I don't care which."

Bridge to Nowhere

Fear & loathing in a game of cards

(Note: I use the word "dummy" in the sense it is used in bridge exactly twice in the writing which follows; those uses should be clear from context. All other uses of the word are in its everyday meaning.)

Dummy's Dilemma 1: How do you talk about something you know relatively little about?

Dummy's Dilemma 2: How do you make incompetence entertaining?

I live in an Institution where, among all the other activities they offer, there is bridge played Friday afternoons. Several volunteers who know the game, including the bridge expert Carl, come in to manually help residents who cannot use their hands, and to dispense advice on how to play the game better.

Carl earns his living teaching bridge, and I am convinced that he is a *savant* in the game. He can, for example, give the barest glance at the hands of the four players and instantly commit them all to memory (at times to be used later to demonstrate some intricacy of play to another gathering.) Then, too, he can look at each hand and tell its holder what the best bid should be. And finally, he can guide the person playing the hand through the labyrinth of tricks in order to make (usually) their contract.

Of course, Carl is not totally infallible; but that is due to certain extreme cases which can arise as part of the game and that are not his fault. (That is, Carl plays the odds.)

I learned to play bridge in our family while I was growing up. Bridge players are notoriously temperamental: the verbal browbeatings of partners because of perceived wrong bids or crossed signals have been known to wreak havoc on friendships and to end marriages. Our family was no exception. Luckily for me and my brother, the histrionics had occurred before we were born; so by the time we were playing, our mother had already worked it out that she would never again be my father's partner. So, since my brother shared my father's temperament, he was our father's partner any time we played; while the two reticent ones -- my mother and I -- enjoyed a peaceful and harmonious relationship as partners.

As can be surmised from the above, my father and brother had a *passion* for the game of bridge which my mother and I lacked. They wanted desperately to win, and they knew that there was always room to improve their skills. By contrast, my mother and I just enjoyed playing the game regardless of our skill level, and we didn't particularly care whether we won or lost. That is, we willingly and deliberately relinquished the urge to improve our playing.

That latter may be desirable in order to preserve family peace, but it is not a good attitude to have when one finds oneself thrust into a bridge environment in which experts watch and analyze one's every move under a magnifying glass.

I found myself so thrust.

Now the question might arise as to why, with my limited sensibilities, I put myself into an adverse bridge environment in the first place. The answer is twofold: first, I've become addicted to Carl's sardonic wit and banter (some of which I don't understand, but that's part of the charm); and second, because I have played a good many of the card games known to man, and I've found that by far the most intriguing and challenging one is bridge.

Unfortunately, I was not up to the challenge. And the reason is due to a few (yes, let's be blunt) little or not-so-little psychopathologies I happen to have brought with me, courtesy of my upbringing. These pathologies extend to every nook and cranny of the game, even the most trivial things that may not seem to hold horrors, but that nevertheless trigger my paranoia. I discuss some of these below.

1. The shuffle:

How much should the dealer shuffle the cards in bridge? This is one of the questions about which I obsess while I am playing.

Everyone seems to assume that the cards should be shuffled at least a little bit. But why? Because otherwise they are not sufficiently random. But what is "sufficiently" random? Unshuffled, the deck of cards would consist of the thirteen tricks from the previous round. In general, each of those tricks contains cards of the same suit; the next deal will distribute these equally amongst the four players. Thus, each player will receive about the same number of cards in each suit.

But I do not want the same number of cards in a given suit as my opponent. I want more -- a lot more! So instinctively I protest against this wretched egalitarianism. Thus do I say: shuffle the cards!

But how much should they be shuffled? Assumedly, each shuffle brings the order of cards closer to total randomness. And the thought of that for me is like gazing into the abyss or being sucked into the maelstrom! It is the prospect of total entropy, of utter disorder. Do you know how many possible hands there are in bridge? About 635 billion (give or take a few million.) Inwardly I cringe at the very thought of such a number.

Best, then, to shuffle, but not too much. How much is "not too much"? I myself know it is enough when I feel myself beginning to get nervous as I sense chaos looming.

2. The deal:

We residents of the Institution cannot deal the cards ourselves. So Carl and the other volunteers do it for us. They assume that one of us is the dealer, and that rotates around the table from hand to hand.

How does a dealer deal the cards? Normally he begins with the person to his left and goes clockwise around the table. In that way, he (the dealer) is the last person to receive a card.

But that's not the way Carl deals. He gives the first card to the dealer and moves around the table clockwise. Thus the last person to receive a card is to the dealer's right.

Well! This means that I have gotten the hand that rightfully belongs to the person to my left. And thus, in a sense, I am looking at what I shouldn't be looking at. This gives me a secret thrill at beholding the illicit, the forbidden. I gaze covertly over at my opponent to see whether she is aware of this violation of a part of her: is she regarding me with envy or mistrust? (Apparently with neither, for she is not looking my way at all.) I feel the smug satisfaction of the *voyeur* -- the one who has access to another's confidential information.

But then I realize with chagrin that this cuts both ways. For the person to my right has the hand that is rightfully mine. Resentment begins to build in me; I feel violated at this intrusion. In my rage I consider the possibility of taking a couple of sneak peeks over at my neighbor's hand. After all, it is really mine!

Fortunately, rationality (a rare thing for me during bridge) rescues me. For (so I reason) if I have the right to do that, then my opponent to my left has the selfsame right to look at my hand. And so on, around the table. In this way each player would know the contents of two hands: their own, and the one of the opponent on their right. Then (I further reason) the bidding might proceed with the purpose of each player attempting to uncover the contents of the other two hands. This could be done using some kind of arcane artificial bidding system of the sort that bridge players love. And the first player to uncover the contents of all the hands could yell something like "bingo!" and be declared the winner of that round.

I wonder what the other players would think of this reasonable idea?

3. The bidding:

The thirteen cards that each player receives are separated by suit and each suit arranged in descending order on two wooden cardholders in front of each of us. Each player counts up his/her points (Ace = 4, King = 3, etc.): a rough guideline is that one can bid with at least thirteen points. And this is where my paranoia begins in earnest.

Let me say something right up front here. I realize that, for the bridge fanatic, bidding constitutes one of the major joys of the game [the other one is playing a hand.] Indeed, the process of bidding, as a sequence of exchanging oblique verbal cues with one's partner in order to find the best contract to be in, can be a beautiful and subtle process. Unfortunately, I cannot draw that kind of aesthetic pleasure from bidding because hanging over my neck like an executioner's sword is the dreaded possibility that I might actually get the bid and then be "forced" to play the hand.

And so (to wax religious for a moment) I pray that this cup, in one way or another, might pass from my lips.

My first impulse is to hope that I should have such a lousy hand (few if any points) as to prevent me from bidding in the first place. In that way I would be relieved of the burden of worry at the very onset that I might have to play the hand. If my prayers are answered, then I shall pass when my turn comes to bid. Over the course of my time here I have developed a number of nifty personas to deal with that eventuality:

the world-weary persona: "Ah me, I suppose I shall have to pass."

the debonair persona: "Oh I think I'll just pass."

the guilt-ridden persona: "I'm so sorry partner, but I'm afraid I need to pass!"

the angry persona: "Dammit, I have to pass again!"

the blunt persona: "Pass."

... and so on, until even I get bored with those sorry excuses for play-acting. At that point I begin to yearn for more; for eventually in bridge, even for me, boredom trumps paranoia -- at least for a while.

So in that bored state I begin to hope for more. In fact, I want the biggest, the fattest cards in the deck! I want so many big fat cards that I will be able to bid a 'slam' (that is, betting that I will take virtually all the tricks if I play the hand) with insolent nonchalance.

107

Of course, with that sort of sudden *hubris* I would have temporarily forgotten that a contract of a slam in bridge is that most rare of entities; and so its playing would become a situation of the utmost pressure on me to succeed where there is virtually no room to fail. Fortunately, the chances of getting such a hand are around one in a few billion (give or take -- whatever) so probability saves me from my own worst instincts. (In general, beware of what you wish for: you may get your wish.)

Eventually, no thanks to the perniciousness of probability, I will get a hand that's at least good enough to 'demand' that I bid. Nevertheless, I continue to pray for the metaphorical cup to pass from my proverbial lips, as follows: I wish that my partner will bid my strong suit first, so that my bid is merely *supportive* of hers. In this way she will have to play both her hand and mine, while I sit back and contentedly watch as the 'dummy' -- that is, the one person who literally does nothing during the playing of the hand.

4. The playing:

I see bridge as a series of coercions against me, the helpless victim. I am "forced" to bid if I have at least thirteen points. I "must" answer if my partner makes a bid and I have at least six points. And, if I do get the bid, I "have" to play the hand.

Regardless of my most strenuous efforts to avoid it, eventually the situation comes about that I "have" to play a hand.

In that case, faced with having to "perform" before The Bridge Virtuoso, I allow myself to go all squishy inside. I become fresh putty, moist clay which invites Carl to mold me as he pleases. In other words (to beat a metaphor to death), I am utterly malleable in his hands.

However, outwardly I give as little hint of this inner Play-Dough character as possible. I adopt the persona of the serious tournament bridge player. In this guise, I am not so much asking Carl for help as *consulting* with him, as one expert to another, on the best strategy. So I might, with a look of great consternation on my face, say something like, "So Carl, what's your opinion on how best to proceed?" -- as if I were General Montgomery talking to General

Eisenhower about the invasion of Europe. The good thing is, Carl is perfectly willing to take this thing and run with it; all I have to do is *appear* as if I am pulling the strings.

And so, for example, I would "guide" him as to the "best" card in my hand to "choose" on a given play -- even though in many such cases, only one card makes sense in the context. But I would still nod my head at the card as if it was the most significant thing in the world, and say in the heavy learned tone of the bridge sage: "the three".

Rather than describe in intricate horror "my" playing of a hand, I have assembled a collection of typical "Carl-isms" and my mystified reactions to them below.

Carl (after I say "pass" on a really crummy hand with few points): "Oh no -- you can't pass with a hand like that! That would be a crime! You've gotta bid! You should bid (names some astronomical number with a suit) at the very least!"

(I "gotta" bid? Here we go again -- coercion!) I am now convinced that this man is a sadist whose one goal in life is to torture me. And even if he does play the hand successfully and make the contract (which he will 99% of the time), he's still a sadist!

(It's a "crime" not to bid? So call me a criminal.)

Carl (as we are bidding): "Oh no, you can't pass now -- you need to go to game!" (Note: "game" is a relatively high bid; but if you make it, you get a lot of extra points. Of course, we are not keeping track of points in our games here; so I have to assume that this useless affectation is just another way for Carl to torture us.)

(But what if I'm not game to go to game?)

Carl (as soon as the 'dummy' lays down his cards): "Now count how many tricks you can take."

(He is sounding an awful lot like my pimp!)

Carl: "Lead this card -- it's always the right choice."

The card is played, and it is immediately trumped.

Carl (who had canary feathers around his mouth even before the card was trumped): "... but not this time." When I ask him about it, he humorously shrugs, "It was still the right choice!"

(How can something be "always right" and wrong at the same time? Is there some kind of higher-order dialectic that I'm missing here? Or are we in some kind of Orwellian situation where "Wrong is Right"?)

Carl: "<u>Now</u> you can draw the trump."

(Why couldn't I draw the trump before? Was there a penalty for early withdrawal?)

Carl: "No -- that's the <u>last</u> suit you want to play at this stage. That can never be the right play."

(Needless to say, I could not see any difference in terms of which suit to play: each one seemed equally hopeful -- or hopeless -- compared to any other. And is he sure that it can <u>never</u> be the right play? Not even seventeen Fridays from now?)

Carl: "Why don't you try this card; maybe you can develop some tricks in that suit."

(What does he mean by "develop"? Is this sort of like building a housing tract? What is the difference between "developing" a trick and simply taking one? How do you know when you're done "developing" and you can start "taking"?)

Carl: "We use the Stamen Convention for bidding."

(As opposed to what -- the *Pistil* Convention?)

... and so forth.

When I was teaching mathematics, I found that my students fell into various learning categories. At the very top were those who were self-starters: these needed very little if any instruction from me. At the next several levels down were those who were capable of learning provided that, in various degrees, I held their hands and coddled them.

And then there were those students at the very bottom: those were the ones, despite all my efforts, who could not learn the subject matter. I called those students "blank slates on which one cannot write."

This is an apt description of my situation in bridge.

We are all aware of the set of books under the generic title, "(Whatever subject) For Dummies" (there is even one called "Sex For Dummies".) One day I asked Carl whether there was a "Bridge for Dummies" book in the series. He said that there was. I inquired as to how it was.

Carl: "Terrible. Awful. Execrable. It is a model of obfuscation. It's the worst introduction to bridge that I've ever seen -- and that's saying something!"

How appropriate -- a dummy looking for a book for dummies which turns out to have been written by dummies.

(16 July 2008)

Confessions of a Basketball Timer

There is an old cliché:

"Those who Can, Do. Those who Can't, Teach."

Now there is another saying that I coined while teaching at a private school a few years ago. I think that, unlike the above saying, it has a sad veracity:

"Those who Can, Coach. Those who Can't Coach, Time."

Private schools, I've found, like to wring as much out of a teacher as they can. So, when I started at one such school, not only was I the Math Department Chairman, but I had to teach five courses. (The normal teaching load for a department chair in a public school is one course.)

And then I was given the job of Basketball Timer on top of all that.

Now I had never done this job before. And, when I was first presented with it, it seemed pretty daunting. It can also be scary because of the obvious public position of the scoreboard.

There are several tasks that one must juggle more or less together. The main two are:

Keep the time clock. This includes stopping it for time-outs and penalty whistles, then starting it again when play resumes.

Keep score. This changes often, of course. It is embarrassing to have the wrong score up on the board, which I did from time to time.

The other tasks, while subsidiary, are still necessary:

Keep track of the number of fouls for each team.

Keep track of the appropriate period.

Keep track of the time elapsed in a time-out.

And, finally, the single most self-important task (I am jesting here):

Blow The Horn when necessary.

The Horn! Who has not heard this sound in a field house and not been stirred by its clarion call to valor and sacrifice? More seriously, who has not listened objectively to this thing and not concluded that it ranks among the most obnoxious sounds ever devised?

The horn is the acoustical equivalent to sowing a field with salt. As soon as it begins to blare, all conversation - all sounds, in truth - are smothered, throttled.

Since this memoir is a confession, I will now confess something: I turned this awful instrument of aural torture to the advantage of our team. Here's how:

When a team calls a time-out, the Timer stops the clock up on the scoreboard, and begins a 20-second private clock, at the end of which the horn blows. Now the Timer has two alternatives here: he can use an automatic device, which ticks off the required seconds and then blows the horn for a discrete second or two, or he can time the interval on his own watch and then manually blow the horn.

I chose the latter, and here's why: I had noticed that, in general, opposing team coaches did not usually respect the 20-second limit:

they would wait for the horn to cease, and then continue giving instructions to their players until the referee ordered them back onto the court. So I timed the 20 seconds myself, and then blew the horn by hand. The coach opened his mouth to give his players the climax of his instructions which were to be crucial to the next several minutes, perhaps to the game itself. But I kept my finger on that infernal button for many, many seconds. And I watched a frantic coach trying to speak, and the panicked looks on the faces of his players who could not hear him. Finally they gave up in despair and slinked back onto the court, their battle plans in disarray.

There are other things that a basketball Timer needs to know, the failure of which can cause undue embarrassment. For example, when a ball is inbounded, the clock is not to be started again until a player has touched the ball. It is especially critical to observe this rule when there is only a second left on the clock. (Fortunately, I learned that before such a situation came about!) I was told that players have been known to roll the ball the entire length of the court to a fellow teammate next to the basket.

I was never able to cultivate the requisite amount of -- objective distance -- from the action on the court. During one game an opposing player fell flat onto his back with a resounding smack. I felt that this young man may very well have broken his back, perhaps even paralyzed himself for life. So I watched with great consternation as the doctors went out to check him over. Then, abruptly, I heard our coach say, "Ted - clock!" I had left the clock running in yielding to the weakness of a human concern. (I estimated that over two minutes of game time evaporated that evening - to whose advantage, I was never certain. But surely not to my own reputation!)

As you can see, the Basketball Timer is wholly at the mercy of events on the court. A basket is made? Raise the score. A whistle is blown? Stop the Clock. It is all quite depressing, this needing to always <u>react</u> to events. (The situation with the horn is admittedly an exception, but these times lasted only a few seconds each.)

Frankly, once I had mastered the juggling of knee-jerk reactions (once, that is, they had become knee-jerk) which form the tasks of the Timer, I began to chafe at this state of affairs. I wanted to be in control of something Big and Overarching and Important. In point of fact, <u>I wanted to control Time itself</u> - or its passage thereof.

Now I know what you're probably thinking: no one, not even God, can control Time's passage. But heretically, hubristically, I found a way of doing this. I only had to make sure it was not detected by anyone.

Abraham Lincoln once famously said, "You can fool all of the people some of the time." So my stealthy goal became: <u>to find those times</u>.

Now when, I asked, does the Timer need to interfere with the inexorable and steady onrush of Time? Why, when one's team is losing, of course! Who hasn't felt the need for more time in such circumstances? (Come to think of it, who hasn't felt the need for more time in a <u>variety</u> of circumstances?!)

The principal problem for any plan of subterfuge concerning time, of course, is the public nature of the scoreboard. At any given moment, a statistical percentage of the spectators is glancing at the scoreboard. Of these, roughly half is looking at the time remaining. Given that, it would not be wise to simply stop the clock for even a few seconds at a time. (although see below)

But ah! Suppose the Timer were to punch little discrete holes in that otherwise-continuous flow of time? Here's the way I determined to do it: allow the clock to run for four seconds, then stop it for a second; then resume that pattern. This can be done by counting so: (on), 2, 3, 4, (off), (on), 2, 3, 4, (off), etc. In this way, what is five seconds in real time registers as only four seconds on the scoreboard. One's team thereby gains a second for every five seconds of play. Trivial? That comes out to five precious extra minutes for a full 20-minute half!

What, you are feeling greedy? Punch more holes in that continuum of time. Shut the clock off every four seconds and you have gained over seven extra minutes per period; stop it every three seconds and you gain ten minutes! But take care: the more holes you punch, the more likely you are to be detected. (Still, I can imagine an ultimate sort of greed in this vein: turning the clock off and on in successive seconds. In this case the clock would take on a slow-motion quality, a sort of southern languidness ('Mommy, is the clock *tired*?') And each period would be bloated to twice its normal length. Certainly suspicion may be aroused in such a case, especially when baby-sitter bills skyrocket!)

There are people, believe it or not, who are indifferent to detection. A friend of mine told me of an away game he was attending. At one point the home team (which supplied the Timer) was behind. The Timer did not start the clock at all after a time-out. It was so obvious that it was assumed to be a *faux pas*. When my friend went over to inform the Timer, the latter told him curtly to mind his own business. This is known as the *brazen* approach to Timing subterfuge (although when it's this obvious, we might better call it *super*-tefuge!)

Such an obvious theft of additional time offends against one's aesthetic sensibilities. Is it too much to ask for a little *finesse*?! All in all, it seems best to cheat on a *modest* scale, as I first suggested.

On the other hand, suppose that the home team is doing so abominably badly that no amount of extra time would allow them to catch up. In that case, why prolong the agony? Why draw out the game and rub salt in the wounds, when all one wishes is to flee the fieldhouse as soon as possible? In such a situation it is up to the Timer to artificially *dissipate* time. This can easily be done at any moment when the clock is supposed to be stopped (remember that injured player?): penalty whistles, time outs -- even half times, when everyone is racing for bathrooms and refreshments (I am kidding about this last, of course: the clock is reset at half-time.) During those "down" times let the clock run: the game will be over before you know it!

What? You want to be a bit more -- *circumspect* -- about it? Afraid some people might notice? Well then, choose those times when they're looking the other way. Penalty shots provide a good time for this. Just make sure the shots are being taken at the basket away from the scoreboard.

Since I have shown that it is possible to alter the clock to one's advantage, the astute reader (with a criminal mind) might ask whether the same -- *bending* -- can be brought to the <u>score</u> of the game. My answer to this eager request is: regrettably, no. And the reason for this is sitting right next to the Timer at the table: it is the Scorer, who, on special paper, keeps track of every play of the game: who made which basket, and so on. On the bottom of the page he keeps a running tally of the game score. And that tally is considered the correct one. (I have had the Scorer correct me on my score up on the scoreboard, which I'd then change right away. And I wasn't even trying to cheat!)

(The Scorer for our games was a student. But, unlike me, he was a seasoned professional at his craft – and one who wanted to do scoring as a career. He had more gravitas than I did (he seemed to have a world-weariness beyond his 18 years.) About two-thirds of the way through a typical game, he would suddenly remark to me, "You know, this game has gotten really ugly!" This would surprise me, for I had not noticed any change in behavior on the part of the players – no fights or more frequent foul calls. It was halfway through the season before I realized that my distinguished colleague just liked saying the word "ugly".)

Did I ever actually implement these sorts of time-elasticity 'experiments'? I'm afraid not on any grand scale. But, I must confess, I did find myself playing around with it a bit, testing the proverbial waters, getting a feel for the lay of the land. What I found was that, given the frantic pace of a typical basketball game, those stopping/ starting regimens are quite difficult to implement. Yes, difficult -- but not impossible. I got the feeling that, with a little practice, I might get very good at such -- *deviant* (literally, since one is deviating the time from its correct passage) -- behavior.

And before you assume that I would be too noble and upright to engage in such a thing, I should confess that, as the banker in Monopoly, I was once caught (I was totally open about it) having embezzled $5000 from the bank. In answer to the shocked inquiries of my family, I justified it thus: "But it's absolutely in the spirit of the game!"

By the way: when I told a cousin of mine who owns a sports club about my plans to bend Time, he scoffed and said, "That's nothing! A <u>real</u> feat would be to figure out how to bend <u>Space</u>!" That is, to be able to treat the court like a giant accordion. "An opposing player drives for the basket and, just as he reaches it and goes airborne for his silly slam-dunk routine, you lengthen the court and pull the basket away from him. Now <u>that</u> would be something!" Sadly, I never did figure out a way to effect this bit of *wizardry*.

P.S. Recently [Summer 2007], the case of NBA referee Tim Donaghy has come into the news. Donaghy is alleged to have made questionable calls in crucial playoff games on which he had bet. Adrian Wojnarowski of Yahoo! Sports writes:

"Privately, NBA officials wish they could've seen a pattern within Donaghy's officiating to suggest that he could've been shaving points, but that hasn't been apparent to the naked eye. He consistently has been graded as one of the league's better officials, which is the reason he was assigned to five playoff games in the past two years."

"NBA officials, sources said, are painstakingly studying tapes from the past two seasons under FBI suspicion (2005-06 and 2006-07). It is believed that more than a dozen games could've been deliberately affected by Donaghy's calls, games where he and the mob associates had bet thousands of dollars on the point spreads."

"The fact that his performance reviews hadn't suffered these past two years reminded the league office how the manipulating of a game can be done in the most subtle of ways (emphasis mine), without alarming even the most educated eyes."

"'Remember,' one league official said Friday, 'the officials are graded nightly on the calls that they don't make, not just the ones they do.'"

Tim Donaghy – a man after my own heart!

The Littlest Jingle Bell

This is the story of the Littlest Jingle Bell. Follow along with me, Gentle Reader, and when you hear the tiny tinkle of the jingle bell, thus: (sound of the most delicate tink-tink), you'll know to turn the page. Oh -- should this narrative become too saccharine, please feel free to throw up in the barf bag provided with this book.

Actually, if you're worried about that saccharine business, you can relax: I will be mixing vinegar in amongst the sugar through the use of an *alternative narrator*. I'll annotate this warm little tale with asides which will serve as a sort of *cold douche* to balance off its excesses.

Anyway, to begin our tale:

Once upon a time, there lived a jingle bell. He was the tiniest jingle bell in all the world, and for that reason he was called "the Littlest Jingle Bell". [tink-tink]

Well, there it is in the opening lines - can you sense it? It's called *anthropomorphizing* - the endowment of a non-human object with human characteristics. There are all sorts of clues that leap out at us: the juxtaposition of "jingle bell" with "lived"; the "he" (how do you tell the gender of a sleigh bell?); the words "tiniest" and "littlest" (rather than "smallest"), which are hyper-precious terms used for living things to make them *endearing*; etc.

Actually, the anthropomorphizing began right at the start with those first four words. I'll show their power by juxtaposing them with the utterly prosaic - the blandest of scientific entities in the blandest prose:

"Once upon a time there was a hydrogen atom. It was the smallest atom in the Periodic Table. That is why..."

We can't escape its clutches - those words arouse our expectations: <u>there will be a story connected to that woeful atom.</u> (Most likely it will be picked on by the other atoms for being so small and puny. "And then one day he met an oxygen atom. It was a match made in heaven, and when the match was lit...")

Ah well. I state all this to let the author know that they aren't getting away with anything here. Besides, an animate jingle bell will be the least of our problems.

He had one fervent wish: he wanted to be one of the bells on Santa's sleigh. [tink-tink]

A sleigh bell that has human characteristics? Why not! After all, he already has a mouth, a tongue, and a palate (a cleft one at that.) Why not go the rest of the way and, god-like, breathe life into this poor little entity. And, by doing this, we will endow him with some essential features of the human condition: a sense of identity, and a longing for meaning. The best thing about this little being is that it - er, he - is low maintenance: he doesn't need to be fed (so: no poop to clean up), and he can't complain aloud (thus, we don't have to *console* him.)

I'm not even going to bother getting into the question of Santa's existence here.

But can you tell where this story is headed? Is there any doubt in your mind?

The Littlest Jingle Bell lived in the quaint little village of Medford in Massachusetts. [tink-tink]

There are some errors in the above account. First off, Medford, Massachusetts is a city, not a village. Secondly, it is fairly large. And, most decidedly, it ain't quaint. (Barring these disclaimers, the passage is correct as written.) Its square is narrow and congested, with rough pavements that are either being repaired or in need of repair. And the parking problem for any thriving business like a Jingle Bell Shop would be horrendous!

What about the past? Well, in the 19th century, Medford was noted for two industries: distilling rum, and building clipper ships. So it must have been a pretty rough place in James Pierpont's day.

Now, Medford is merely *prosaic*.

(Still, there are at least two pleasing vistas in Medford. One can be seen from the Winthrop Street bridge, with the Mystic River meandering through meadowland in the foreground, and the spires of St. Joseph's, Richardson's Grace Episcopal, and John Pierpont's Unitarian churches towering above the trees in the background (though, truth to tell, Pierpont's church was a different building on that site.) The other vista, the green ornate wrought-iron foot bridge reflected in the Mystic in the center of town, can be spotted from the Main Street bridge.

From either of these vantage points, one can pinch oneself and believe that Medford is, in fact, "a quaint little village".)

Medford is the place where "Jingle Bells" was written many years ago by James Pierpont. [tink-tink]

That James Pierpont wrote "Jingle Bells" (notice that I am confident that this ditty is universally known) is an undisputed fact. As to the Medford birth of that song, I shall let the reader decide from the following salient details of his life:

1822: James Pierpont born. His father was an abolitionist Unitarian minister in Boston.

1836: Runs away to sea at age 14.

1845: Returns. Marries, has two children.

1849: Father becomes minister at Medford Unitarian Church. James leaves wife and kids in the care of his father and ships off to California to cash in on Gold Rush.

1850: James's business burns in San Francisco. He returns to Medford (via Cape Horn, of course.)

1851 (We are now treading a thin line between fact and legend here. I quote here from a history online): "James Pierpont goes to the boarding house of Mrs. Otis Waterman, who let him play a piano there belonging to William Webber, a Medford music teacher." (We should be most suspicious when histories start getting this specific!) "Mrs. Waterman owned the Seccomb Boardinghouse, which became better known as the Simpson tavern (more James's sort of place?) and was eventually torn down. After he had played the piece for her, Mrs. Waterman declared that it was a *very merry little jingle.*" (Ha - the very word to inspire the lyrics!) "James then wrote the lyrics about the one-horse open sleighs - also known as 'cutters' - that young men raced on the one-mile route from Medford to Malden squares." Does it not seem fairly clear that "Jingle Bells" had its genesis in Medford? Do you have any doubt? What, you want <u>proof</u> - letters, diaries and the like? O ye of little faith!

1853: He goes with his brother, John, (also a Unitarian minister) to Savannah, Georgia, where James serves as organist and music director in John's church. His wife and children are again left behind with his father. James has his first songs published in Boston, including "The Colored Coquette" (should we lament that it is lost?) and "Wait, Lady, Wait" (no doubt dedicated to his wife.)

1856: Tired of waiting, his wife dies.

1857: James marries a woman with whom he had already had a child three years earlier. "One Horse Open Sleigh" (the title is later changed to "Jingle Bells", or "The One Horse Open Sleigh") is published in Boston. It does not sell well in either edition.

1860: The Unitarian Church in Savannah closes due to its abolitionist leanings. James's brother returns to the North. James, however, stays in Savannah.

1861: James Pierpont volunteers in the Confederate Army (even as his father serves as a chaplain in the Union army.) But you need not fear for his life: he served as a company clerk. He also wrote music for the Confederacy, including "Conquer or Die". (Notice how easily certain composers, safe from the fray, can call on others to give up their lives!)

1866: James moves his family to Valdosta, Georgia, where he taught music and, we are told, was involved in a local scandal...and so on.

He is rather - *interesting* - isn't he (even Michael McGlynn, the present Mayor of Medford, called him 'a bit of a rogue.') And it seems that Savannah has sought to put forth a rival claim to Medford's as to the origin of "Jingle Bells". Lacking more concrete evidence, we will never know for sure which town to give the credit to - which doesn't stop us from trumpeting Medford. After all, it *hath the virtue of convenience*!

But here is a question each of us can answer individually: Which would you rather be, a successful man who is forgotten not long after he dies? Or a bit of a scoundrel who does a bunch of things not very well, but who is remembered forever after his death for a song everyone loves to sing? Would you not perhaps opt for a tiny bit of immortality?

He lived with lots of other jingle bells in the Jingle Bell Shop where he was born. [tink-tink]

As a resident of Medford I have long harbored a desire to open a so-called Jingle Bell Shop as near to the (supposed) site of the composition of "Jingle Bells" as possible. It would be a family affair, I reasoned: my mother-in-law could write and illustrate books on "Jingle Bells" and "Over the River and Through the Woods" (another Medford ditty); my brother-in law could act as the maitre d' up front; while I would labor in the back forging (or is it casting?) the various jingle bells to be sold (including sterling silver ones for our high-end customers.) Items in this noble emporium (or would it be a tourist trap?) would be a bit on the expensive side; but the customer would be mollified by receiving with each purchase a <u>Certificate of Authenticity</u> which testified to the fact that the sleigh bells so bought were in fact acquired at that venerable Shop.

Well, my brainchild never reached fruition: there is no Jingle Bell Shop in Medford (a waste of a marvelous business opportunity, in my view.) But let us for a moment try to imagine bringing into existence such an entity.

The site (sorry - *alleged* site) of the composition of "Jingle Bells" in Medford (marked by a plaque) is on High Street just a few doors away from the square. An office building fills up the whole block, and its individual stores have been renovated in the cold blandness of steel and tinted glass. So if we would want the Jingle Bell Shop on the very sacred site of composition (and of course authenticity is our goal *whenever possible*), all that steel and glass would have to be torn out. And in its place would be something that would appear to be as Old and Venerable as the famous ditty itself.

The inside walls and shelves and floors would be built of old wood which had been left to weather outdoors for a long time. Worm holes could then be *interpolated* into the boards. Spiders would have to be *imported*, the better to spin their webs between ancient-looking beams. Dust would be *blown into* the back rooms. Mildew would be cultivated in special petri dishes and then *introduced* into the walls. In short, a sort of *faux* Old Curiosity Shop - totally contrived but then, paradoxically, *genuine*.

There would be paned windows on the front of the Jingle Bell Shop. Would these have fake ice crystals painted on them? Bite your tongue! The window casement would be constructed of refrigeration coils. So the ice on the windows would be <u>real</u> crystals all year round. The only bizarre thing about this would be that in the summer the ice would form on the (air conditioned) <u>inside</u> of the panes.

There would be, of course, only one Jingle Bell Shop: it would be irreproducible, utterly unique. (True, eventually we might have some vague plans to open a sister Jingle Bell Shop in Savannah, Georgia somewhere down the line. But that, too, would be unique, one-of-a-kind, irreproducible. And: it would double our revenue!)

At night, after the people had left, all the jingle bells would gather around James Pierpont's piano and sing "Jingle Bells." [tink-tink]

I have no doubts that this would make for a horrid tintinnabulation! For jingle bells have little resonance and no real pitch, although I assume they do have a slight relative pitch dependent on their size. (Let us hope they have a rhythmic sense!) So using the word "sing" here is rather an excrescence on the normal understanding of the word. (Another thing: if bells shake and there is no one there to hear them...)

As for that piano:

Halfway into the Jingle Bell Shop would be the so-called Tunesmith's Corner. There would be a fireplace, of course, with a cheerful fire going. (NB: Why are fires in fireplaces always "cheerful"?

Why not "abstracted" or "moody" or even "cantankerously spiteful"?) Near the fireside would be an old upright piano (Pierpont's? Who knows. But it would "become" his by virtue of the "Law of Juxtaposition"), upon which would sit a piece of manuscript paper (artificially aged, like the rest of the establishment.) And upon that manuscript paper would be inscribed (by me) the opening of the famous ditty. It would be as if the composer had just been there in the act of composition.

The first six notes, of course, are all the same. And what, pray, might be those opening words scrawled on that ancient-looking parchment? It seems a bit facile and obvious to put the actual finished words there. Why not show what very well might have been an initial inspiration:

"Jangle bells, jangle bells..."

It does grate a bit, doesn't it. But, it must be admitted, the *germ* of the central idea is there. Once that opening is corrected, he might have proceeded thus:

"Jingle bells, jingle bells, Jingle all to bed!"

Do you see? No doubt his first impulse was to rhyme this with "sled". And so originally he sought to sing about the joys of sledding (and maybe bedding too!)

Well, whatever. The important thing is to have something on that damn piece of pseudo-old manuscript paper.

It would be *insinuated* that this was the very spot where "Jingle Bells" was written. And who is to say it isn't? (This is an example of what I call "seizing the historical perspective": state your own history first, thereby putting everyone else in the position of having to disprove it - usually an all-but-impossible enterprise.)

The Littlest Jingle Bell lived in the dusty back room of the Jingle Bell Shop with other jingle bells that were odd and all but forgotten.

The word "odd" is intriguing, isn't it.

There would be two rooms in that venerable Shop. These correspond to the Ego and the Id in Freudian psychology.

The front room, well-lighted and cheerful (that fire!), would contain everything desirable relating to jingle bells. There would be beautifully bound books with handsome illustrations on vellum paper. There would be large, glittering brass and silver jingle bells in cherry presentation cases lined with green felt; and other smaller ones arranged in careful size gradations on oiled leather harnesses. All the jingle bells would have "JBS" elegantly engraved on them. Of course there would be the Tunesmith's Corner, subtly sanctified by using deep cranberry-hued velvet ropes to set it apart (as Mozart's fortepiano is in Salzburg.)

The back room, by contrast, would be dark and hot and musty. On one side would be the furnace in which the various jingle bells are cast. There would be tables for finish work and the like. On the other side would be various shelves containing the widest variety of finished jingle bells to be found anywhere.

Now once it is established what exactly is to be produced, any business like this one reaches a steady state wherein one's activity is in the main devoted to the mere *replenishment* of what is sold. Is it conceivable, then, that this business might become a bit *boring* to its owner after awhile? This boredom would have front- and back-room implications.

In the back room I would begin to *experiment* with size and shape. Could I turn out an oblong jingle bell? A double one with two jinglets? One with undulations? I would *challenge* myself to produce the largest jingle bell in the world; and the smallest (no doubt the latter would give "birth" to the Littlest Jingle Bell.) In short, the back room would contain all the - *extremes* (I was tempted to say 'freaks', but desisted) - of the jingle bell world. (It also was a far more interesting place than the front room, which relied in the main on dazzle and glitter.)

In that front room, boredom might cause me to begin to stretch the truth a bit about what I purported to sell. I might, for example, feign the title of *restless traveler* (although in truth I hate traveling) in search of unusually engaging sleigh bells. In particular, I could pretend to seek those of unique importance in history: Bells from the sleigh Napoleon used as he fled Moscow! Bells from the horses of the hussars who rode the Charge of the Light Brigade! Hell, the original bells from that Medford One-Horse Open Sleigh immortalized by James Pierpont!

(What, you are skeptical that I could find such bells? So am I, frankly! Where potential fraud is involved, no matter how kindly one's intentions, one cannot be too careful. After all, a lawsuit against The Jingle Bell Shop would cast an unfavorable light over the venerable *Certificate of Authenticity*, and then where would we be? No -- better to undertake all this by *allusion*, as it were: we could speak of bells "*similar to*" those used by Napoleon; bells "*of the sort*" found in the famous Charge; and even (I realize I'm cutting it rather closely here) "the very jingle bell *sounds* heard by James Pierpont as he was sitting down to write his famous ditty.")

(See how careful I am? Sleigh bells, of course, can be easily tested for their age. But how could the experts carbon-date a <u>sound</u>? They can't, of course!)

(Well, and why not nail down a connection by juxtaposition viz.: "Napoleon Bells"? If someone questions this, I could reply indignantly as one whose honour has been impugned, "I didn't say 'Napoleon's Bells'!")

Is boredom at the root of all creativity?

It is Christmas Eve night, and it is snowing in the village of Medford. The harness of brass sleigh bells on the door jangles merrily and Santa himself enters the Jingle Bell Shop. [tink-tink]

Yes, let's cut to the chase: it is snowing in Medford. The sleigh is sitting out in front of The Jingle Bell Shop (let us hope there is not a fire hydrant there.) The reindeer are pawing the snow (and the loose asphalt), impatient to be on their way. And Santa is fiddling around in a bell shop. (When the owner's wife rushes to the back room to tell her husband the exciting news as to their visitor, he replies irately, "I don't care <u>who</u> it is, we should have closed half an hour ago!") Perhaps Santa had just had a double-cappuccino at the Bestsellers Bookstore Cafe (itself a Medford anomaly) across the street. Certainly he needs the caffeine; and he cannot start his deliveries until everyone is in bed fast asleep. So he has some time to kill.

But why that store in that town? Is he really just wasting time, or does he have a nobler motive for being there?

Unfortunately, the original manuscript of the children's story breaks off here, and so we will never know for sure what the author intended.

I can just feel the ire of my readers bearing down on me, accusing me of something like *contrivance* in all of this. So I would just like to reassure everyone on this point: I am merely the editor of this petit tome - don't shoot the messenger!

At the same time I feel an obligation to bring this story to a fitting resolution. But what is "fitting"? (Are the ones that don't quite 'fit' the most interesting?)

Actually there are many possible endings for this tale, but most are anticlimactic. Santa stands at the door, gazes around for a few seconds, then leaves. Perhaps he is panicked as to the time. Maybe he's sick of jingle bells. Maybe he's just plain sick and throws up in the gutter.

If he does decide to enter the shop, he could be seduced by the glitter and extravagance of the front room, so that he never enters the back room at all. He could be bored (how many Christmas Eves has he taken this trip?) and have no interest in where he is or why. He could be drunk and boorish (it began as a warming against the cold night ahead and got out of hand.)

But of course none of those makes for a very compelling story. They seem irrelevant, we feel cheated – why? Because this tale is called "The Littlest Jingle Bell". No tale worth its salt would leave its title character out of the final climactic scene, would it? (Actually there are many such cases in literature, not least of which is Shakespeare's "Julius Caesar", whose title character dies fairly early on. But the present story isn't a work of literature – is it?)

So we seek closure in this story. Santa must enter that back room! And so we concoct a more "fitting" finale for this tale:

In this version of the story, Santa is all-wise and all-knowing. He is a connoisseur of everything for the sleigh which is good and noble. His musical sense is as finely attuned as that of the best conductors. And he's not one to endure the acoustical status-quo for very long - he's a *restless* man. So each year he is in search of that bell which will change the timbre of the sleigh sound ever so slightly. And he's an egalitarian, so that any bell has an equal chance of being chosen over any other.

When he pauses on the threshold of the Jingle Bell Shop, one contemptuous glance tells him of the glitz and glitter of the front room, the sham of the Tunesmith's Corner. He strides resolutely through all that nonsense to the back room. There he finds bells of the sort he has never seen before.

He begins trying them one by one, patiently picking them up and jingling them. And then what?

In one heartbreaking version, Santa doesn't see the Littlest Jingle Bell at all. (Why not? Because that bell is too small, there's too much dust, the room is too ill-lit - whatever.)

That doesn't seem like the sort of ending we wanted either. Santa must find the Littlest Jingle Bell. He must find him, pick him up, hold him up to his ear, and shake him gently.

This is the most important moment of that little entity's existence - it is the one thing he has dreamed about. He knows he must give the performance of his life! So (I'm winging it here, obviously, but I think I know the author's style by now*): he closes his eyes as tightly as he can* (though of course he has no eyes to close); *he clenches his little fists as hard as he can* (though he has no hands to clench); *and he gives the best rendition of his "tink-tink" that he can* (though he has absolutely no control over his jinglet.)

And then what? We are at our last binary fork. Even now there is the possibility of two endings - one heartwarming, the other gut-wrenching.

In the heartwarming ending, Santa exclaims, "The very bell I've been looking for – I never dreamed I'd find one so deliciously little!" and chooses the Littlest Jingle Bell for his sleigh. (As he pays the inflated price for the bell, he waves aside the bogus Certificate of Authenticity with a barely hidden look of disdain. For what is more authentic than Santa's *imprimatur*?) Outside he attaches the Littlest Jingle Bell to the harness on the reindeer nearest him, knowing that this is the location from which the bell's delicate "tink-tink" can be heard to its best advantage. And then off they all go, flying into immortality. *And they lived happily ever after.*

As for the gut-wrenching version (which I hesitated to publish here: it is so cynical I am wont to weep out of pity): Santa picks up the Littlest Jingle Bell, holds him up to his ear, and, shaking him gently, listens closely. Almost imperceptibly, a frown steals over the ancient countenance. For a moment he regards him carefully. Then with the devastating words, "Nope – much too small!" he tosses (in a rather perfunctory way, I'd say) the Littlest Jingle Bell back onto the dust heap of the shelf (and of history itself, I suspect) and leaves the shop forever.

Well! Which ending would you choose? Before you do, however, let me make a case for the second (gut-wrenching) ending:

A friend of mine who is a science teacher idolized Linus Pauling all his adult life. One day the friend found himself at a conference where the renowned chemist was to be the keynote speaker. After the speech he stood in a long line to meet Pauling. Eventually he reached the famous man. They shook hands, my friend told him how much he admired his work, and a picture was taken. All that lasted less than a minute. But for years afterwards my friend would talk in glowing terms about that moment of meeting his hero.

Just so our tale here: the Littlest Jingle Bell met the personage of his dreams. Admittedly the meeting did not give him what he most wanted. But in time it will be <u>The Encounter itself</u> that he will see as important. Over the subsequent years he will begin to change elements of the meeting in his mind: Santa did not toss him back onto the shelf, but rather *laid him gently down*. Perhaps he even *caressed* him. Then, too, Santa's words would not be blunt and dismissive, but rather *kind and hopeful*. Perhaps he would praise him by telling him how *beautiful* he is. And he might say something like, "I'm sorry I have no room for you now, but *some day I will come back here and fetch you - I promise!*"

This version of an ending for our tale is capable of generating many stories precisely due to its imperfections. That, in my view, makes it by far the more interesting, the more – *human* - of the two.

So will you choose the gut-wrenching ending? What - you still want the fairy-tale one? You are hopeless! Just remember – that bag is available should you ever need it!

By the way, I lived in Medford some twenty-six years, and I have no recollection of it ever snowing on Christmas Eve.

Many Happy Returns

Training with the Master

There was no doubt about it: I was terrible at it from the very beginning.

When my brother and I were growing up, our favorite store in our hometown was the Five and Ten. One evening just before dinner in early December, when our ages were still single-digit numbers, we found ourselves in that emporium wiling away the time while our mother ran some errands nearby.

There were all sorts of wonderful things there for a boy in the early 1950s: these included hobby kits to build antique model automobiles (my interest), and stamp albums along with packets of stamps from around the world (my brother's preference.)

But today we were looking for something (more specifically: something that I could afford) which I could get my brother for his birthday. We looked at such wonders as plastic model DeSoto taxicabs whose doors and trunk opened up. He finally chose a yellow water pistol in the shape of a machine gun.

Then he left the store; for it would not be seemly for him to see me in the act of purchasing his own birthday present. I took one of the pistols off the shelf, brought it over to the main counter in the center of the room, handed it to the man standing there (whom I knew to be the owner), and said with an emphatic certainty that belied my usual reticent demeanor, "I'll take this." The man said something I've never forgotten:

"Water gun for fifty-nine."

He took the pistol from me and wrapped it in brown paper. I paid him. Then I left the store with that warm cozy feeling one gets when one has done a good deed for someone.

It was already dark at that time of day at that time of year. My mother and brother were parked in the Kaiser waiting for me right in front of the store. Holding the package, I got into the back seat with my brother. And at that point my feelings of altruistic bliss turned quickly into the torments of hell.

Brother: "Did you get that stupid water gun? I didn't want that!"

Mother: "Teddy, why did you buy that for him? Can't you see that he doesn't want it? You're going to have to take it back! Ugh -- your father will be home any minute!"

I begged not to have to do this but I was given no choice: I had to go back into the store -- and quickly. With a heavy heart I passed through the door.

The owner saw me and asked, "Can I help you with something?"

I was feeling terrible. Here was a man who was in the business of selling things to people; that is how he earned his living. Furthermore, he just expressed a desire to help me. And what am I about to do? Dash his fondest hopes -- and his livelihood -- to the ground! I felt like the lowest heel.

"I -- I have to bring this back." I handed him the package.

The man's brow wrinkled: clearly I was already causing him pain. He began to unwrap it. "What seems to be the trouble?"

I was stuck there: did I want to tell him what had happened with my brother and my mother? Not on your life -- I would have sooner crawled over broken glass! On the other hand, I had not prepared myself for that question. So I blurted out the first thing that popped into my head: "The trigger's broken."

The man looked at the trigger and tried it for a few seconds. I saw his brow begin to darken: now he was growing angry. When he looked up at me and spoke, his voice had an eerie calmness about it:

"This trigger is fine. You lied to me. I'll give you your money back. But I never want to see you in this store again!"

I took my money and left the store forever. Inside the car I began to tell my mother and brother what had happened; but I was so upset that I burst into tears. At that display my brother began to mock me, while my mother yelled at me because of my behavior in the store. Once home, my father yelled at me some more. Dinner was not pleasant.

And thus ends that charming little tale. I can see that there are some deep currents at work in the above scenario: a brother's betrayal, a mother's lack of understanding, deflected altruism, and all the rest. These provide fertile ground for some future memoirs.

But I've decided to take a more modest tack here and spin a fantasy based on the banal obviousness of the following phrase:

I realized that I was terrible at taking things back.

I knew that I never wanted to be in that sort of horrible and embarrassing situation again. (Unfortunately, for my favorite store it was too late.) Admittedly, there wasn't much I could do to control my mother and my brother. However, there was one thing I could work on for improvement: my skills at returning things.

As it turned out, there happened to be someone else living in our house who was a veritable genius at taking things back. I would seek his advice. So a few evenings later I swallowed my pride and summoned all my nerve to approach my father while he was reading the *Newark Evening News*. I began thusly:

"Dad -- Dad -- I -- I -- the other night -- I -- that is, you..."

My father did not have much tolerance for such mealy-mouthed behavior: "Come, Teddy, what's the trouble? You can give it to me straight -- spit it out, I won't bite your head off!" So I summoned all my courage and rhetorical skills as follows:

"Dad, no doubt you recall what happened to me in the store the other night. That was really terrible and I never want to have it happen again. So I -- I want you to teach me the way you take things back to a store. I have observed you, and I've noticed that you're very good at it; in fact, I'd say you were a natural." (Needless to say, I didn't mention how much he embarrassed our family while we were in various stores.)

My father bit off my head: "Geez, wazzamaddawiya?! How are you going to learn to become a man if you can't stand on your own two feet?" He had been born before the turn of the century, and as a result he was a great advocate for the idea of self-reliance as found in the works of Horatio Alger, his favorite author. (I was glad that he wasn't the one who taught us swimming, with his sink-or-swim attitude!)

But I flattered him so much (while hiding my disgust) and begged so shamelessly (from which he didn't bother to hide his) that he finally agreed to take me on as an apprentice back-taker.

He told me that there were three essential things I needed to master in order to become an expert: Body-language (as he called it -- he seems to have anticipated the expression by a few decades, the Statement, and the Reason(s). He told me that he would bring me with him to a store over the weekend to begin my lessons.

1. Body-language:

When I told my mother about our conversation, she laughed and said to me, "You can learn a lot about that just by observing your father as he watches the prize fights on Friday nights!" I knew well what she was talking about: he would go to a sort of belligerent trance. He would sit on the edge of the couch and then, as the fight progressed, become more and more agitated. A wild look would come into his eyes, and he bared his clenched teeth. Meanwhile he was flailing away with his fists. For all intents and purposes my father was fighting every Friday night.

The next day my father took me to a store where he "needed" to return something. He said to me, "I'd like you to stay out of earshot and to just watch my body-language this first time out."

Now although I was only nine years old at that time, I had already witnessed my father returning things innumerable times. As I said before, I remembered how embarrassed we all were because he always seemed to be belligerently accosting store personnel about something or other. (He was of medium height and build; so I think that he cherished a context in which he, a physical nonentity, could be the aggressor in a public confrontation.) In fact, so much did he like returning items that I sometimes suspected him of deliberately buying things he didn't want just so he could later indulge himself in the pleasure of bringing them back.

But at those times I have been embarrassed because I was a member of his family. Now I had a newfound scientific interest in his behavior: I was doing *research*. If my father's back-taking was a canker on the body of our family, I was beginning to inject myself with some of its venom.

I observed him at the store. As he went up to the counter and approached the manager, he became transformed in front of my very eyes. No longer was he the rather pathetic little public man of my acquaintance. I noticed that his body assumed the crouched posture of a welterweight boxer; in fact, with his navy watch cap, he resembled what I imagined to be a scrapper down on the Jersey City docks. And, in the way he leaned towards his adversary while bobbing his head, he was a coiled serpent which might lash out at any moment. In doing all that, my father had intuitively compressed his behavior during the prize fight into a subtle collection of vaguely menacing gestures. It was a masterful bit of acting.

The manager never had a chance.

2. The Statement:

That evening my father called me into the living room and wanted to hear what I would say first in the event I was bringing something back. I stammered out my first attempt:

Me: "I -- I wonder whether you would allow me to return this item?"

Dad: "That is the most wishy-washy thing I've heard all week! You are "wondering" whether they would "allow" you to bring the item back? You are almost begging them to refuse! No -- you need to get rid of the namby-pamby pandering and just say what you want."

Me: "I'd like to return this item."

Dad: "You put it in some kind of hypothetical form, as if it's not real that you're standing there with the bloody item in your hand. In short, don't beat about the bush -- just say it!"

Me: "I want to return this item."

Dad: "Of <u>course</u> you 'want' to return it -- why else would you be there? Can you leave your wants out of it and just state what you are literally doing?"

Me: "I am returning this item." I paused, exhausted.

Dad: "Bravo! Do you see how clear and chaste that is? No manager can argue with that simple statement of fact."

Me: "But it's so direct, so aggressive, so -- brazen..."

Dad: "Yes. And there's something of a threat in it as well: it seems to want to continue with the words, '... whether you want me to or not!'"

Me: "I still don't see how one can succeed with that, it is so blunt and obvious!" I was of the school of thought which assumed that the best way to get someone to do something was by cajolery and flattery.

My father thought about this for a moment. Then he said:

Dad: "A few years ago I ran a series of informal experiments on this very idea, and they taught me something very interesting. Here's how it all started: one afternoon while I was down at the plant, I was waiting in line to make a blueprint when I was called to the phone. It was your mother needing me for an emergency at home. I had to have a blueprint as soon as I came back. So I did something that I never had done before (well, at least not since my school days): I cut into the front of the line while saying, 'Excuse me but I wonder if you would allow me to make my copies now? I have an emergency at home which I have to attend to right away!' Thankfully, the line parted for me and I was able to make my blueprints."

"I thought about this incident over the next few weeks. Something gnawed at me: was I allowed into the line because of my sob story, or was it due to something more basic? Like a good engineer, I had to find out. So a few days later I cut into the blueprint-making line again, this time with the words, 'I wonder if I might cut in? I am in a hurry and need to make copies.' To my surprise (and delight), the line parted like the Red Sea and I was allowed once more to make blueprints early."

"Well -- I couldn't stop there -- I had to carry things to their logical conclusion. I had found out that the sob story wasn't necessary; I wondered whether any excuse was? So I allowed another few weeks to pass and then once again I cut into the line using the words, 'Excuse me -- I need to make copies.' Wonderfully, miraculously, the line parted for me."

"Do you see? No *bona fide* excuse was necessary, only a literal statement of intention (I wonder whether any statement, no matter how irrelevant, might have sufficed, such as 'Excuse me -- it's raining out!'?) The only criterion is that one must make the statement with absolute confidence, in such a way that no one feels they would dare argue with it. Of course it always helps to ask to be excused!"

3. The Reason(s):

My father knew that he had to gradually ease me into learning the art of returning things to a store. He told me that he would start me out in the simplest possible sort of public situation, something "to break the ice": the Returns counter at Korvettes. He described it thusly:

"At those stores there is a counter, labeled 'Returns', which is solely dedicated to that activity. One stands in line, and when one's turn comes, one simply hands the goods one wishes to relinquish to the girl behind the counter. And here is the great thing: one does not have to even say the hated words, "I am returning this." For that's the whole purpose of that counter! Does the girl care about the fact that you are returning something (perhaps she owns a sizable chunk of Korvettes stock)? Not a whit! The only things she cares about are her salary of $0.93 per hour (or whatever it is), and being able to find the right bin in which to toss (with utter indifference) said returned items."

"True, one must interact with the girl in two ways. First of all, she will ask for a sales receipt; without it you can not receive a refund (though I have a couple of ways to get around that too.) Second, she will ask you for the reason why you are making the return. This would seem like a moment fraught with the most danger: give the wrong answer, and you will be scourged, mocked, and then run out of the store on a rail. Are you worried? Relax! Wonderfully, unbelievably, this is one of those rare situations in life where <u>no answer is wrong</u>! No doubt the purpose in collecting these responses is for the management to determine which products are undesirable and in what ways. (There is probably some lower level functionary whose sole job it is to pour over those entrails and attempt to make rhyme or reason of them.)"

"In short, Korvettes is the perfect place for you to start honing your back-taking skills."

So my father drove me to Korvettes on the next Saturday. He began the process of my initiation by purchasing, seemingly at random, six items: an extra-large man's shirt, a woman's dress, a pair of boots, a frying pan, a very large velvet 'painting', and a water gun. On one of these he held back the sales receipt; but he told me what to say when the girl asked for it. He gave me a small pep talk:

"Remember: no place can argue over a personal preference. (If you say you don't like something for whatever reason, what can they do?) And don't forget: with a firm statement you can get whatever you want."

"Now go up to that counter and have fun! Stay loose! Give your imagination free reign! Let this outing be *cathartic* [I didn't know this word but he explained it to me] for your past trauma! Remember: no answer is wrong!"

I took the six items up to Returns. I could hardly see over the counter. At first the girl didn't notice me (she was filing her nails until I piped up in my high-pitched voice, "I'm returning these!". Then she said in a flat bored tone without locking: "First item please." She held out her hand.

I handed her the extra-large shirt along with the receipt. She checked the two to ascertain that they belonged together. Then she drawled: "Reason for return?" She was already poised with a Bic pen over a standard form they used there.

"I don't like the color," I replied with the firm emphasis I had learned from my father. The girl dutifully checked the appropriate box on the sheet ["Wrong Color."] She took the shirt and tossed it back into a bin behind her. She never compared my size (I was a small thin lad) to the size of the shirt; or if she did she didn't care. This served to embolden me.

Women's dress: "It doesn't fit me." ["Wrong size"]

Work boots: "I don't have the receipt, because they were a gift, but I know they were brought here because I saw them on the shelf." ["Gift return."]

Frying pan: "I don't cook -- and neither does my wife." ["Cannot use item."]

Velvet 'painting': "Originally I had shoplifted this; but my conscience kicked in and anyway I had gotten tired of it. So I forged a sales receipt, and here I am." ["Dissatisfaction with item."]

Water gun: "The trigger's broken." ["Item defective."]

And that was that, the purging of all my paranoia.

Over the next several months my father would lead me through a graduated series of intricacies in back-taking at various stores (the 'final exam' was the successful return of an item from a 'No Returns' sale), to the point where he proudly deemed me to be 'an expert'. But that first session at Korvettes was by far the most fun and liberating.

By the time I was ten, I was actually *relishing* the prospect of returning something -- just like my father.

Addendum: I recall one situation in which my father did not take an item back to a store employee. He had bought something or other that he wanted to exchange -- it was really quite insignificant, small enough to fit into a small paper bag. I remember (I was with him at the time) that he simply walked into the store, went back to where he had gotten the item, took it out of his bag and put it back on the shelf, plucked the item he wanted off the shelf and dropped it into his bag, and then proceeded to leave the store.

Or tried to. There was a store detective at the door who stopped him and demanded to know what was in the bag. Luckily, my father had the sales receipt from the old item; and the new item cost exactly the same. So he was just admonished by the detective to "go through proper channels next time!"

Do you see what my father was doing? From his standpoint he was just being efficient. But he was doing what I could only dream of doing in my early years: he was eliminating the middleman.

(6 June 2008)

Mother Goose

A tall tale whets an appetite

(The following is a transcription of a telephone "conversation" which I had around 30 years ago. My wife, Dorothy, who was standing next to me all the while this was going on, will testify as to its veracity.)

One evening, at exactly 6:45, the phone rang. The caller asked, "is this the massage parlor?" I replied that it wasn't.

I thought nothing more about what I ascribed to be a wrong number. But the next evening, there was another call at exactly 6:45 asking for the massage parlor. And the same thing the next evening.

We finally came to the realization that there was probably an incorrect phone number printed in some publication (no doubt the *Boston Phoenix*) for a massage parlor. I decided to have a little fun. So the next evening when the phone rang at 6:45 p.m., I answered in a low, unctuous voice, "Mother Goose Massage Parlor -- may I help you?"

A male voice replied, "Yes --can you tell me what services you provide?" He seemed to emphasize the word "services" in a very suggestive way.

"Services?" I said. "Yes, we have all sorts of--services! What kinds of services did you have in mind?"

But he was keeping it purposely vague: "Well, uh, what kinds of services do you have?" The word "services" hung in the air suggestively like a ripe peach.

"Services? Do we have services! You won't <u>believe</u> the services we have! Do you want me to describe our run-of-the-mill services? Or should I tell you about the kind of *unique* services we have that no other massage parlor has?"

He said he'd like to hear about the "unique" services.

So I began: "In other massage parlors, they use their hands to rub you down. But, as far as I know, the Mother Goose Massage Parlor is the only place in which we *rub you down with a live goose*."

To my surprise, he responded with "Uh-Huh..." This was said in that tone of voice expressing genuine interest, as if to say "Tell me more!", rather than the incredulity I expected. I quickly pushed through to the punch line:

"So, whereas those other parlors are merely giving you rub-downs, at the Mother Goose Massage Parlor we give you *down-rubs*."

I expected that my caller would get my little joke, give the obligatory chortle (or groan), and hang up. But once again he responded with "Uh-Huh..." His appetite had just been whetted, and he was eager to hear more. I found myself placed in the position of having to improvise on the spot:

"Then, after you've been given your down-rub, we leave the room and allow you to be alone with the goose to do whatever you want with it."

"Uh-Huh..."

I was winging it by the seat of my pants, but what else could I do?

"*Once the goose is dead*, we retrieve it from you, bring it into our kitchen, and prepare you a complete roast goose dinner with all the trimmings. And the cost for everything -- the down-rub, the personal use of the goose, and the banquet -- is only $100." (Note: this was quite a chunk of change for the year 1978. On the other hand, look at what he would be getting for that paltry sum!)

And what was my caller's response to this obvious bit of -- to my way of thinking at least -- reduction to absurdity?

"Uh-Huh..."

What could I do? It was obvious that the caller was intrigued by my idea of a unique massage parlor. I simply could not get him to hang up! Thinking quickly, I finally told him that there was someone at the door -- could he hold? He said that he would. I put the phone down for about 30 seconds; then I picked it up again and said:

"Sir, are you still there?"

"Yes..."

"I'm afraid that was the Massachusetts Society for the Prevention of Cruelty to Animals. They tell me that they have been looking at my little, er, operation now for some time."

"So what does this mean?"

"Quite frankly, it probably means that my goose is cooked!"

"Uh-Huh."

(By the way, if someone spends all their days in a massage parlor without getting any natural light, do they develop a *parlor pallor*?

(16 March 2008)

The Old College Try

Better Late Than Never

From the first moment I was in school, my parents talked about me going to college. It was, you might say, an unwritten assumption. After all, they had both attended college (my father was an engineer, while my mother was a teacher.)

So I did not worry about college while I was in high school. It would happen, I knew, when the time came. People (my parents, the guidance counselor, etc.) were looking out for me, as they always had.

My parents each had the notable distinction of being the first in their families' lineage to graduate from college. My father's father worked as a machinist, while my mother's parents were farmers.

We did not know that things had changed since my parents went to college. My father had graduated from Newark Technical School, a forerunner of the Newark College of Engineering (no doubt it has changed its name yet again since my day and age), in 1921; he had attended at night while he was working. So he had probably walked in off the street, registered, and began attending classes on the spot.

Likewise my mother, who attended the state "Normal School" (Teachers' College -- now SUNY-Cortland) in the next town and graduated in 1928. No doubt she walked in the day before classes were to start and registered.

My parents were also naïve. They had almost no friends socially, and those they had were strange people connected to my father's workplace. So they were not in touch with the parents of my classmates, who knew what was what. Those kinds of parents were the sort who would call the guidance counselor and even the principal every other day to find out what the status of their kid was on the College front. They were a pain in the butt, but they didn't care, because they knew that the squeaky wheel gets the grease.

All of that is intended to form a backdrop to my little tale. It was December of my senior year in high school. I was sitting in homeroom one morning, half listening to the announcements while I did some last-minute cramming for a test that day. I heard one which said:

"Congratulations to Mark Strauss on his early admission to Dartmouth!"

I had heard those sorts of announcements for the last few days and hadn't thought much about it. But now I was curious. I nudged my friend sitting next to me and asked, "What is that? What does it mean?"

"Oh it means that he got into college early."

"How does one get into college?"

And then my friend said those immortal words that I will never forget:

"You have to do something called 'apply'."

"And how does one apply?"

"You have to have them send you an application."

"How will I know which colleges to apply to?"

"You should go and see Miss Howell -- she'll tell you."

Miss Howell was the Guidance Counselor. Naïve and ignorant though I was, I was able to surmise that my parents weren't the only ones to drop the ball here -- as far as Miss Howell was concerned, I wasn't even on the radar screen.

She gave me the names of three men's colleges to apply to, all of which were in Pennsylvania and not terribly far from our town in New Jersey. They were: Lafayette, Lehigh, and Franklin & Marshall. By comparing notes, I later found out that she recommended those same three colleges to all the boys that she didn't know what else to do with. Likewise for the girls. Miss Howell only knew the names of about eleven colleges or something.

So I wrote away to those three schools and got their applications and then went through the onerous task of filling them out -- with help from my mother. (I remember that she was mystified over how to answer the question "Father's Profession:" I recall being more mystified over the fact that she was mystified!)

We had the applications in the mail by mid-January. By early April I had heard from two of the three schools. Lafayette had put me on their Waiting List, while Franklin & Marshall was making my acceptance contingent upon a personal interview. I did not hear from Lehigh at all that month.

So during April vacation, my mother and I embarked upon a trip down to Pennsylvania to look at those schools -- the sort of odyssey that the Responsible Students had taken a full year before.

Before we left for our college tour, I was able to get a hold of a valuable pamphlet called "Helpful Hints for the College Interview." For once in my life I was going to go into something prepared beforehand!

Unfortunately, this pamphlet was written for the Admissions Person doing the interview. So all it said was: "Browbeat the candidate! Make him realize that you hold his future in your hands, that you have an enormous amount of power over him!"

Luckily, I had the intelligence and the good sense to see this for what it was. And with that bit of insight, I assumed that I had passed the first step of the interview process -- namely, to know that I was the one to be interviewed.

I did get a hold of a pamphlet I wanted and needed. Forty-eight-years later, I still recall a part of the first point, and I provide it below; the rest is a logical extrapolation from that.

Helpful Tips for the Student Undergoing a College Interview

1. At the start of the interview, the admissions person might offer you a cigarette. <u>This is not a trap</u>. If the act of smoking puts you at your ease, helping you relax and think better, by all means take one.

   a. Things you should say: a modest "Thank you" or "No thank you" is enough.

   b. Things you should avoid saying; Things such as "Thanks -- I would've had a nicotine fit if I had gone much longer without a weed!"; or "What are you trying to do -- kill me off before I even start coming to this dump?"

2. During the course of the interview, the Admissions Person might offer you a stick of chewing gum. <u>This is an inverted trap</u>. They are well aware that [in 1961] the chewing of gum is forbidden in virtually every high school in the country. At the same time, most colleges want enterprising students who are willing to push back against silly petty little rules (as long as they are not <u>their</u> silly petty little rules.) So you <u>must</u> accept the gum. On the other hand, it is the kiss of death if at any point you take the gum from your mouth and stick it under an article of furniture in the room.

3. At the start of the interview, the admissions person may offer you a plug of chewing tobacco. This in itself is not a trap; but you are expected to accept it; and <u>how you deal with the sputum will be a test</u> (there will be no spittoons in the room) to see how enterprising you can be.

a. What <u>not</u> to do: swallow the sputum in the mistaken belief that it makes you look self-effacing, as if you are "taking a hit for a larger good." What it actually does is make you look stupid and without imagination.

b. The sort of thing you <u>can</u> do: shoot a gob of tobacco juice at the beautiful antique Oriental rug of the Admissions Person, and then toss off these words: "The cronies of Andrew Jackson were allowed to do that when he was in the White House; and as he is considered to be one of our best presidents..." This shows, first, that you know your History, and second, that you do not fear to choose the most audacious of solutions -- the kind that is comparable to Cutting the Gordian Knot.

4. At some point the Admissions Person will refer to your "tepid" grades or your "lackluster" recommendations and ask you what "might" account for them. (They will avoid at all costs the word "weak", since they could wind up recommending you for admission, and no college wants to accept what they themselves call a "weak student.") <u>This is a trap</u>: you are not expected to give a purely truthful answer (notice their careful use of the word "might", which gives the candidate license to improvise.)

a. Possible response 1: "I'll level with you because I know that you value honesty. I slacked off for no really good reason, other than that I was busy reading action comics while I was sniffing glue." See how horrible the truth is? The candidate's basic assumption would be wrong here: the college does not cherish honesty so much as it values <u>the illusion of reasonable extra-ordinary circumstances</u>. The answer you gave here would be enough to single-handedly sink your candidacy. If you need to confess, go to Confession.

b. Possible response 2: "I think that I can plead extenuating circumstances if anyone can. When both my parents were killed in an auto accident just before last Christmas, I was left with my seven younger siblings to care for. Needless to say, I had to take on two jobs to support us all and buy the kids' presents, and these ate up all my time and energy." This is what is known as "The Laying It on With a Trowel" excuse. It is so melodramatic and over-the-top that it is easily detected (Christmas always seems to make an appearance in these sorts of excuses; and the number of helpless siblings is invariably seven) and as easily debunked. (If you put your parents' phone numbers down on your application form, your goose is cooked -- unless, that is, your little tale is true. But in that case the Admissions Person will ask a follow-up question: "What do you plan to do with the seven kids while you are away at college?")

c. Possible response 3: "Right after school started last Fall, my parents started having awful fights. My mother would scream at my father all the time, and he would either scream back at her or clam up and stay out late. I couldn't do my work in that house, but every time I asked to go to a friend's house, my mother would accuse me of wanting to desert her too. Actually, I'd rather not talk about it if you don't mind." There you have it -- the perfect excuse in all its crushing banality, an apt description of at least half the families in America. The Admissions Person has not heard it before -- it's too embarrassing a thing to admit (which is why it will work every time.) And there is no way that he would ever call your home to check your tale. ("Pardon me Madam, but could you tell me whether your family is as dysfunctional as your son says it is?") You can then add the knockout punch: "I can't wait to get away from that house and into your college library where I hope I will be able to study in peace and quiet!" At this point the Admissions Person is practically checking the "Recommendation to Admit" box on his form.

5. At some point every interviewer, whether for college or for a job, will ask the following basic question: "What do you think is your greatest weakness?" This is a trap: the Interviewer does not want a direct answer to this question. Do you think that he is sitting there and asking questions in order to find out how weak someone is? That would be a distinct waste of his time: he sees as his job the admission of strong students, not weak ones. Therefore the Candidate must turn the question inside out and give an answer which expresses a strength.

a. Examples of unacceptable responses:

"I tend to gossip instead of studying."

"I have two felony convictions because of my temper."

"I masturbate a lot and I'm not ashamed of it!" (Etc.)

b. Examples of acceptable responses:

The granddaddy of them all:

"I tend to work too hard."

"I tend to take notes that are too detailed."

"I tend to place too much trust in authority." (Etc.)

6. There will come a time when the Admissions Person will ask

147

you, "Why did you apply to our school? What was it about us that you found attractive?" This is not a simple question, and it has no one right answer. However, common sense will tell you what sorts of responses the Interviewer is looking for: he wants you to flatter his college. He wants you to tell him how beautiful and verdant his campus is. He wants you to tell him what splendid facilities he has there. He wants you to praise his distinguished and educated faculty. Yes, all these things seem obvious. But is it possible that they are maybe a little bit <u>too</u> obvious, and therefore boring? The Admissions Person has heard all that stuff a million times before. Is it possible to answer this question in a more creative way? We offer the following as a modest proposal in that genre:

Creative Response: "How can I put this as delicately as possible? Let's face it, my grades and recommendations <u>are terrible</u>!" [The student would have used the word "suck", but the word did not exist with that usage in 1961.] "But my guidance counselor gave me a sage piece of advice: 'You Want to Go to College? Fear Not! No matter how bad you are as a student, there is always a college somewhere which is worse (meaning: which will accept you.) He talked about everyone else's Safety Schools being my first choices. And then he said something particularly interesting: 'So that means that your so-called Safety School is going to be pretty much the bottom of the proverbial barrel -- the kind of school which asks you for only two things: your father's checkbook, and proof that you have a pulse -- in that order!'

"Well, I thought long and hard about what he had said: it seemed as though my college future was secure; and I felt good about it for a few days. But something gnawed at me which I could not get rid of, and that was the unabashed and unbridled cynicism of his proposal. It got so I couldn't sleep at night, because I kept asking myself whether this was the future I wanted for myself, of always taking the easy way out. I finally decided that it wasn't. So the next day I marched into that guidance counselor's office and demanded the name of another college. No, not one of those garbage colleges and not even another safety school. What I asked for, and received, and irregardless of my chances of getting in (which I knew were probably nil) was the name of (as I put it) 'One Noble Institution of Higher Learning which can hold its head high in calling itself a True College.' And that school is the one in which we sit at this very moment."

[Note: *the* candidate was admitted on the basis of that one response (which showed that he had a pulse) -- and his father's checkbook.)

7. When the interview is concluded, the Admissions Person will rise, smile, and shake your hand. (Caution: do not wipe off your hand after you've shaken his.) Once in a great while, that person will ask whether he can kiss you. This is not a test. The candidate should view this the same way as with the offer of a cigarette at the beginning: if it seems like the natural culmination of the interview, a nice way to wind things up, then by all means accept the kiss. On the other hand, if you think that it is not an appropriate gesture at that time and place, you should politely decline. (Caution: you should resist any temptation to kiss the Admissions Person back: it is considered too aggressive. On the other hand, responses like "gross!" or "yuck!" are needlessly hurtful and should be avoided.)

And so, armed with the above information, my mother and I drove first to Easton, Pennsylvania, the site of Lafayette College. It seemed like a decent enough school, although I had nothing to compare it to. I did not have an interview there; and it may well be wondered why I did not request one. The reason should be obvious: I was both shy and ignorant, and as long as the one could mask the other, I was fine. But put me in a position where I was expected to speak in a semi-coherent fashion, and all bets were off. So I did not go out of my way to get interviews.

So we left Easton and drove to Lancaster, the site of Franklin & Marshall College. (Why we skipped Bethlehem and Lehigh is a mystery to me even now. Perhaps we assumed that, since we hadn't heard, that it was a hopeless case.) I do not recall anything from the interview at F & M other than that I seemed to acquit myself well enough (I would have remembered any disasters), and I was not offered a cigarette.

And that was it -- my one interview. The final tally was: rejected by Lafayette, and accepted by Lehigh and Franklin & Marshall. Which of those two schools did I wind up accepting and attending -- the one which cared enough to meet me in person and then accepted me on that basis? Or the one that was as silent as the Sphinx right up to the bitter end when they had to make a decision?

Postscript: it was nearly the end of Freshman Week at Lehigh when I asked someone there: "How does someone get into the Glee Club?" He replied: "You have to go through what is called an 'audition'." There was a pause and then he added: "As a matter of fact, today is the last day of auditions!" Some things never change.

(1 February 2009)

Organist

Introduction: Organists

I was an organist for many and sundry denominations over the course of a long (and chequered) career.

Now organists, I've found, seem to run the gamut from A to Z in terms of character types.

At one extreme there are the pious ones - those who in all sincerity believe that their playing is undertaken toward the greater Glory of God. My first three instructors on that instrument - Dot Pfeiffer, Frank Scherer, and Clyde English - each fell into that category of modesty and piety.

But then there is the other extreme - those who have no moral scruples and to whom nothing is sacred. I knew a fellow once who disdainfully referred to the Dean of British Organists as "E. Sour Pigs". He told me that once, while altar boys were releasing incense into the cathedral during Mass, he played variations on "Smoke Gets In Your Eyes". See what I mean? Not only to do such a thing but to brag about it as well - not a shred of decency!

Now I myself fell somewhere between these extremes as an organist. Those who know me may guess where that might be. But for those harboring doubts, I have attached a document, the origins of which I explain forthwith:

As most of you know, I was the organist at a certain church (I am being purposefully vague to protect the innocent - and the guilty!) in Massachusetts for many years. One day I got a call out of the blue from the Chair of the Music Committee at the Church. She asked me to write up a job description for Organist and send it to her. I agreed.

But after I put down the phone I began to ask myself, Why would the Music Committee need a job description from me? After all, I know what my job entails, and they know that I know that. And then the True Reason hit me like a bolt from the blue: Of course! They need the job description to show to a new person. And this is because they are planning to fire me!

Now I know that this seems like paranoia to many of you. But, as the saying goes, "Just because you're paranoid don't mean they ain't out to get ya!" So I said to myself, "You want a job description? O.K., I'll write you a job description to end all job descriptions!" I have appended it below.

PS: My paranoia was just that and nothing else; they were perfectly happy with my work and I was soon to receive an "Excellent" job rating. I never found out why they wanted the write-up.

PPS: I was told that the document caused much merriment in the Music Committee and beyond.

PPPS: Just to clarify something: to the best of my recollection, my remarks with regard to the Choir Director were undertaken in a spirit of Mischief rather than Malice. (the latter does not form the basis for my sort of humor.) And this feeling is bolstered by the fact that this person and his wife remain our close and devoted friends to this day.

I have also included a couple of other documents. One is my decidedly unromantic description of the organ as an instrument. The other is an account of an encounter after a service in a church where I was playing.

Organist Job Description

1. The Organist plays a Prelude, Offertory, and Postlude at each service during the regular church year.

The **Prelude** is a relatively extended work of solemn import, normally lasting from 3 to 10 minutes. The extra-musical purpose of the Organ Prelude is to, metaphorically speaking, lay down an emotive carpet which "ushers" the parishioner into a quasi-religious ambiance via harmonic-tonal suggestion.

The **Offertory**, by contrast, is undertaken out of relatively crass motives. A short work of about 1 1/2 minute's duration, it is in essence a many-to-one mapping from musical tones onto the wallet of the parishioner. A Tristan-like ecstatic tension is set up which can only find release in the offering tray.

The **Postlude** is a very short, upbeat work denoting victorious finality, of such dazzling briefness that even those whose sole wish is to flee at all costs the sanctuary's confines will feel a bit cheated by its brevity, if not wit. It should have the effect of an uplift so profound that no listener need put their feet on the floor upon leaving.

2. The Organist accompanies all Choir rehearsals on Thursday evenings (8:00-9:30 PM), Sunday mornings (9:15-9:45 AM), and accompanies the Choir during its non-a cappellational renditions on Sunday morns. It might be assumed, then, that superb accompanying skills are the *sine qua non* for this position. How misguided and misleading such an assumption would be. Sure they're important, but so are clothes: the lack of either can cause undue embarrassment! What, then, is the crucial factor governing a successful Organist/Choir dovetailing? Simple - the relationship of said Organist to the Choir Director. Bluntly put, this must transcend absolutely the usual-banal meaning of the expression "professional working relationship". In plain fact, the Organist must be nothing less than the Yin to the Director's Yang (but at all costs NEVER the Yang to his Yin!) (S)he must be Walter Mitty to his Attila the Hun, Steve Martin to his Maximilian Schell - well, you get the picture: contrasts – complements.

3. The Organist plays any other incidental musics for the Sunday service as the minister, etc. might desire and require: Hymns, "Spirits (and/or Elixirs) of Life", Doxologies, Responses, Amens, Codices, Spirituals, Nunc Dimittises, Matins, Vespers, Inbetweeners, Swell to Seeyas, Nice to Greetyas, See ya Latahs. The Organist should be prepared to play any such musics at the drop of the proverbial organ shoe, his-or-her sole motto being, "If I get it after the service, it's too late!"

4. The Organist should be adept at playing suitable musics for any sort of extra solemn service such as Weddings, Funerals, or Ordinations ("Marry 'em/Bury 'em/Query 'em".) It is at the discretion of the Organist as to whether (s)he desires to play such a service, but professional courtesy requires that (s)he be granted Right of First Refusal. In other words, the Organist holds all the trump cards in this one.

5. The Organist should have a minimal knowledge of the physical workings of the instrument which (s)he plays on a weekly basis. At the very least, said Organist should be able to tell, by whatever means, whether any part of the instrument is broken, out of tune, or even just Out of Sorts on a particular day. The notoriously temperamental nature of such instruments makes a sympathetic Organist a virtual necessity. The Player should be able to reassure his/her instrument, to comfort it when necessary, and to give it brief-if-erotic massages if needed after a long and grueling service.

Two Sundays

I was organist at the Lutheran Church of the Redeemer in Woburn, MA from 1974 to 1978. I'd like to talk about two "adventures" I had there.

1. We had been up late one Saturday night toward the end of October, having an intense political debate with another couple (it was the year I was in the Labor Party.) We were living in Brighton at the time – a long drive from Woburn.

Nevertheless, I arrived at the church at 7:00 A.M. as usual. The first service was at 8:00 A.M., so this gave me plenty of time to play through my music once more, to familiarize myself with the hymns, and so on.

The organ had been made in Sweden, the home country of most of the parishioners (there were lots of Eric Ericksons and the like in the congregation.) Like an elephant, the organ had a big body and a small brain.

The "body" was the console: it dwarfed anyone who sat behind it. It sat out there solitary and alone like a huge roll top desk, an island on the left side of the sanctuary. As it faced the congregation, I found it to be an excellent place to hide – especially during sermons. (I think I read several of the lesser novels of Thomas Mann during such times when the minister was emoting about speaking in tongues [yes, he and his wife did that at Pentecost] and the "handle" for his CB radio [it was "PTL".])

This giant "body" of the organ was deceptive as to its "brains". True – there were plenty of stop tabs with all sorts of fanciful names such as 'diapason' and 'bourdon' – names known only to the province of organ builders and organists. But many of those were borrowed from others: the 4' dulciana could be using the same set of pipes (an octave higher, of course) as the 8' violina; and so forth. So that in reality, this organ only had seven ranks (sets of pipes): those were half-visible in a little case bolted to the wall up to the left of the organist. It was a pitiful size – about as small as any church instrument could be.

What made such borrowing possible was the fact that this was an *electro-pneumatic* instrument. From Wikipedia:

"The basic operation of the electro-pneumatic system is as follows: when the organist selects a stop and depresses a key, an electric circuit is completed, causing a low-voltage current to flow from the depressed key, through the stop-tab switch, and on through the cable to the electro-pneumatic relay. The relay interprets the command from the console and sends an electric current to the appropriate solenoid. The solenoid is energized, causing the pipe valve connected to it to open, which emits compressed air into the pipe, allowing the pipe to speak."

(This does sound like a Rube Goldberg device, doesn't it! In fact, the whole process, from depressed key to open pipe, is instantaneous.)

This sort of instrument is to be contrasted to the *tracker*, or direct mechanical action organ:

"In a tracker organ there is no pneumatic or electrical assistance to the keyboard action; instead each key is connected directly by a thin flexible wooden strip called a tracker to activate the air valve under the corresponding pipe. The result is an instrument that responds more directly and sensitively to the skill of the organist."

[By the way, I think that the business about "more sensitivity" is nonsense: a key is depressed, a pipe speaks. That's what we organists care about.]

Due to the direct mechanical action, a tracker organ cannot borrow from other ranks of pipes. Thus, every stop is genuine, a new rank.

In general, you can tell a tracker organ by the clickity-clack sound of its trackers; and by the fact that the keyboards are almost always facing the pipes.

My own take on this dichotomy is as follows: an electro-pneumatic organ is to a tracker organ as power steering is to unassisted steering. That is, the former allows you to drive in effortless comfort – if you like that sort of thing. On the other hand, if you want more of a feel-of-the-road, then you won't like power steering.

The drawback with tracker mechanisms is precisely its direct-mechanical action: the more stops you have on (and keyboards coupled), the harder it is to press down the keys. (Sometimes, as while parking, one yearns for power steering!)

The drawback with electro-pneumatic mechanisms is the opposite of the above: the effortless ease that it takes one to play, no matter how many stops are engaged. So, on a very large instrument (scores of ranks), one can become heedless of the tremendous sound forces one has unleashed, with the result that (depending on the acoustics) the product may resemble a giant acoustical slush box.

Anyway, I was presiding over a pitifully small *homogenized* instrument; but not one so small that I couldn't use it to do what I wanted it to do – with a bit of ingenuity. (The church would eventually add a *krumhorn* – an exotic reed stop - to the organ while I was there.) So I became clever, resourceful, seeking out and trying every possible combination of stops.

I had finished my practicing. The time according to my watch (which I reset and wound each morning) was 7:49. This really left me no time to leave the organ and perhaps mosey outside to enjoy a bit of the early spring weather. (When I was living and studying in Morgantown, WV, I would see my nattily dressed organ teacher Clyde English on Sunday mornings standing by the side door of the Methodist Church where he played, nonchalantly enjoying a pipe smoke before the service began.)

I had timed the Prelude music: it was exactly seven minutes long. So I would have to start my playing at 7:54: this allowed me to run over the time and finish at 8:01, thus allowing a minute's grace (but no more!) for latecomers.

So I began. I was playing a piece by Alexandre Guilmant, a 19th century French organ composer who wrote hundreds of wonderful little occasional pieces with such fanciful titles as "Will 'o the Wisp". I had worked hard to strain the resources of this pipsqueak of an instrument, employing different stops for solos and using the swell shades for subtle balance.

I was playing for my Ideal Listener. This was, I posited, a parishioner who not only knew who Guilmant was, but who knew this particular piece intimately. (Of course, no one in the congregation – with the possible exception of the choir leader, Peggy Butt, – had ever even <u>heard</u> of Alexandre Guilmant, nevertheless knew any pieces by him.) This Listener would thus be able to appreciate all the many nuances of my preparation and playing. It was like cooking a gourmet meal for a connoisseur of fine food.

But there was more. There are times when I might make an error while playing: a wrong pedal note here, a slightly botched entrance of a voice there. After all, I am only human! But what of my Ideal Listener then? Amazingly, by some wonderful coincidence, they would lose their concentration for just that exact moment. Thus, conveniently, they would only hear what I wanted them to hear: they would be utterly attentive or carelessly indifferent as the occasion demanded.

And so I played exquisitely (when I did) and they listened (or not) until the end. At that point I knew there would be an Invocation by the Minister, to be followed immediately by the opening Hymn. So I had the hymnal open beside me on the bench, ready to place up on the music rack.

But there was no Invocation. Indeed, when I looked over toward the pulpit, I did not see Reverend Pearson at all. What could have delayed him? Was he ill? Had he collapsed in the sacristy? I had no idea.

I realized that it was incumbent on me here to provide musical filler through on-the-spot improvisation. Why? Because unscheduled silence in a place like a church (that is, where every event is completely scripted – with a detailed printed program to boot) is a sure sign that something is wrong. It is like dead air on a radio show: something – anything - must be enlisted to break the silence. (Indeed, the organist at my home church in NJ would even provide music for the congregation to *sit down* after they had sung a hymn!)

Now improvisation is an art pretty much confined these days to organists and jazz musicians. (In the Classical era, this was not the case. Mozart, for example, left a space at the end of the movements of his piano concerti for the pianist to improvise a cadenza. But that practice ended with Beethoven's Second Piano Concerto. [He knew he could write one better than anyone else could improvise.]) Any organist worth their salt not only can improvise on the spot, but *relishes* the chance to do so.

There is, in fact, a grand tradition of improvisation on the organ, especially in France. There is a story about the great 19th century Belgian/French composer/organist César Franck, who, in the exams at the Paris Conservatory, was given a choice of two themes to improvise on. Franck improvised on each one in turn; and then, as a finale, put the two together simultaneously – a stupendous feat. More recently (1972) I attended a recital by the legendary French organist, Marie-Claire Alain, who, at one point, asked for a theme from the audience to improvise upon on the spot. (By the way, the "theme" was a terrible one; but she coped.) However, I have never seen this done at any other organ recital; and I fear the practice may well die with Marie-Claire.

The one part of church services in which organists are almost sure to improvise is during Holy Communion. There the parishioners are sufficiently distracted by the goodies (wine, bread) being dispensed to them, as well as by suitable thoughts (hopefully transcending a later golf game), that the organist can hone his/her improvisatory skills at will. This usually involves a vague wandering about in a quasi-Wagnerian harmonic wilderness, thus depicting musically the soul's thirst for a Higher Power; or a long series of excruciating suspensions illustrative of the Savior's suffering. Being a non-believer, I would usually refuse communion. But sometimes a challenge in multitasking was too much to resist: could I feed myself (with my left hand) the Precious Body and Blood, whilst simultaneously continuing to make up semi-coherent music on the spot (with my right hand and feet)? (The jury may still be out on that.)

But, let's be blunt here: improvisation is the musical equivalent of *bullshitting*. Just as in speech, some can do it better than others.

Today I improvised quietly on the first hymn tune. I did not have a large palate of far-flung chords at my disposal (as a wonderful organist named Bill Whitehead did.) But I was able to wring variations on that melodic material quite adequately.

(And what would my Ideal Listener think of this effort? Sadly, their attention would probably wander quite a bit.)

How long would I have to improvise? I had no idea. It might be only a few minutes; but I had had situations where I had to 'fool around' for an extended period of time. (My record? 45 minutes, on the occasion of a wedding when the Best Man had left the rings back at the motel and had to return to get them. However, then I was playing various pieces from my repertoire using the music. So I was not so much bullshitting as *filibustering*.)

Anyway, I indulged in musical improvisation for awhile – until it dawned on me that someone should have come out and let me, if not the congregation, know what was going on. So even as my fingers wandered, I hiked myself up and managed to look over the ramparts to see what was happening with the congregation.

Nothing was happening. The sanctuary was empty – and dark. No one was there, for the simple reason that (as it finally dawned on me) everyone else had remembered to turn their clocks back to get out of Daylight Savings.

2. It happened on a Sunday in late April (I suppose you can already see where I am going with this) at the same church. We were now living in Arlington, a community much closer to Woburn. So of course I arrived at the church at 7:08 – that is, a few minutes later than I wanted to. (There must a 'Paradoxical Law of Inverse Distances' somewhere, which states that the closer one lives to one's work, the later one arrives.)

But when I got there, the parking lot was full of cars. Was there an early congregational meeting I didn't know about?

I walked into the church. And, as I approached the sanctuary, I heard something I'd never heard at that church before: someone else playing the organ. In fact they were playing the first hymn, which the congregation was singing.

And then it hit me: we'd forgotten to set our clocks ahead for Daylight Savings.

What does one do in such a situation – one who has such a

position of great public responsibility? Well, if something like that were to happen in a dream, the trauma of the lapse would no doubt cause one to awaken – maybe sit bolt upright, perhaps even scream out loud.

But when it happens in reality, as it did here? Well, I can tell you what actually happened: I smiled and shrugged my shoulders; after all, what could I do? (Indeed, Peggy Butt [who was playing], the choir, and even the minister found my lapse to be quite amusing!)

P.S. During the time I was at Redeemer Lutheran, I was subjected, Jesus-like, to two huge temptations to leave. One was from a church that had a brand new magnificent 23-rank Casavant organ (they also offered my wife a paid soloist position.) The other was from a church that had no organ at all (and no paid soloist job.) I think it is obvious which temptation I yielded to.

If you said the one with the magnificent 23-rank Casavant organ, you would have been wrong. That was a Baptist church (a relatively conservative denomination) in Winchester. When I saw that the mean age of the congregation appeared to be about 80, I surmised (correctly, as it turned out) that that was a dying church. (The organ was destroyed in a fire a few years later; and the building was converted into condos.)

I left Redeemer Lutheran after four years in order to take an "organ" job at First Parish Unitarian/Universalist Church in Arlington – even though that church did not yet have an organ - or even a real sanctuary (they were rebuilding from a fire.) But I was attracted to two other things about the church: its liberal religion; and its excellent location, on the nexus of Cambridge and Lexington, to give concerts.

But after five years we did acquire an organ – a wonderful little 1869 E.& G.G. Hook: this was a tracker organ which was twice as large (it had 15 ranks) as the one in Woburn.

I did leave a very loving congregation in Woburn. Before I left, more than one person took me aside and beseeched me to take care, as they had heard that the Unitarians were "godless humanists". (I solemnly promised to so take care.) And then, a few weeks after I'd left, I received a call from choir director Butt. After hemming and hawing for a bit, she told me that they'd held a prayer service at the church in order to ask God to bring me back. Was I interested in returning?

I was very touched by this, and told her so. But I added that I would probably stay where I was.

Oh yes - I was never too early, or too late, to a church service again!

Vox Humana

Before I begin my little true-life narrative, I need to define two terms:

The **Vox Humana** ("Human Voice") is an organ stop invented in the nineteenth century (of course.) Each note consists of not one but two pipes which are tuned just a wee bit different from one another. This causes a slight interference of the two sound waves, which is heard audibly as beats and a tremor. The effect is intended to simulate the Human Voice. What it actually is, is one of the most cloying and obnoxious sounds ever devised by man; its equivalent in literature is Dickens's Little Nell.

The **Schübler Chorales** of Johann Sebastian Bach are six organ chorale-preludes, each one arranged from a vocal solo in one of his cantatas. "Wachet Auf!" ("Wake Up!") is the most famous (by default?) of these pieces.

And so on to our tale. I was Organist at the Christian Science Church in Champaign, Illinois for a year. Now Christian Science, like any organized religion, has its pluses and minuses.

Minuses: excruciatingly boring services. There are no ministers in the CS church, only lay readers (who move like automatons.) All CS churches thoughout the world read the same two texts (one from the Bible, the other from Mary Baker Eddy's <u>Science and Health With Keys to the Scriptures</u>) on a given Sunday. No opinions are expressed (except those of Mrs. Eddy, who died in 1910), no anecdotes are told, no witticisms offered. Yes, boring!

Pluses: the psycho-sexual imagery in many of Mrs. Eddy's hymns. One, e.g., speaks of being chained to a rock in the middle of a raging sea and Christ coming to her. Good stuff which you won't find in any Unitarian hymnal.

Anyway: part of my responsibility in this church, as in any other, was to play a Prelude before the service began. One Sunday, I decided to treat the congregation to something special: I would perform a couple of the Schübler Chorales in both their versions - with voice, and then with organ alone. In this way my listeners could hear the two versions juxtaposed - an aural treat.

So I brought my singer-wife, Dorothy, with me that Sunday, and we performed two of the Schüblers twice over. After the service I expected to receive kudos for my enterprising programming. Instead, two women of grim demeanor appeared at my organ console.

One of them intoned, "Did you know that there is a bylaw in the Christian Science Church which expressly forbids the use of a vocalist in the Prelude music?"

I did not know this, of course. (Indeed, I knew of no such rule in any other denomination.) I realized that I needed to justify my actions, but how? I thought quickly, and then I replied:

"That's all right - I was using her as <u>an artificial Vox Humana stop</u>!"

The two ladies were not amused by this clever rationale. And so I had to quickly reassure them that a) I was acutely aware of the gravity of my offense; and b) I would most certainly never perpetrate such a dastardly deed again!

PS: As the above is an account of my <u>worst</u> experience as organist after a service, I think it only fair to include the <u>best</u> one as well. Once long ago, in another denomination in another town, I played "Litanies" by Jehan Alain - a hyper-modern work requiring astonishing virtuosity (something I was thankfully able to bring to the performance) (he said in all modesty.) Before the minister began the sermon, he declaimed that he had "heard the voice of God in this piece". Then, after the service, a woman came up to the console and pressed ten dollars into my hand. "You have given me something", she said in the voice of one greatly moved, "and I want to give you something in return!" "Oh, I couldn't take this!" I protested as my hand closed over the money.

From then on I tried to program "Litanies" often!

PPS: While I was at West Virginia University, I taught the organ privately. One day three nuns came to me and asked to be my pupils. I inquired if any of them had a particular piece in mind to study. One replied, "Yes - I'd like to learn 'Washit Off'".

Pathétique

At the start of my freshman year at Lehigh I got my own classical music program on WLRN, the student radio station.

The only downside was that The Ted May Show aired on Sunday afternoons from 2:00 to 6:00 P.M. This was a sort of graveyard shift, for many students went home for the weekend and had not yet returned. Indeed, there were not any other station employees in the studio during that period of time: no engineers, no program directors - no one. I cued up my own records and gave unprepared, inane blatherings about the various composers and their music I played. (I did not even resist doing voiceovers of classical pieces I was playing: "This has been "Marche Slav". Thank you for listening to the Ted May Show today!")

Now the radio station was located in the basement of Packer Hall, the building in which the dining hall resided as well. At that time (1961) there was a rule in force that a tie and jacket had to be worn at dinner. I never seemed to remember to dress for dinner before I came to the studio; as a result, I had to run back up to my dorm to dress up after I finished my show.

But one Sunday I had a brilliant idea: I would put on a recording and then, while it was playing, run up to my room to dress and then rush back before the record had finished. After all, I reasoned, one side of a record takes about twenty minutes to complete...

So I cued up the opening of Tchaikovsky's Pathétique Symphony, gave my silly spiel about the poor doomed composer

163

gulping a cholera-infected glass of tap water as he was finishing the symphony ("<u>That</u> is why it is called 'Pathétique'!"), started the turntable - and bolted for the door.

I arrived at my dorm in good time and was tying my tie ("That is why it is called a 'tie'", I would have said on my program) (and, who knows, I may have been right!), when I had a grand inspiration: I would listen to my own radio show live in my dorm room!

So I turned on WLRN. And I heard the following: the first one-and-a-half bars of the famous theme from that Tchaikovsky symphony, followed by a click - and then a repetition of that - *ad infinitum*.

Yes, the record was stuck. And I realized that I was at least seven minutes from the studio, with no one there to rectify the situation for me.

I rushed back, unstuck the record, and at the end gave my listeners a pathetic rationale, viz: "I wanted to demonstrate what happens when a composer gets writer's block." Yes, pathetic!

But do you know the most pathetic thing of all? I never heard about this - *faux pas* - from anyone. No - apparently, no listener ever called the station to complain, for my superiors never mentioned the incident to me. I was forced to draw one conclusion: <u>no one (except, ironically, for my inept self) had been listening to my show that afternoon</u>. Or, if someone was, they didn't care enough about what happened to complain.

I got the message. And, despite my obvious talent for this sort of work, I quit my radio show at the end of the first semester.

Student Daze

I was once forced (if that is the word for it) as an adult to simulate being a high school student over an extended period of time. It wasn't pretty, but it was necessary. Here is that story:

In the beginning of my teaching career in the late '60's, I had taught at the college level full time. It was possible to do that in those long-ago days with just a masters degree. But after taking the time to get a bachelors degree in another field, I found that the job market in higher education was now closed to me. And, as I hadn't yet gotten certified to teach in Massachusetts, public school jobs were also unobtainable.

So I took a job as a "tutor" at Lexington High School. This was, in reality, a helper in a self-contained classroom. The pay was $7.50 per hour for a 30-hour week.

That was the fall of 1976. Our daughter had just been born and so we were in need of additional funds to pay bills. I was eating my lunches in the cafeteria and paying the faculty price for them. As I recall, teachers paid around $1.25 for their meals, while students paid $0.50. The difference over a 180-day school year was $135. That was a significant amount in those days.

I asked whether, because of my low pay, I could get my lunches at the student rate, but I was told that I couldn't.

So it became clear what I had to do: I had to simulate being a student in the cafeteria. I would have to give a daily performance which would fool the cafeteria workers - or at least the woman at the cash register.

How difficult, I wondered, would that be?

I paid faculty rates in the lunchroom a couple of more days while I closely observed the student human comedy there.

The first question was: could my face look like a student's? The answer I came up with was: most decidedly. I had always had a youthful face: I did not really start shaving until I was out of college (Brahms's voice didn't change until he was 25, but that's another story.) In particular, I had (still have) "baby cheeks" with scarcely a hint of beard (I'd like to think this to be an indication of androgyny.) I was 32 now, but my face hadn't aged all that much (having no conscience, I never worried.) I saw several examples of students there with faces which looked much older than mine: grizzled veterans who looked like they had to shave thrice per day; wizened sages wrinkled before their time; etc. So I seemed fine in the face department.

The next question had to do with clothing. I soon realized that I had nothing in my wardrobe which even remotely resembled what I saw in the lunchroom. I would have to import the clothing I would wear. So off I went to a Goodwill store, where I purchased: a pair of worn bell-bottomed jeans; a Jim Morrison T-shirt; and a pair of Ked hightop red sneakers.

I tie-dyed the Jim Morrison T-shirt. As for the jeans: worn as they were, they were not nearly worn enough to belong to a student. So I took them down into the basement, where I placed a 2x4 up inside each leg. Then I used a power sander to wear away the material in the knees and thighs until they were threadbare. I also cut off the bottoms of the legs so that the material would fray there.

The sneakers were fine as they were.

I now began to consider what *demeanor* I wanted to present to the world (i.e., the lunchroom) whilst attired in that *habiliment*. This I divided into two parts – the non-verbal, and the verbal:

In the case of the non-verbal, I first thoroughly tousled my hair until it was wild and down over my eyes. I made sure I was chewing gum – with my mouth open, of course. (Gone were the halcyon '50's of my own youth, when chewing gum in school was the arch-crime. Now, on the tail of the drugged-out '60's, gum was the least of the worries of principal and teachers.) I cultivated a decided slouch, and developed with practice an awkward insouciance, which would turn into a nervous swagger whenever I seemed to be feeling my oats. I practiced avoiding eye contact with adults, leaving them with the impression that my insolence took the form of indifference. And then, as a final touch, I tucked a Marlboro cigarette behind one ear. (In those days, students were allowed to smoke at school, albeit in a special cordoned-off corner of the parking lot.)

As for the verbal: on my reconnoitering missions I had noticed that the quickest way to be ignored in the lunchroom was to behave in an overtly absurd fashion. The more obnoxious one was, the more one blended in.

So I sought to be overt and obnoxious. I dressed up in my "scholarly" attire and tousled my hair. I sauntered in and took a tray. (I made sure I always held the tray with my left hand, so that my wedding ring was hidden. Of course I had laid out the money beforehand.) I went through the line, snapping gum and avoiding eye contact. I slouched, resembling a coiled spring. Then, just when I reached the checkout lady (that is, The Crucial Point), I suddenly yelled out into the lunchroom (I was not yelling to an actual person, but the cashier didn't know that), "Hey Joe, waddcha get on that math test? The old bag gave me a D! I'll fix her tomorrow with a good wet spitball!" The last word was scarcely out of my mouth when the cash register rang. I glanced at the amount: it was $0.50. She hadn't even hesitated.

Only once did I see a look of suspicion in a cafeteria worker's face. I saw her staring at me (perhaps she had seen my ring) while I was eating. I had heard it said that desperate situations call for desperate measures; this was clearly one of those situations. So, out of the blue I began to laugh hysterically and flail about. In the process, I knocked over my milk.

I glanced slyly over at the suspicious worker. She had turned away in disgust. That's when I knew I had done it. I had carried it off. I had arrived.

Gradually I was able to wean myself of the bizarre outfit. As for my demeanor, I maintained the traits of a surly youth for a while, but gradually I phased those out too. My hair was combed; the gum disappeared; and I ceased to slouch. I even made eye contact! It was as if I had been taken in hand by a kindly aunt. Finally all that was left was the hint of a frown (a compact reference to everything else), which I could invoke should the need ever arise.

I learned my lesson from all this: I needed a decent-paying job. So the next fall I started taking courses to get certified to teach.

P.S. For some reason I cannot fathom, I did not ever consider packing my own lunches. Why not? Perhaps because doing so would have deprived me of playing a daily dramatic role which, for whatever reason, I needed and wanted to play.

P.P.S. The reader who found the above exercise in surreptitious frugality amusing might also want to read "Wine & Cigarettes".

A Tale of Two Domes

How does one tell a story the details of which one knows very little about?

Well, I suppose one could admit (i.e. come clean about) one's ignorance in the beginning, tell the tale as best one can, and hope that the reader feels enough goodwill towards the author (because they were honest with the reader and all that) to overlook the deficiencies. That is, an implicit but unstated *quid pro quo* is set up between author and reader. This is called "the laying of one's cards out on the table" method. The problem with this approach is the fact that ignorance in and of itself is not very entertaining -- on the contrary, it is almost always a real turn-off. For the entertainment and artistic enjoyment of a text comes precisely in the richness of detail.

Well then, I suppose one could tell the skeleton of the story as best one knows it, and then "flesh it out" by filling in the gaps with another story -- perhaps a totally different one unrelated to the first. This is what is known as "the alternative narrative method of distraction". Of course, success with this method depends on how good the story is that is meant to distract from the other. So we are back to the need for richness of detail in a story.

Or: one could have a narrator tell the skeleton of the story and fill in the gaps by "shooting the bull" (perhaps it sounds better if I speak about 'making jazz riffs') about various elements of the story and his/her take on them. This is called "the filigree method of distraction". In this sort of telling, the focus shifts from story to narrator, who becomes the main object of interest.

Can you tell which method I chose?

Time: Sometime within the last few decades.

Scene: Sitting room of a large Southern mansion of the Greek revival sort (i.e. the usual cliché: long gracious shaded front porch with huge pillars and rocking chairs facing a lawn with trees hung with Spanish moss and a river in the distance.) Two women in their 30's are having late afternoon iced tea spiked with Southern Comfort. One of the women, the trophy wife of an aging Southern congressman and matriarch of the mansion, is speaking:

"The nahce thang about Beaurahgahd's job is that he mates such intrestin papel. Now take yesterdee for example: he brought home a colleague that ah thank is about the most fascinatin of any ah've met. His background is so -- intriguin, not least because the beginnin of his 'career', if you want to call it that (ah don't know what othah wahd tah use) was supposed to be his end -- ah mean the absolute end of his entirah life. He told the whole storah to Beaurahgahd and Beau told it to me so ah'll trah to get the details straht."

"This man was originally an Eskimo, if you don't mahnd me usin the word. (ah know, ah should problah use a word lahke 'Inuit'. Goodness knows it's hahd enough to keep ahead of the Pay-Say police, especiallah when you learned somethin lahke 'Eskimo' in school. [She laughs uneasily.] Ah suppose theh want me to use somethin lahke 'Aleutian American'... oh hail, I'll just stick with 'Eskimo' and if you don't tell, naithah will I.)"

"Anyway, as recentlah as ten years ago this man was livin in an itty-bitty igloo with a whole bunch of othah Eskimos in the middle of absolutelah nowhah in the fah north. He was the oldest person in that extended family sorta situation, and in Eskimo terms he was reallah old, although in normal human terms like us, he wasn't reallah all that old (it's sorta like dogs or somethin.) I guess he wasn't able to go off huntin and mushin on a dog sled or fishin no more."

"So one naht, while outside a big snowstorm was ragin, these Eskimos was sittin around the fire in the igloo. (Ah know what you're goin to ask -- it was the same question ah had: why don't the fire melt that li'l ol igloo? The answer is -- let's see if ah can remembah this -- it does melt it some, but it's -- well dern it, theh ah've gone and plumb fergot!) Anyway, everyone in this big family was lahke gnawin on some raw walrus blubbah, or whatevah it is those people eat up theh. (Mah husband prefehs his steak so rah that, goodness gracious, it almost gets up and walks off the plate! And ah also know that those oriental foods lahke sushi and that kinda thang with raw fish are considahd delicacies. But you won't get me tryin them, no siree -- no wigglah worms crawlin around insahde me, thank yah verah much!)" [She humorously wriggles her body in an imitative grimace.]

"So they're sittin around the fire in the igloo gnawin on blubbah. And the thing to know is, there weren't nearly enough blubbah to go around (I guess they left it off the shoppin list that week -- ha ha.) The old man was gnawin on his shahe when he suddenly realized that evrabodah, right down to the itsy-bitsy babies, was starin at him. (Did that sorta thang ever happen to you, Mabel? It did to me once: ah walked into a room fulla people jabberin, and evrabodah -- and ah do mean positivelah evrah last soul -- stopped talkin when they saw me. Ah mean, as in frozen in mid-sentence. Let me tell you, that is the creepiest thang that's evah happened to me! It turned out that word had leaked out -- I can't imagine wheh from -- that Beaurahgahd and ah was engaged. So it was a good kinda creepy!)"

"Givin somebody the starin treatment in that Eskimo society must be pretty darned serious. Apparently it didn't just mean that they was mad at him; it was more lahke some kinda evil eye or somethin, and everybodah knew what it meant, includin the old man. So he silently handed off his blubbah to his eldest son (ah guess that li'l Eskimo society was just as patriahchal as the one down South here)" [sighs audibly] "and just walked outside into the blizzard and, as he put it to Beau, what amounted to 'certain death'."

"(Beaurahgahd told me what the word is when you banish an old person to their death, but of course ah forgot it already. (Ah swear, Mabel, ah got a mahnd like an absolute <u>sieve</u>!) It sounds somethin like 'gerundectomy' -- ah know that much. Of course it's a terrible thang, especially if you're the old person. You have to admit though: if you're goin to do it anyway, then that snowstorm is mighty *convenient* for the purpose. Thank about it: it not only kills you, it buries you in the bargain. Outta saht, outta mahnd!"

"(Ah mean, thank about what kinda problem you'd have if you lived in a place lahke Florida. Whaddle ya do -- leave somebodah out in the hot sun until they dah of heat stroke or somethin? That ain't outta saht, and it sure as hail ain't outta mahnd because Honah, you got a public health problem on youh hands! Ah suppose the nearest equivalent situation in Florida to the Eskimo would be to put the old goat in a li'l boat with an outboahd motor and about thirtah miles wortha gas and say 'Bon Voyage!'. But then you ask youhself: whah waste a perfectlah good boat and motah?"

"[Laughs uneasily] (Mah oh mah, how ah do go on with these pressin social issues! The excitin thang is, ah get to do more than just thank about these sorts of thangs; ah actuallah help Beaurahgahd craft legislation. Ah mean -- and this is strictlah between you and me Sweetie -- he consults me about absoluteleh <u>evrathin</u>!)"

"But ah'm gettin away from mah story about the old Eskimo. He told Beau that he silently walked out the door of the igloo into the blizzard. (Whah 'silently'? Well, thank about it: if you were the old man, what would you say in such a situation? 'Thanks for all the good tahmes'? 'Sorry we couldn't work somethin out'? Ah mean, if it were me, ah'd at least trah a li'l bitta negotiation: 'I'll tell y'all what: ah'll just eat snow until you gahs kill another walrus.' As for the others, did they say anahthang to him before he left? How bout 'No hard feelins, okay?'_or: 'Hosta la vista baby!' But why not just be blunt: 'Chill out, Grandpa!' See what ah mean? It's gotta be silent.)"

"(You know what ah'd do if it were me havin to walk outta that place? Ah'd at least slam the dooh after me! You know, make the Grande Exit. Except that ah guess igloos problah don't have a dooh you can slam -- most likelah it's just a big animal skin hangin down. Too bad! So I'd just bang that big ol hide a few times on mah way out -- you know, to fill the igloo with all the dust mahtes and mold spohes and mange pahticles and peskah fleas and whatever else those animal skins would be full of. So ah'd be saying in essence, "Since things ain't goin to be none too good foh me, ah'll make sure they ain't exactlah the best foh you neithah!"

"(You know what else ah'd do? Ah'd grab a nahce warm jacket to put on. I suppose they'd call that hedgin your bets; it's problah in violation of some sorta social code those kinda people have -- you know, when you're sent out to freeze to death, it's problah not koshah to trah to prolong the agonah in the hope that you can last out the storm. But as a matter of fact, ah happen to know that them there Eskimos are prettah darn good at withstandin cold: ah once saw a movah where an Inuit ran for mahles and mahles ovah ahce and snow while being absolutelah buck stahk naked (no Mabel, I weren't watchin no Eskimo porn!)"

"Anyway, whether or not he slammed the door or grabbed a coat, this old guy was out of that igloo and smack into the ragin blizzard. He said that he walked or staggahd a coupla hundred feet before he collapsed into the snow. And at that point he was thinkin: 'I'm done for!' That's what he told Beaurahgahd: 'I thought that ah was absolutelah a dead man!'"

"But as luck would have it (I would call it a bit of a miracle mahself), there happened bah just at that exact moment in that exact place some kinda all-terran vehicle which was on patrol from a neahby ahmy base or somethin. They saw the old man before he was covered ovah with snow, rescued him, and brought him back to the base tah thaw him out."

"That's when he stahted whaht he called his 'odyssey' -- his gradual wanderin south from the fahthest point north (I guess there ain't no other direction to wandah if you're that fah north!) He worked odd jobs havin to do with fish, from mendin nets to cannin factories, tendin to gravitate toward population centers. He learned English and became fluent by chattin up people around pot-bellied stoves in general stohes."

"He became what is known as 'a crackah barrel philosophah' (which, just between you and me Honeh, is just a fancy name for a first-class bullshit ahtist.) His fame began to spread, and people came from mahles around to hear him. Beaurahgahd said somethin verah funnah to him about that: 'Theh you were, a lahftime in distance and culchah awah from the existence you had led as an Eskimo, and you'ah rahght back to chewin the fat!'"

"Eventually some influential people persuaded him to run for Congress. He did that -- and was elected!"

"Anyway, yesterday was this man's verah first day in his new job. Of coahse he was nervous and all; but Beaurahgahd was functionin as a sort of mentoh for him, to introduce him to the rituals of the place and all that. He entered the House chambah and was dismayed to see that theh were onlah three other congressmen waitin theh to heah his maiden speech. But he gave it anyway -- Beaurahgahd said he was quahte eloquent, considerin that it was in suppoht of this totallah mundane bill that provahded so-called eahmahks foh his constituents. In fact -- and this is what made Beaurahgahd sit up and take notice -- the man called for fundin of pohk barrels -- I mean, literallah, barrels of pohk! -- for his Eskimo friends back home. (That'll give em a lotta fat tah chew on!) Beau thought this was a rahyot!"

"Aftah that rathah shoht session was ovah, Beaurahgahd brought the man back here to, as he put it, 'lick his wounds'. He had our nahce negro butler bring them mint juleps out on the verandah. The man was lamentin the dismal turnout foh his maiden speech. Beaurahgahd looked at him in disbelief and asked him: 'You mean you don't undahstand?' The man said he didn't. And then Beau said somethin that, ah sweah, will crack me up til the daih ah dah:"

"'It weren't important tah them cause you don't yet have the powah tah wheel and deal.' When the man still looked mystifahd, Beau added: 'Don't you see? *You have no* senoritah!' "

"Now ain't that about the funniest thang you evah did heah? Beau said that it's one of the best examples of *ahronih* he ever encountahd. We both was laughin til our sahdes was bout busted, and fahnallah the man came to see the humah in it hisself and had a good laugh at his own expense."

[Looks at her watch] "Mah goodness, Mabel, how tahme does flah! That was a long storah and mah pooh li'l throat is absolutelah pahched from all the tellin of it. So ah do bahlieve ah have earned anothah glass of ahwe infamous ahced tea!"

(18 November 2008)

The Unraveling

A Gauche Undertaking

(First, the factual tale. Around 1929, the refined French composer

Maurice Ravel (1874-1937) received a request from the Austrian pianist Paul Wittgenstein (1887-1961), the brother of the famed philosopher Ludwig, to write him a concerto for the left-hand alone (the pianist had lost his right arm in World War I (1914-1918).) The composer studied virtuoso pieces for the left-hand alone by such eminent predecessors as Saint-Saëns, Czerny, Alkan and Scriabin. As he later wrote: "In a work of this sort it is essential to give the impression of a texture no thinner than that of a part written for both hands." The completed work, *"Concerto pour la main gauche"*, is described by Ravel's biographer as follows: "This is Ravel's most dramatic work, combining expansive lyricism, tormented jazz effects, a playful scherzo, and driving march rhythms, all of which are scaffolded into one movement of modest dimensions." (Ravel was familiar with jazz, having taught George Gershwin orchestration in 1927.) Wittgenstein played the world premiere with the Vienna Philharmonic in 1932. Ravel wrote another piano Concerto -- a normal one for two hands -- in tandem with the one for Wittgenstein. These were the last two pieces in any form that he wrote.)

(Second, the fictional tale. The following is an extrapolation of four connected entities: "Ravel", "Wittgenstein", "Concerto for the left-hand alone", and "1916". It is all intended to be logical; however, as no research was ever done, most of what is written below may be at least inaccurate, if not downright wrong. The author apologizes in advance for any accuracies. As for his use of the arch-politically-incorrect c-word [he lives in an institution wherein every single resident is a "c" and yet the word dares not speak its name there], his natural [and probably only] defense is that he is a "c" himself.)

One day in 1916, out of the blue, the distinguished French composer, Maurice Ravel, received the following curt note postmarked from Vienna (a total surprise to him, since that city was part of a country which was at war with France at the time [but you know the post office: "Neither snow nor rain..."]):

"I am in need of a piano concerto for one hand alone. Do you know anyone who might like to write me such a piece? -- Paul Wittgenstein"

Ravel recognized the name as that of a young hotshot Austrian pianist. The last thing Ravel had heard was that Wittgenstein had gone into The Great War as cannon fodder for the enemy. Now here he was, asking for a piece for one hand. But why? And why the oblique request? "He's acting just like his brother!" exclaimed the composer, not without irritation. He was referring to the philosopher whose writings were so abstruse that only a handful of people could understand them.

Of course the composer was not fooled for a second: he knew that Wittgenstein could not ask him directly to write him a piece since their countries were at war; so the pianist had to play it coy and pretend as if the French composer was the furthest thing from his mind.

As a matter of fact, Ravel was greatly intrigued by the challenge of writing a concerto for one hand alone. The problem was, he didn't yet know which hand he would be writing for; and he didn't know what the exact situation was concerning the other hand: was it missing, or was there something else going on here?

Ravel reread the letter and noted that it did not specify that anything was missing. So in the beginning the composer had to puzzle out as to why a pianist would want a piece for just one hand alone. What could this mean? He finally assumed that on the piano Wittgenstein was technically deficient in one hand, and that he wanted to cover up that fact by playing only music with that hand eliminated -- a sort of stunted cop-out piano music. So Ravel began to ask critics and other knowledgeable experts about the pianist: did they ever suspect him of having a "lazy", "sloppy" or even downright "slovenly" hand, quite apart from the fact that he was "a dirty Austro-Hungarian against whom we in France are fighting trench warfare at this very moment?" But the critics all told Ravel that Wittgenstein had a "superb technique in both hands -- quite apart from the fact that he has used those hands in an attempt to decimate the flower of French youth."

So Ravel was led to conclude that Wittgenstein was missing something. But what? He looked at the letter yet again: it had said "... for one hand alone." So he was missing a hand; and it must have been the left hand since the handwriting in the letter was so beautiful. Well, that wasn't so bad! The fact that the pianist still possessed (what the composer assumed to be) a viable stump of a left arm as well as a fully functioning right hand, left plenty of room for creative music making. The stump could be used for boogie-woogie-type "vamping" at the very least (Ravel was open to new trends from America), while the right hand could fill in with all sorts of elaborate filigree. Yes, not bad at all!

Ravel had no way of knowing that Wittgenstein was left-handed and so wrote fluently with that hand -- and therefore was missing the right-hand, not the left. "Aha," you cry, "But Ravel should've been able to tell from the slant of the handwriting that it was written by a lefty!" Indeed, it is well known that left-handed writers have handwriting that slopes backwards, as if it is reluctant to proceed across the page.

What only Wittgenstein's closest friends knew was that the pianist, by dint of hard work and perseverance, had managed to train his handwriting to slope to the right, thereby appearing eager to march across the page. (Unfortunately, this change induced in him a tendency to stutter.)

So Ravel proceeded to write the piece he thought Wittgenstein wanted. One afternoon he was in a café and there met another composer named Claude Debussy. Ravel bragged to his older colleague that he was hard at work on a piano concerto "for right-hand and left stump". When he told him whom the piece was for, Debussy exploded in his most elegant French: "Tu imbécile! Wittgenstein lost his right hand, not the left one; in fact, he lost his whole bloody (pun intended) arm!"

Ravel was understandably devastated by this news. Now he was going to have to throw all his hard work away. Worse, he was going to have to rethink the whole piece.

The prospect filled him with dread. For one thing, the left-hand was in general the weaker of the two hands: this was particularly true of pianists, for the reason that the demands on the right-hand in the repertoire were greater. So his piece would be doubly stunted:

because it would be for only one hand; and because it was the weaker hand.

Then, too, in general almost all the playing that the left-hand does in the traditional repertoire is on the bottom half of the piano keyboard. In this regard, middle C. has functioned since Beethoven as sort of a "Maginot Line" which is very seldom crossed by the left-hand except to make brief "forays" into "enemy" territory for quick "skirmishes" with the right hand.

The prospect seemed horrible: he was going to be mired in the bottom half of the keyboard ("like trench warfare!" he noted to himself grimly), forced to write a turgid, lugubrious, muddy sort of music. The Bolsheviks were poised to take over the Russian government; now people would assume that they had taken over his piano concerto as well!

Fortunately, Ravel was not merely a good composer, he was a great one. So he did what any truly great composer would do -- namely, ask another first rate composer what <u>he</u> would do. So he contrived to meet Debussy at a café. (This wasn't difficult: they both always went to the same café every day -- partly to pick up any stray ideas floating about. As Ravel was attempting to do here.)

Debussy was his usual restrained, refined French self:

"Crétin -- and I mean that in the kindest possible way -- you can have the left-hand enter the upper register any time you want!"

"But the right-hand -- it will get in the way..." ?

"Dégénéré!" [Debussy had a fondness for this particular epithet because it allowed him to use so many accents agues in one word.] "There won't be a right-hand to get in the way! So you can give the left-hand carte blanche!" Except that Debussy did not actually say those last two words; rather, he translated the words into English as "free rein", as any well-educated Frenchman at the time would do to idiomatic expressions which were spoken in French in foreign tongues.

Debussy did give Ravel more advice: "The piece should be fairly short, the reason being that people begin to get tired of music for the left hand alone once the novelty wears off. I'd say fifteen minutes tops."

And then Debussy gave Ravel this final cryptic advice: "In a work of this sort, it is essential to give the impression of a texture no thinner than that of a part written for both hands."

Ravel came away puzzled by this pronouncement: what did it mean? He had said, "... a texture no thinner than that of a part written for both hands"; but which part of which piece? It seemed like an awfully general statement to make! It could be made to apply to the vast majority of music, from the most anemic pieces by Eric Satie to the most cluttered by Beethoven -- and none of those pieces could be played by the left-hand alone. And then, too, Debussy had used the word "impression": what did that mean -- a slight [or slide?] of hand?

For the first time in his creative life as a composer, Maurice Ravel was paralyzed to write a piece. Finally he decided to drop it and write other music, which he was able to do successfully. Did he write back an answer to Wittgenstein? No. After all, the pianist hadn't had the courtesy to ask him for a piece directly. Besides, he was a dirty little -- well, you get the idea.

Time passed. Debussy died. The War ended (Europe lost.) Ravel became even more famous as a composer and teacher. He taught the young (of course there was never a time when he wasn't young) George Gershwin orchestration; and, in gratitude, the younger composer wrote "An American in Paris."

And then in that same year 1927 -- that is, 11 years after he received the last one -- Ravel received the following note:

"I had sent you a previous letter on this subject, but it must have gotten lost in the War. So I will repeat here what I said there: will you write me a piano concerto for the left-hand alone? -- Paul Wittgenstein."

Ravel was a little miffed at Wittgenstein for bending the truth here about having asked him outright for a piece before; and he was a little bit suspicious that so much time had passed since the last request: had the pianist been trying to drum up other commissions before his? And so he was sorely tempted not to reply to this note either. On the other hand, the pianist <u>was</u> asking him for a piece now, and such a thing was always flattering for Ravel. Finally the composer decided to write an affirmative response, and even hubristically suggested a first performance date in Paris two years hence.

But immediately Ravel began experiencing the same psychological blockages that he had had before: he could not find a way to write the piece. Unfortunately, Debussy had died, so he was not there to give Ravel the kind of sage (and mysterious) advice he had dished up in the past. He even tried writing a second 'normal' piano Concerto in tandem with it: this he did with great success. But the one for the left-hand alone eluded him. Finally, he wrote what he could and hoped for the best.

The first performance in Paris was plagued by scandals. The very printed program for the concert contained an embarrassing 'error': the name of the piece was listed as a "Concerto pour une pianiste gauche". No doubt the work of some hack in a printing office still embittered by the War, it implied not only that the pianist was rude, but that he was effeminate to boot.

Then, when Wittgenstein came out on stage, he was roundly booed and hissed. As he sat at the piano, his empty jacket sleeve was clearly visible to the audience. They began to yell out epithets too horrible to write here, such as "cripple!" and "freak!" as well as the usual "German Pig-Dog!" and the like. It seemed clear that, for this audience at least, the War had still not ended. Finally, stagehands had to turn the piano around so that Wittgenstein's intact arm was facing the audience. Of course then they couldn't open the piano lid, and so the whole performance had a muffled sound to it.

But those weren't the worst things. Tragically, as we said, for the only time in his creative career, Ravel had gotten composers block while he was trying to write the piece against the deadline. And so, of the three sections (Introduction, Improvisation, Jazz), only the first was truly Ravel's work. (and that sounded a bit like a boilermaker factory in the fledgling Soviet republic.) As for the second section, Ravel was hoping -- perhaps even praying -- that

Wittgenstein could turn in a credible performance as an improviser, much as Gershwin had improvised a large amount of "Rhapsody in Blue" with such brilliance in the first performance of that work.

Unfortunately, Wittgenstein could not improvise his way out of a paper bag. What he turned out in the performance sounded like a fairly-talented nine-year-old kid fooling around on the piano. This pathetic performance only landed more catcalls and boos upon the hapless pianist as well as the do-nothing composer.

But the worst was saved for last. The third section began, and some truly wonderful jazz -- perhaps the most wonderful most people in the audience had ever heard -- emerged. All the jeering stopped in the fascination of the moment. It looked as though Ravel's reputation would emerge intact after all. The bubble was only punctured by someone suddenly yelling out: "Hey -- that's Gershwin's 'An American in Paris'!" Unfortunately for Ravel, someone in the audience had just returned from America where they had heard the first performance of that new work.

(Did you hear the one about the composition student who had to have a movement for a symphony written and turned in by Friday? In desperation he wrote out, backwards, one of the movements from his teacher's Symphony, and handed it in. He received an "F" -- on the grounds that he had plagiarized Beethoven's Fifth.)

Well, Ravel and Wittgenstein were driven out of the concert hall by a barrage of tomatoes. They ran to a café to lick their wounds. Ravel was in despair, and he poured out to Wittgenstein the tale of his compositional blockage. The pianist thought for a moment; then he said: "There is a psychologist in my hometown who might be able to help you -- I think he gave Gustav Mahler a hand when he was having trouble writing back around the turn of the century. His name is Dr. Sigmund Freud."

Ravel said that he had heard of Dr. Freud as the famous inventor of psychoanalysis. So he traveled to Vienna by train, and Freud agreed to meet with him. He began by telling the psychologist that he had heard about him having helped Mahler with his music. Freud scoffed:

"Mahler never needed help writing music -- he could do it in his sleep! No, goodness knows, that was the least of his worries. Of course I would never betray a professional confidence -- though, just between you and me, the poor man was married to a young nymphomaniac; and, believe me, that is no bed of marital roses!"

So Ravel went into psychoanalysis with Dr. Freud, and, in short order, a sordid little tale from Ravel's childhood emerged. It seems that his father and brother were left-handed, while he and his mother were right-handed. From this seemingly trivial little dichotomy, his mother built an absolute one: that the right-handers were "good", while the left-handers were "bad". (You doubt that this could constitute a viable family situation? I used my own family that I grew up in as a model!) Ravel had always wondered why, for example, he had never married: was it a coincidence that all the girls he met were left-handed, automatically rendering them ineligible? Did he ever suspect that people were whispering behind his back that he was a 'mama's boy'?

As a therapy, Freud introduced Ravel to one of his "stable" of "available" "society" "women". (I used quotations because with Dr. Freud, you were never quite sure <u>what</u> you were getting!) This was a big blonde softig, left-handed Fräulein. Soon, Ravel was able to begin working on his piece from scratch again. And, as he worked, his "new friend" would sit next to him and, in sultry tones, repeatedly mouth the words "Right-hand good, left-hand <u>better!</u>" into his susceptible ear. In this way was he able to finish the whole Concerto, including the scoring, in one effortless month.

This time, the première of "Concerto pour la main gauche" (the correct title) was in Vienna in 1932. Wittgenstein was given a hero's ovation, and the audience demanded that the dangling right sleeve deliberately show on their side. The pianist played flawlessly. As for the music (for the usual large orchestra, including percussion and harp), here is how a critic put it the next day:

"This is Ravel's most dramatic work, combining expansive lyricism, tormented jazz effects, a playful scherzo, and driving march rhythms, all of which are scaffolded into one movement of modest dimensions."

I don't know about you (or, for that matter, the critic), but I find the above to be the clearest and most concise description of sexual awakening in music that I have ever read.

(25 December 2008)

Vinnie & Ritchie

Vinny

Was it the richly appointed sitting room of a Florentine palazzo? Or the "greeting" room of a Sicilian bordello?

I remember the drive over to Medford with the real estate agent the first time: it felt interminable, as if we were going into uncharted, alien territory. The agent was gushing over the place we were about to see -- something that made me suspicious. (Memo 1 to real estate agents: your taste may not correspond to someone else's. Memo 2: The fact that you get a commission if you rent the place renders everything you say -- even "Excuse me while I use the restroom." -- immediately suspect. Memo 3: We all know that the intensity of your effusions is inversely proportional to the quality of the property being effused about. For example, if you were about to show us Versailles, would you rave, "Wait until you see this next place -- it's a real beauty! And they did a good job on the landscaping too!" So stop the effusions -- they only make us nauseous. Memo 4: When you tell us to look at something [Example: "Nice ceilings!"], we will know that it is a diversionary tactic to keep us from looking at everything else.)(Unfortunately, we tend to behave like lemmings and so we will probably dutifully gaze up at the ceilings.)

The house was a brick duplex, one of those pseudo-Tudor designs with a peak over each door. Actually, it could've been quite appealing, except for the fact that there was nothing living above thigh level in height within 100 feet of the house. (Note 1 to homeowners: it is desirable to have a mature tree or two on the sunny side of a house upon which the sun relentlessly beats, heating it up to 120° inside. Note 2: Bark mulch is organic but not living. It is a cheap way of preventing weeds -- and every other living thing

-- from growing around a bush, a sort of benign Agent Orange. It is ugly and dull. Note 3: How can you own a house so much lacking architectural unity that its so-called designer felt compelled to stick a pointy-thing over each door?)

The agent was continuing to emote over the interior appointments we were about to behold. (Yet another memo to real estate agents: saying that something's true doesn't make it so. I suggest you enter politics.) We stepped over the threshold and entered the living room.

We were struck dumb by the sheer audacity of it all. Quite literally, it took our breath away.

There was a deep, funereal twilight created by at least two sets of thick opaque draperies -- one set to block out virtually all the light, the other to be tied back from the first to give it contrast and depth. There were tufted chairs and love seats upholstered in matching pastel silks. A palm tree stood in the corner. We had the strange sensation of opulence multiplied incessantly by itself, an effect due to one-foot-square mirrors covered with gold specks affixed to every wall.

The whole effect, in fact, was of something balanced precariously between elegance and kitsch -- with a decided leaning towards the latter. It seemed like a first tentative approximation to Citizen Kane's Xanadu.

In the dining room were two huge hutches that appeared to have been carved out of solid marble. You could see the pink grain suffusing the sturdy columns on either side. I wondered at how such massive constructions could have been gotten into the house. (Positive note to homeowner: nice job hiding the use of railway sidings to get marble monuments into house.)

Covering every square inch of those two rooms was a baby blue carpet. Perhaps this was meant to suggest the pure sparkling azure of the Adriatic Sea, mirrored by the sky-blue ceilings up above.

The kitchen and bathroom were both decorated in black-and-white: this included wallpaper extending onto and covering the ceilings, and shag rugs covering the floors. There was even a black wall phone in each room. Oh yes -- the kitchen counters were black bathroom tiles. (Important note to homeowners: it is potentially very dangerous to mix up kitchen and bathroom!)

As we prepared to go upstairs, we noticed that what we assumed had been a fine gumwood banister had been replaced by a white, wrought-iron one. So one could stand halfway up the stairs, lean over this romantic balustrade, and admire the sumptuous room below.

The master bedroom contained a large round bed with a custom-made round red velvet spread. And yes, above the bed, on the ceiling, were pasted more mirrors.

We were, as I've said, stunned by all that we saw and beheld there. It was so unlike our taste, so contrary to any way that we thought we wanted to live. So for several minutes, we were rendered speechless. No doubt we were ashen in countenance, for the real estate agent began a sort of filibuster as we were leaving. (Aside to real estate agents: if you say it enough times, we may finally start to believe it. But in some cases you're going to have to say it a <u>huge</u> number of times!)

So the logorrheal agent drove our silent selves back to our apartment in Arlington (that is, civilization), and we told him that we would call him "if we are interested" -- almost always a bad sign. As soon as he left, my wife and I looked at one another and laughed out loud. Of course the place was absurdly impossible and impossibly absurd! And we promptly forgot all about it.

Well, not quite. Over the next couple of weeks, as our search for another place grew cold, little facts that we had ignored began to gradually seep into our consciousness. For one thing, that apartment was essentially a two-story three-bedroom house, well built of brick and with gumwood woodwork. What had offended us were superficial furnishings and doodads that were not part of the essential house itself. I began to fantasize about what we could do with them: drear drapes could be *ripped down* from the windows, and rugs *torn up* from the floors; a tacky wrought-iron railing could be *wrenched unceremoniously* from its moorings on the staircase, and gold-spattered mirrors *scraped* from the walls.

Then too, a map showed us that the house, far from being "out of it", was very near Medford Square -- a quick walk for a glass of wine in the evening.

Finally, the rent was very reasonable compared to Arlington.

So when that hapless real estate agent called back in two or three weeks and asked in the forlorn tone of the hopeless case whether we had any interest in the Medford apartment, I'm sure that he was as shocked as we would have been a few weeks before if we could've heard our reply: "Yes we are very interested -- in fact, we'd like to take it!" (Aside to real estate agents: you might think from this case that once in a while it pays to sound forlorn. You would be wrong: the pathetic never sells, except in bad dramatic productions.)

I met the vacating resident of our new abode on moving day: he was a little behind schedule and so there were still some of his things in the house. I encountered him in the sunroom, with its garish red rug (he had used the room as a den; it would become my study.) He was a bit frantic and apologized for the delay (I told him it was okay; but I was careful not to say "Take your time"!) He told me his name was "Vinny", that his wife had gone back to live with her mother, and that as a result "things are all haywire." (I wondered whether she was in rebellion against his bizarre decorating ideas; but I finally realized that this (the decorating) had to have been a joint venture -- it was too perfect to have been erected in conflict; and that, thus, the breakup must have come for other reasons.)

I wandered out into the living room. The lush drapes had already been taken down, and I saw how much it had helped the zealous real estate agent for us to see this rug in that hushed twilit gloom: too late the harsh light of day revealed many stains and spots -- and, no doubt, a multitude of unseen hairs -- left by recalcitrant pets. Like the Adriatic, this rug was polluted.

Two of Vinny's friends were carrying out some of the larger pieces from the house. At one point I saw them lugging one of the marble hutches from the dining room. I shook my head with disbelief at their strength -- until I saw the piece from the back and realized that those huge edifices were empty shells, constructed of

185

cheap light wood painted to resemble marble and weighing next to nothing.

My second (and last) encounter with Vinny occurred in the basement. There he was supervising the unhooking of the washer and dryer by two of his cronies. We didn't have a dryer; and I noticed that his was essentially new. I casually asked him what he planned to do with it. He shrugged:

"Oh, put it in storage along with all the other stuff." It did not escape me that Vinny had lumped all of his elegant furnishings under the catchall word "stuff".

I asked whether he was willing to sell it. He said maybe -- "for the right price". I asked what that might be. He replied with flat finality: "Sixty bucks".

I could not quite believe my ears. Here was a brand-new dryer hooked up to the gas, and he wanted that paltry sum? I was so happy with his reply that I felt I just had to negotiate:

"How does forty dollars sound to you?"

Vinny: "Keep unhookin' it guys!"

I gave in, of course. "Okay, that's fine. To whom should I make out the check?"

Vinny: "Uh -- cash."

And with that one word I saw in a flash that those hollow, faux-marble hunches were metaphors for Vinny's world. Indeed, in the coming weeks we would find out, from the various creditors appearing at our door looking for him, that Vinny's whole lifestyle was in all likelihood a façade built on debts he could not pay.

The owner permitted us to take down the mirrors from the walls and the wallpaper and mirrors from the ceilings. But we had to live with the rug and the white wrought-iron banister. And when we asked him whether we could plant a tree or two on the hot, sunny side of the house, he thought for a moment before he replied: "Well, maybe a dwarf tree..."

Richie

A few short years after we moved into our rented faux-Tu
my brother-in-law bought the house five doors down the ~~street from~~
us. Living next door was a man named Richie, his wife, and their
young son, Little Richie.

The previous owner had made the front of the house open and
inviting, with a quaint flagstone path meandering up to the door. But
then, one day, Richie had a brick wall topped by thick, iron spikes built
around the front yard, with iron gates for both the walkway and the
driveway. By dint of a subtle narrowing and the placement of a step
at the beginning of the walkway, the house became psychologically,
as well as physically, intimidating for any would-be visitor.

At that moment, my brother-in-law conceived his first *inkling*
about Richie. But he shook it off as a sort of prejudice.

But there were no walls or definite boundary lines in the
backyards. And, as it turned out, Richie was a very expansive and
generous sort of fellow when it came to his neighbor. Often when
my brother-in-law would be working in his yard, Richie would come
over, throw his arm around his shoulder, and ask if his sons or nieces
would be interested in something he had in his garage. He would
roll up the door and reveal a building chock full of something or
other. One time it was comforters (my nephews didn't have much
use for those; but my daughters each picked out one); another time it
was major league baseball hats -- hats from every conceivable team
in both leagues, boxes upon boxes piled from floor to ceiling with
nothing but hats. On still another occasion he invited my brother-
in-law into his kitchen, where the latter saw four or five microwave
ovens stacked up (he was not offered one of those.)

What sort of cook needs five microwave ovens? What sort of hat-
wearer needs a crate full of hats from each major league team? My
brother-in-law, who was an enterprising cook as well as a sometime
hat-wearer (though not, I hasten to add, of the Major league variety)
did not know the answers to those questions. Should I add that
another *inkling* about Richie entered his subconscious? This was not
so easy to brush aside as the first had been; but he finally concluded

that the man was in some kind of wholesale business, and was using his garage and even parts of his house as warehouse space.

One morning when I was on my way to a temporary teaching position in Winthrop, I inadvertently found myself following Richie to (assumedly) his place of work. He was picked up in front of his house by a stunningly beautiful, black Mercedes-Benz. It was one of those automobiles that you know just by looking that it is custom-made; for it was a little longer and a little sleeker (while, paradoxically, at the same time being understated) than your average run-of-the-mill Mercedes. And so I "followed" them quite a way toward the coast north of Boston. We only parted ways when Richie's driver turned off for Revere.

When I told the gist of this to my brother-in-law, I saw a slight suggestion of a shrug of his shoulders, as if to say (as I would): "Some of my best friends -- musicians and teachers -- live in Revere." Yes, he would shrug it off, even as he was thinking: "But how many of them work there?" And inwardly he would feel too many inklings now fast morphing into a sort of *hunch*.

Richie would sometimes say strange things to my brother-in-law. One day he took him aside and said in a conspiratorial undertone, "We're goin' away on vacation for a week. If someone comes up to you and asks whether he can go up to your second floor and watch my house, tell him he can't -- okay?"

The dominoes were falling faster now. My brother-in-law found his hunch rapidly becoming a *suspicion*.

One early fall day just before lunch, my brother-in-law got a call from the school. They told him that there had been an injury to his older son: he had been hit in the head with a baseball. The father picked the boy up and brought him home. The lad was weeping profusely and was nearly inconsolable.

A nasty goose egg was already manifesting itself on the boy's forehead. My brother-in-law first made up an ice pack and applied it to the welt. He then gave his son a perfectly ripe peach which he had been saving for his own lunch. Finally, he carried his son into his bedroom for a nap.

My poor little nephew was lying sprawled on his bed, his shoulders heaving with sobs. His father was rubbing his back and singing to him:

"Baby's boat a silver moon
Sailing in the sky..."

The lulling of his singing and the softness of his caresses were having an effect: the sobs were slowing down.

"Sail, baby, sail
O'er the deep blue sea;
Only don't forget to sail
Back again to me."

Then from deep down in the pillow he heard his son murmur, "I love you Daddy."

This is it, my brother-in-law thought, this is what makes life worth living! Is there strife and hunger in most parts of the world? Of course. Did strong, powerful men prey upon those who were weak and powerless? To be sure. But right at that sublime moment he was willing to suspend disbelief and think that all mankind was in perfect harmony; that the world was one big beautiful whole.

He was moved almost to tears by his own thoughts and feelings. He raised his glazed eyes to gaze out the window in order to confirm for himself that the world outside was imbued with the self-same harmony as he felt within himself; that that world was as good and fresh and pure as he instinctively knew it to be.

Two men were standing next to the open trunk of a Cadillac in Richie's driveway only a few feet from the window. One was Richie, and his suit jacket was off. He was wearing a shoulder holster with a gun in it.

My brother-in-law asked himself: What kind of man who is not a police officer or a detective would be carrying a gun? His mind raced over all the professions he could think of -- until he alighted on one that beggared the very use of the term "profession". For a moment his body became tense, as what had been but a suspicion in his mind became all but a certainty. He felt his vision of a harmonious world beginning to crumble around him.

But then he relaxed as he recalled the famous words of the poet:

"Good fences make good neighbors"'"

Watermelon

An endangered species?

Some of you remember how it was in the so-called good old days when we were kids. We'd be at a family picnic on a hot summer day, and there'd be watermelon for dessert. Inside the melon there would be big black seeds which could be neither chewed nor swallowed. So they had to be spit out in some way. Well, viola, an instant harmless weapon suitable for use on one's unwary cousins and siblings!

And so we would spit seeds at one another for a few golden moments -- that is, until one of us who was a little more enterprising than the others would suddenly have two insights: first, that it took a lot of energy to blow those seeds far enough to reach one's adversaries (it was also unsanitary, but that did not seem to bother us -- on the contrary); second, those seeds were each coated with a sort of natural slime which allowed them to be placed under great pressure using lips and/or teeth, and then suddenly -- and soundlessly -- released at great speed towards one's target through curled-up tongue.

Have you eaten a slice of watermelon lately? (This reminds me of those ads on TV: "Have you driven a Ford? Lately?" Correct response: "Well, yes -- and it felt like just as much of a clunker as the Tin Lizzy that I drove back in 1923!")

If you have eaten that slice lately, you may have noticed something interesting: chances are there were no big, black, hard seeds inside of the type we used to spit and 'slither' at one another. Instead, there are a few poor, little, pathetic, stunted, soft, white seedlets (I will not dignify them by calling them "seeds".) We soon discover that these drear little entities are good for absolutely nothing. They can be swallowed; but as they do not seem to have any food value (I am convinced that nothing that anemic-looking could have any), what would be the use? Besides, do I want one of those stuck in my throat to bother me the rest of the day?

(A challenge to food companies around the world: see if you can mash the seedlets and market them in the form of a putty-like paste which could be spread on crackers as a sort of depressing appetizer [would paprika help?].)

Then, too, those bland little nothings are useless for spitting at someone: they have no mass of any consequence, and thus they can not be propelled an honest foot.

So what are they good for? I asked myself this question many times over, but could not answer it to my satisfaction. It took me a while before I realized that I was asking the wrong question. The real question should have been: why are they there to begin with?

Apparently to replace the black ones. I guess the marketers of watermelon failed to understand how much fun we were having with those big bad black bullets. They must've thought that they were a pain for us to deal with; so they substituted the wan, white, wimpy ones.

But how do you make such a substitution?

Here are some guesses by one who is unfamiliar with modern technologies, but who usually can rely on his hunches:

a) Special needles with strong vacuum devices are inserted through the skin of the watermelon. These "suck up" the black seeds. The wan white seedlets are then "blown" back in using a reverse process.

(Problems with this theory: it is unclear why, if the goal was to make the watermelon easier to eat, they would go to the trouble of inserting the little white seedlets. Perhaps they wanted them there as a sort of sentimental reminder of what was lost; but it is unclear as to whether the effect is worth the effort. The other caveat has to do with the physical possibility of being able to suck up the big, hard, black seeds through the pithy fruit; or, if that is accomplished, to withdraw the large, hard seeds through the tiny needle holes. I will not bother to speculate on the possible existence of needles that suck and blow.)

b) Inject a powerful, undetectable drug into the watermelon which "ages" the big, black seeds, turning them, within days, into withered, old-fart, white seedlets.

(Problems with this theory: the white seedlets are not withered, they are smooth. In fact, they appear to be immature, or proto-versions of the mature black seeds. So maybe I should change the above to: "Inject a powerful, undetectable drug into the watermelon which infantilizes the big black seeds..." Of course, the old caveat about why we would want the white seeds in there still holds. Plus, all of this business of injecting individual melons is beginning to seem mighty labor-intensive!)

(Another problem with this theory: this would mean that, in essence, they had discovered [sorry, Ponce de Leon -- re-discovered] the Fountain of Youth of mythical fame -- at least for this one, tiny, little corner of nature. But even if this were true, it would still be a far cry to finding a drug which works on the proverbial laboratory animal, to say nothing of humans.)

c) They grew a new kind of watermelon -- the kind that has little, anemic, white seedlets instead of big, robust, black seeds.

(Examination of this theory: at the risk of sounding like a broken record, why would anyone in their right mind want to put those white seedlets into the melon? Answer: maybe they can't help it. I'm sure that scientists would tell us that they are trying like the dickens to eliminate all the slight little white seedlets, but some keep slipping through [this is called "leakage" or "seepage" by plant growers -- or at least should be.] So when we use the term "seedless", we will understand it to mean "near-seedless".)

Well, that clears that question up! Now we know: the seed switch is what is known as "A Miracle of Modern Science." As everyone knows (so why am I bothering to say it? Because I know damn well that everyone doesn't know what I'm about to say, and I'm just trying to browbeat any readers who are uncertain of themselves on this subject), in order to get a new plant, one plants a seed from the fruit of an existing plant of the same type. So, in order to get a plant which bears fruit containing those little, anemic, white seedlets, one must plant one of those little, anemic, white seedlets.

(Okay, I'll confess, the above is not always true [in general one must be highly suspicious when one encounters the words "one must..."]. But, in order to get the right dramatic effect, I took the liberty of stating the situation in that form now. I plan to reveal the slightly more complex truth below.)

There is only one problem with the notion of white, seedlet plants begetting other white, seedlet plants: I can tell just by looking at those little, white wimps that they are constitutionally incapable of growing anything whatsoever. They are, in fact, a veritable insult to the whole notion of "seed".

"But daddy, they look like seeds."

"In a superficial sense, yes. But looks can be deceiving in this sort of situation."

"What do you mean 'this sort of situation'?"

The father decides that this is the opportune time to give his son a biology lesson -- even though he himself never did particularly well in the subject.

"Let's dissect each type of seed and observe the difference."

Somehow the father is able to find one of the old, black, watermelon seeds -- don't ask me where or how -- I think he was hoarding them; or perhaps the family had had watermelon of both types that evening for dessert. He cuts through the black seed with a knife.

"Do you see the green and the flesh, the moisture and the sheer -- fecundity of it all? You just know that it can grow something!" The father is astonished at his own eloquence; but at the same time is a bit embarrassed for conjuring up imagery that might provide difficulties should his son bring it up. The boy nods dubiously, but luckily says nothing. The father then picks up one of the little anemic white seedlets: it is so puny that he can hardly get it between his fingers. He cuts through it.

"What do you see? Do you see anything at all? No? Well, neither do I. There's just some more of the pitiful, white stuff. You can tell with near absolute certainty that this can't grow anything whatsoever. In other words, it is what they call in the growing business 'reproducibly void'." He had made that last bit up out of whole cloth, not only to impress his son, but also to avoid certain other words. (Need I add that he has a fondness for euphemism?)

Indeed, he was extra proud of the fact that he had invented that method of dissection to tell whether a seed is fertile or not right there on the spot (even though he just told his son that "looks can be deceiving".) He expected his son to be impressed; instead the son says:

"But aren't the seeds of a cantaloupe small and white like those others? But they're not -- what do you call it?"

"Reproducibly void?"

"Is that another name for impotent?"

Well, there it is -- yet another word that dares not speak its name -- at least not on evening television commercials.

That is one precocious kid! We shall see that he has not only already had a good science education, but that he asks the right kind of questions. And you can bet that the next thing he'll want to know is, how can you produce a viable plant from the impotent fruit of another? That is, how can you get a so-called seedless watermelon from another so-called seedless watermelon?

You can't, of course. The so-called seedless watermelon is the end of the line. Nothing can be produced from it.

I don't know about you, but this makes me very nervous. For it seems to me like they are breeding watermelons whose destiny is their own extinction. (When I refer to "they" in the previous sentence, I am talking about those who tend to play fast and loose with nature.) I could tolerate this result for any number of fruit-growing plants for which I have very little feeling (the kumquat? I wouldn't care a fig if they all died out tomorrow!) But the lordly watermelon, the Leviathan among fruits? I find that impossible to conceive (so to speak)!

"So, daddy, why don't watermelons which can't reproduce themselves die out?"

"The growers must have other ways of producing them."

"How?"

The father has only a vague notion of the answer to this question. He gave his last answer by the seat of his pants -- that is, something between inspiration and bullshit. Now he has to come up with something and fast.

"By engaging two other types of watermelon plants in what could be called 'non-invasive, alien intercourse'."

"Is that the same as cross-pollination?"

"Yes, basically."

"So the seedless watermelons are produced by fertilizing one kind of watermelon plant with pollen from another kind of watermelon plant?"

"I guess so..."

"What is an example of invasive, alien intercourse?"

(Thanks to his use of suggestive language, the father has opened a whole can of worms -- if not Pandora's Box itself!)

"It must be between unlike species of animal -- a donkey and a horse, for example, to produce a mule."

"Is that called mating?"

"I suppose it is."

"Isn't a mule impotent?"

"Yes it is."

"Do you think it's possible to produce an impotent chicken by mating a rooster with some other bird like a pigeon?"

(dubious) "I suppose theoretically..."

(seemingly out of the blue): "Is it true that bones in chicken bother us as much as seeds do in watermelon?"

(Wondering where this is all going): "Probably more so, because we can't shoot the bones at one another!"

"Well then, if cross-breeding is how they produce seedless watermelon, then that must be how they make boneless chickens!"

(Feeling like he's been caught in a logical trap): "What? Oh, I -- I guess so...."

After the boy is in bed, the father brags to his wife about the great biological discussion he had had with their son. The woman scoffs: "Then, all I can say is, there must be a whole lot of helpless, pathetic chickens out there who can't stand on their own, nevertheless flap their wings or stick out their necks to so much as feed themselves; nervous wrecks wallowing and flailing about in the dust of farm yards while they are waiting to get fat enough to be slaughtered."

But we need to leave that happy family situation and return to the subject of watermelons. Ultimately, the survival of the watermelon depends upon our ability to grow new plants. Here is what I think we know at the moment:

a. Watermelon plants are grown from the seeds of watermelons; but

b. Watermelon plants cannot be grown from the seedlets of near-seedless watermelons; therefore

c. Watermelon plants must be grown from the seeds of watermelons with big black fecund seeds. And, because, in general, only seedless watermelons are being produced, it follows that the total number of those big black seeds must be more or less constantly decreasing.

So the big question seems to be: Where are the good (i.e. big, black, potent) seeds, and who is in charge of them?

It seems to me that there are two possible answers to this question:

1. They are spread around the world, willy-nilly, amongst

anonymous amateurs who are unaware of their true value and who thus, caught up in the mad rush to produce impotent watermelons, might inadvertently allow the good seeds to be frittered away; or

2. They are quietly bought up and hoarded by unscrupulous speculators, against the day when they can corner the market and drive the cost of watermelon so high that it would be considered a delicacy at a family picnic.

Of the two choices above, which is worse? You might be tempted to say the first situation of total anarchy, since no one knows what anyone else is doing, and, before you know it, all the seeds will have disappeared because no one cared or was keeping track.

But consider this: imagine picking up a newspaper one day and reading the following:

FIRE DESTROYS SEED WAREHOUSES; BUILDINGS BELIEVED TO HOUSE ALL REMAINING WATERMELON SEEDS

I don't know about you, but that headline sends shivers running up and down my spine.

Is anyone out there minding the store? And, now that I think of it, what about those seedless (aptly named in this case) grapes?

Appendix: A short glossary of botanical terms:

cross-pollination: using pollen which are out of sorts
grafting: bribing a grower to mess with his trees
impotent: like sterile, except dirtier

(15 December 2008)

Wine & Cigarettes

Writing Under the Influence

I went out to write and drink and smoke for 14 years.

After my back-to-back political immersions with Herbert Brun and the Labor Party, I had a lot of pent-up political ideas to get off my chest. And the best way to do this, I decided, was to write political essays. I recall that I was reading a translation of Theodor Adorno's *Minima Moralia* at the time, and these social critiques affected my own writing (I even called my pieces "Minima" for awhile.) I was also reading Marshall McLuhan's *The Mechanical Bride* – a wonderful and humorous book of critical examinations of (mostly) magazine advertisements. (His given first name was "Herbert", by the way.)

So in 1977 I began going out at night to write. My search for a venue was tricky: it had to be a place that would not mind my sitting there for two hours or so while ordering very little. And it would have to be a place that allowed smoking. (By the way, I was a "sissy-smoker", in that I could not bear to draw smoke into my lungs.)

Filthy habit that it was, smoking got me out at night to places where I would not be interrupted by friend or phone. Indeed, I only smoked after 9:30 P.M. At the hour when most people were beginning to yawn, I began to feel the pangs of nicotine-dependency. As a result, I got an immense amount of writing done.

My searches brought me to *Howard Johnson's* at the Fresh Pond traffic circle in Cambridge. This was open 24 hours a day (hence no disconcerting last calls); it was spacious (hence no guilt about taking up a seat); it was attractive (I happened to like the deep red Naugahyde seats); and it was informally anonymous (hence no one to bother me).

My first evening there I tried coffee with my cigarette. But, unlike so many people, I did not take to the mixture of two stimulants. The next night I tried wine, and that was it. I would go on to mix those two ingredients, wine and cigarettes, 365 days per year (including Christmas) for the next 14 years.

At that time HoJo's had a goblet of burgundy for 65 cents. This provided enough wine for a whole evening of writing. If the ordering of wine constituted my "rent" of that space in a Naugahyde-covered booth for an evening, then the "rent" was cheap indeed.

I got an abundance of writing done there, mainly short, political essays. During the day I would carry a little pocket notebook around with me. Whenever I would think of a subject to write about, I would inscribe it in the notebook. (I think that at any given time, I'd have thirty or more topics listed in that little book.) When I arrived at HoJo's each night, I'd take a seat in a booth and there begin a series of carefully choreographed actions. First, I'd open my writing tablet and take out my (Bic) pen. Then I'd remove the little pocket notebook and lay it out in front of me. I'd choose a cigarette as I was perusing the list of possible topics. And then, simultaneously, three things would happen: I'd light the cigarette, a waitress (they were all well-trained after a few weeks) would bring my goblet of wine, and I'd put my finger on one of the topics and exclaim, "That one!" I'd take a drag, the nicotine would kick in, and my hand would begin to write automatically.

Thus was I able to practice instant gratification and write a complete essay each night: these became a collection which I called "Impreachments". (The title being a recognition that I had a tendency to take myself too seriously.) At that restaurant I also wrote hundreds of aphorisms, which I collected under the title "Apercus"; and the quasi-poetic linear notes for The Percussion Group recording of my drum piece, "para-DIDDLE". So this seemingly-prosaic place was very good for my work.

Unfortunately, after two years, we moved further away from HoJo's, and so I needed to seek a new venue for my escapades. Eventually I wound up at *Carroll's Diner* in Medford Square. There I realized how lucky I had been at HoJo's, for at Carroll's the wine cost more than twice as much for a glass only half as large. So now I needed two glasses of wine for a normal evening's work.

At Carroll's my "rent" had become prohibitively expensive.

I finally hit upon a solution to my problem: I would buy the first glass of wine from Carroll's, and bring in the second with me. I did this as follows:

1. I purchased a gallon of Carlo Rossi Burgundy for $4.99 at the liquor store;

2. Before going out, I filled a medium-sized, plastic, medicine bottle with the cheap burgundy;

3. I put the bottle in my vest pocket, after insuring that the cap was tight. (Nevertheless, I soon had a maroon stain on the tan corduroy vest pocket.)

4. In the restaurant, I would pour the wine into the wine glass, thus giving myself an extra glass of wine - and halving my evening's "rent"!

Of course it would not do for the waitress (or anyone else) to see me engaging in this activity. So the pouring would have to be done gradually and surreptitiously.

It seemed clear that I shouldn't drain the original glass of wine. For, once the waitress saw that, she would need to believe me to be someone comparable to the loaves-and-fishes practitioner if she were not to be suspicious when, somehow, magically, the glass filled itself again.

I found that the optimum level of fullness (notice I do not say 'emptiness') - the lowest level in the wine glass that would not trigger the suspicions of a waitress, and thus the level most ripe for refilling - was somewhere between two-thirds and one-half (okay, seven-twelfths, but who can estimate that?), but closer to two-thirds (to a waitress, the glass is never half-full, it's always half-empty.)

Once that critical level was reached, the process of 'pourage' was commenced, as follows:

First, a *façade of normality* had to be maintained for my activities. Of course I could not write during this process, but as long as possible I simulated writing. I affected a studious look to my countenance, even going so far as to raise my fingers to my lips in a pretense of deep thought.

And then, whilst pretending to that sort of industry, I would, with the utmost studied casualness, reach over to grasp the wine glass. Of course it had to appear that that wine glass was the furthest thing from my mind, that I only reached over out of mere habit. (Needless to say, the reaching over should not be so casual that I would inadvertently knock over said glass!)

At that exactly crucial point in the process, I would raise my eyes to the heavens, as if I sought inspiration for my writing from a higher power. Anyone watching me would, in a sort of unconscious mimicry, tend to look up as well.

It was at that precise moment, when I had deflected the eyes of any spectator in an irrelevant (if not irreverent) direction, that I would, ever so slowly and casually, slide the wine glass off the table with my left hand and lower it to my lap, placing it carefully to rest on the seat between my legs. (Caution: do not allow glass to topple to the floor!)

At that same moment I would lay my pen down on the table. In doing this, I would affect a weariness with my toil, to which my closed eyes and knitted, furrowed brow would attest.

And now my right arm would creep stealthily down - down to the pocket of my vest, from which it would remove the bottle containing the ruby elixir. My left hand would unscrew the top. And then came the Achilles' heel of the whole process, since it is the one time I had to look down: I would pour some of that ambrosia into the wine glass. (Caution: do not pour wine into lap!) How much, you might ask? The answer is: enough to add a significant amount to the glass without filling it completely (for that would cause suspicion.) How much is meant by "significant", you ask? My reply is: don't be so quantitative! "Significant" is "enough", and you'll know it when you see it.

The last step is to raise the wine glass again. (Caution: do not smash glass against underside of table!) I thought I might as well raise it all the way to my lips, thereby bringing the level of wine nearer once again to that magical point where "pourage" could begin anew.

Needless to say, I had to go through this process, these simulations, several times in the course of an evening. I am aware of the fact that this seems to be a time-consuming and nerve-wracking series of events to carry off once, to say nothing of two or three times. But I ask in good faith: <u>does anyone have a better idea how to save $1.73 (that includes tax) every single night</u>?!

Eventually, of course, it had to happen: my machinations

would be detected, permeated, seen through. Or at least I thought and assumed they were. The following is a complete and accurate transcript of the "conversation" with the waitress on this topic (if indeed it was on that topic):

> She: "I wish you wouldn't do that."
> Me: "Do what?"
> She: "What you were doing."
> Me: "Oh – okay."

(I challenge the reader to take this petite exchange as a model to be expanded upon, namely: How far afield can this "dialogue" be taken and still have, as its "substance", merely an allusion to something never mentioned?)

Now I was wont to point out to that waitress (though I didn't) that her busybodyness was detrimental to her employer's best interest. For, if she discouraged my wine-pouring, I might not be able to afford to go there any more. Thus, the owners would lose the revenue on one glass of wine each night. She should have been fired, in my non-prejudiced view (but she wasn't).

I never did find out what she <u>thought</u> I was doing.

I guess I continued going to Carroll's while swallowing the extra cost – until one evening, around 1987, when I came and found it closed. (I later learned that it had been sold to a developer for well over a million dollars.) I was at a loss as to where to go, when I remembered that Mr. Carroll also owned a place down toward Boston called Memory Lane. So I drove there. The place was huge, but I didn't see any customers inside. However, there was a group of waitresses, some of whom I recognized from Carroll's, standing over by the bar. When I entered, they broke into a cheer, crying, "It's Mr. Burgundy!" Apparently my pouring fiasco hadn't gotten around; or, if it had, it had long been forgiven and forgotten. Now, I was an object of nostalgia.

I sought a new venue for my adventures. Eventually I found the Rosebud Café in Davis Square, Somerville. This was a low-class bar, but it had its charms. From the outside it looked like a sleek, black diner. Inside there was a row of wooden booths along the windows, and a bar along the opposite wall. It was ill-lit, dirty and raucous, and it appealed to me immensely. For all its semi-sleezy aspects it was a safe place (I was never aware of any reputed drug deals there) and even welcoming (the barmaid would occasionally give me a free glass of wine "because you don't cause any trouble"). It was not like the bar down the street where, the one night I was there, a woman slashed her lover's face with a broken bottle.

The problem was, as time went on, the Rosebud became less and less reliable. First of all, they began running out of wine: first burgundy, then rose, until one evening, bizarrely, they had no wine at all! Then, too, I'd find them closed on various nights (those drug deals). I sought a fallback option and found Christopher's in Cambridge. There I would order a half-carafe of burgundy and hang the expense! (Needless to say, the Rosebud did not serve their [non-existent] wine in carafes.) Christopher's was the first bar/restaurant I'd written in that had a smoking section (a small one around the other side away from the fire).

During that period it was not unusual for me to frequent these two places on alternate evenings. One was imbued with the esprit of things Cantabrigian, while the other was soaked in the sweat of Somerville. And I cherished the contrast, the counterpoint between the two. The following things overheard should give a taste of their respective (if not necessarily respectable) patrons:

CHRISTOPHER'S: "Is there some way to impose the system of Wagnerian Leitmotifs on Joycean stream-of-consciousness techniques?"

ROSEBUD (over a blaring jukebox): "F – U – H – H – H – H - C K !!"

I think it is obvious as to which establishment I preferred to frequent. Unlike Christopher's, the Rosebud lacked all pretense, and I found that refreshing. There was an edge to the Rosebud that I found exciting. The bar was a long tube where anyone entering had to encounter everyone else there, even if only with a look or a glance.

I grafted the romantic image of the maverick with a cigarette onto this. For one (and only one) time in my life, I played the game of engaging a complete stranger with a look and then staring him down. At least that is the way the "encounter" happened in my own mind: what is more probable is that my "adversary" was not even aware that an "encounter" was taking place. A complete account of this "encounter" is given below:

I sit in a booth facing the door.

I take a long drag on my cigarette.

The door opens and a man stops at the threshold.

Our eyes lock.

Slowly and coolly I exhale the smoke.

The stranger's eyes fall.

Defeated, he slinks by me into the bar.

(The reader is invited to spin variations on this "theme" (I myself produced twenty at one point). For example, the stranger could wink at me, causing me to choke on my smoke. I even imagined a meta-confrontation, wherein the stranger dictates the narrative to me and I dutifully write it down.)

Well, it was bound to end eventually, this going out to smoke and drink and write. For one thing, I had long since exhausted the list of topics to write on: toward the end, I was mainly writing in my Journal. There was also the question of money: during my Christopher's phase, I estimated the cost of wine plus tip and cigarettes to be around $2000 per year – a not-insignificant amount.

But the main reason for halting may have been my health. One time I began coughing in the car on a family outing. My wife said to me bluntly, "Do you want to live to see your kids grow up?" I got the message: sissy smoker or not, I quit for good. That was in 1991.

And of course now there is no bar or restaurant that allows smoking. I had gotten in on the tail end of it.

As for those places I frequented, only Christopher's still exists (sans smoking) as it was when I went there to write. HoJo's has lost its red Naugahyde charm and is now a Ground Round. Carroll's was razed and a medical building now stands on the spot. But the most depressing transformation has been the Rosebud: on the outside it is the same. But, like Bill's Beer Hall in Bilbao, it has become a clean, well-lighted place serving fairly decent food to the bourgeoisie (I wouldn't have dared to eat food at the old Rosebud, had they served any). In short, it has become respectable. Yes, terrible and depressing!

Firing Lines

Muskingum

Introduction

I was fired from my first job - that as Assistant Professor of Mathematics at Muskingum College in New Concord (I called it "New Corncob") Ohio - back in 1968.

New Concord was a small village of about 1000 souls which had achieved a brief sort of fame just before I arrived there in 1967: it was the hometown of astronaut John Glenn. (I was told that, when they wanted to profile the village on the news, they had to rebuild a bridge just to get the sound trucks in.) New Concord was so small that Coleman Knight, the Chairman of my Department at the College, was also the Mayor of the Town (a useful connection for fixing parking tickets - except that there were no parking meters). Main Street consisted of a drug store, a small grocery store, a truck stop diner - and little else. I myself lived scarcely a block from campus.

In such a small, insular place, it was inevitable that everyone should know everyone else's business. There was no such thing as an anonymous or private life there. New Concord may not have been Peyton Place, but the arch-magnification of every real or imagined personal *peccadillo* made it seem so.

Add to this the fact that Muskingum was a small Presbyterian college, which was still somewhat in the throes of religious stricture (there was, e.g., a rule that one could not walk across the campus while smoking. True - this could not match certain rules at Bob Jones University, such as the one which purportedly said that a boy was not allowed to walk with a girl and carry a blanket at the same time) and you can see how such an environment could seem - *limiting* (*stultifying?*) - to a young bachelor of 24.

And so I proceeded to commit the arch *faux pas* of that *milieu*:

I contracted a "relationship" with a student. Now before you condemn me to utter perdition, ladies and gentlemen of the jury, allow me to defend myself as follows: a) this "girl" was in reality a 22-year-old woman; b) <u>she</u> was not taking a math course from me or anyone else (she was an organ major - no wisecracks!); c) <u>she</u> was the experienced one; d) I had not yet met the woman who would become my wife; and e) the only single female on the faculty who was anywhere near my age was, in my mother's quaint expression, "as homely as a mud fence."

So I ate the apple, tasted the forbidden fruit, plucked the plump pomegranate. And then, just to be sure The Authorities knew about it, I committed a <u>public indiscretion</u>.

Marsha (for such was the student's name) and I had met up one cold, late-December evening on campus. As we were both pianists, we were anxious to play four-hand duets. But the only pianos were in the chapel, which was locked. So we jimmied a window and climbed in and proceeded to our dueting - that is, until we were interrupted by a night watchman eager to learn what we were doing there. We told him the truth, hoping that he would be sympathetic with two musicians' need to play. But apparently he did not find our cravings compelling enough, for he turned our names in to the administration.

Now I know what the reader is probably thinking: "actions unbecoming a college professor," or some such. (Then again, perhaps the reader knows college professors well enough to realize sadly that such behavior is all too normal for them.) Such a moralist would fail to appreciate how desperately young keyboard artists yearn to find instruments to play. (As an organist still in my teens I used to walk into random churches in strange towns, uninvited, and play their pipe organs. Yes, the life of a "musical second-story man" came naturally to me from early on.)

I would also like to point out one ironic fact to the jury: that, while Marsha and I could have been at my apartment that evening (where there was no piano), we chose to play duets instead. So, while we admittedly did bend the law a bit, our behavior that night was essentially <u>moral</u>.

Anyway, after Christmas break I was summoned into the office of the Academic Dean, a stuffy (but probably well-meaning) fellow named Howard Evans. Thanks to me, poor Howard had on his hands what is sometimes referred to as "a situation of some delicacy" (which of course is usually a situation of the utmost <u>indelicacy</u>). Was I called on his oriental carpet for breaking-and-entering? Hardly - that was small potatoes at Muskingum. No - I was to be read the riot act because of my relationship with Marsha.

Now I must say that I resented a person like Howard Evans attempting to dictate my personal behavior. After all, he had this plush-cushy job wherein he could sit in judgment on other people. I also knew that he had a wife - a comely *zaftig* blond German Frau named **Charlotte**. He had *imported* his wife with him into this provincial backwater, yet I was expected to behave as a sort of monk just because of some arbitrary rule he chose to impose.

Anyway, I left the office - and resumed my relationship with Marsha right where we had left off. Why? Was I making a personal/political statement and thumbing my nose at Dean Evans's arbitrary rules? I'd like to think so, but that just wasn't the case. Quite simply and utterly more basic, the Spirit was ambivalent; while the Flesh was decidedly weak.

I didn't change my behavior, and so I was let go. The official reason given was that I didn't have a doctorate; but a colleague told me it was because of Marsha. I got a job at another college in a thriving metropolis where my teaching was appreciated and no one cared what I was doing in my personal life. So my firing from Muskingum was a blessing in disguise.

Below are two accounts of that fateful meeting with Dean Evans. The first is, to the best of my recollection, our "conversation" (really, essentially a monologue by Herr Evans, with a few dutiful responses by me), together with my inner thoughts on our remarks. The second is the conversation as I would have liked it to have been.

This dual presentation - of actual and fanciful events - is a lode which I may well choose to mine elsewhere. After all, I have had enough mini-disasters in my life to keep me busy for quite some time. And what is more fun than to recast events in our lives so as to come out exactly as we wish they had? Or do the demands of Art trump even our most fervent wishes about the past?

(12 April 2005)

Marsha

I was ushered into the opulent/decadent office of Dean Howard Evans, a smug, self-satisfied, vapid philistine (do my prejudices show?)

Dean Evans: "Hi, Ted - thanks for coming in."

(As if I had had any choice in the matter - as if I had come in out of the *goodness of my heart*! Yes, and how - *magnanimous* - of him to thank me!)

Me: "No problem."

(Actually, it presented a serious problem: I had to drag myself there - and that was decades before I had MS. Of course I had to affect a casual, devil-may-care air, as if there were nothing I'd rather be doing.)

DE: "So how was your Christmas break?"

(What a relief - here I thought he was calling me in because of Marsha. And how flattered I am that he is interested in my puny little vacation.)

Me: "It was fine. I drove East to visit my parents in New Jersey for a few days."

(Yes - a very few days. After which, despite the immense attractions of the Garden State, I rushed back to be with Marsha most of the time.)

Me: "How about you?"

(Of course there was nothing I cared less about than the vacation doings of stuffed-shirt Howard Evans! But I felt I had to *simulate* interest in his life, on the assumption that it might create a sort of bond between us and thereby foster a *sympathy* for me on his part.)

DE: "It was very satisfying, a great time to recharge the batteries."

(Oh God, I hate it when these administrators use those sorts of facile metaphors, as if he were some sort of automaton. Actually - accurate metaphor, Howard!)

DE: "We went down to visit my wife's family and had ourselves quite a feast."

(Where was that - Lower Bavaria? And do the rest of her family exhibit the same - *sumptuous* - attributes as your voluptuous wife?)

Me: "I hope you didn't eat too much."

[As was all too evidenced by the fact that he was bursting out of his waistcoat. Clearly this was my attempt to put this little conversation on a humorous level - an ill-advised move if the Dean did not view his own bulk with the requisite - *lightness*.)

DE: "Well, once or twice a year won't hurt, I hope."

(The triumph of Hope over Experience?)

DE: "Speaking of Christmas break,"

(Nice *segue*, Dean Evans. There I was, thinking that we were just going to continue chatting about our vacations, when wham! you turn the conversation to the Unfortunate Subject I have so dreaded. And of course you have me over a barrel: as we have been so friendly up to this point, I cannot stop being friendly now, can I?)

DE: "I received a report from Buildings and Grounds..."

(I find that hard to believe: I've never seen a building yet that could issue a report; or grounds either, for that matter.)

DE: "...that I found a bit disturbing."

(Just a bit, Howard? Are you sure you weren't *livid with rage*, like all of the Morals Police?)

DE: Can you tell me exactly what was going on?

(Do you really want me to be exact? Okay - we played through Debussy's "Petite Suite", and then the Schubert "F-Minor Fantasie".

In other words, a nice mixture of the Germanic and non-Germanic - like your marriage! Marsha took the top position while I - no, forget that!)

Me: "Oh, nothing - we were just playing."

DE: "Playing?"

(Ugh - bad choice of words.)

Me: "Duets. Piano duets."

DE: "Well, be that as it may, you should be aware that your relationship with - what was her name again?"

(Is he telling me that he doesn't know the name of the student I was with? Of course he knows it! So the question is purely rhetorical, and he's being coy with me: he's making me say Marsha's name, so as to incriminate myself! I need to avoid falling into his trap, but how?)

Me (meekly): "Marsha."

DE: "Yes - Marsha. Well, as I said, you need to be aware of the fact that there is a rule in effect at this college which expressly forbids faculty to date students. Are you aware of that rule?"

(Why of course I am - I'd been apprised of it *ad nauseum* by several of my fellow faculty members who were concerned for my welfare.)

Me: "No."

DE: "Well, let us agree that you are now aware of it. And I'm sure you'll also agree that you wouldn't want to do anything to put your teaching position here in jeopardy, would you."

(So there it is - the veiled threat. This is the perfect time for me to retort: "How dare you attempt to legislate my personal life! This is My Life To Live, Sir, and your silly arbitrary rules have no place in it!")

Me: "No, I certainly wouldn't."

DE: "Good, so we understand one another. Thank you for

coming in, Ted. (Peers out the window, brightens): Well, it looks like the sun may be trying to peek through the clouds out there."

(Who cares about your stupid sun? I hope it stays behind the clouds for the next hundred years!)

Me: "Oh great!"

Charlotte

I was ushered into the office of Dean Howard Evans (DE).

DE: "Hi, Ted - thanks for coming in."

Me: "No problem."

DE: "So how was your Christmas break?"

Me: "It was fine. I drove East to visit my parents in New Jersey for a few days. How about you?"

DE: "It was very satisfying, a great time to recharge the batteries. We went down to visit my wife's family and had ourselves quite a feast."

Me: "I hope you didn't eat too much."

DE: "Well, once or twice a year won't hurt, I hope! Speaking of Christmas break, I received a report from Buildings and Grounds that I found a bit disturbing..."

Me: "Oh?"

DE: "Can you tell me exactly what was going on?"

Me: "Oh, nothing - we were just playing."

DE: "Playing?"

Me: "Yes. Playing."

DE: "Well, be that as it may, you should be aware that your relationship with - what was her name again?"

Me (barely audible): "Charlotte?"

DE (starts): "What?"

Me: (doesn't respond)

DE: "What did you just say?"

Me: "Oh nothing."

DE (clearly disturbed): "No - I heard a name."

Me: "I don't think you did".

DE: "No - I really think I did."

Me: "What sort of name?"

DE: "A particular sort."

Me: "What sort of name is a particular sort of name?"

DE: "The sort of name that I thought I heard."

Me: "Well - what particular sort of name did you think you heard me say?"

DE: "I'd prefer that you repeat it so that I can be certain of what I thought I heard."

Me: "If I don't recall saying a name to begin with, it'd be hard for me to repeat, wouldn't it?"

DE (getting agitated): "Why don't you try repeating what you thought you didn't say, and we'll see what happens."

Me (calmly): "Why don't you try repeating what you thought you heard me say, which I don't necessarily recall saying, and then we'll see where that leads."

DE (giving up): "Very well, if you choose to be difficult: I thought I heard you say the name (swallows hard, whispers) 'Charlotte'."

Me: "I'm sorry, I didn't hear. Can you say it a bit louder?"

DE (gasps, louder): "Charlotte".

Me: "Is that what you thought you heard me say?"

DE: "Yes, I think I did."

Me: "You admit that you could be wrong."

DE: "I'm pretty certain I'm right."

Me: "What makes you so certain?"

DE: "Because that is a name that I am particularly attuned to."

Me: "Perhaps you are a little bit <u>too</u> attuned to it."

DE: "Let's just say I know it when I hear it. And I will swear I heard you say it just now!"

Me: "Well, and what if you did? I'm sure that there are plenty of Charlottes to go around."

DE (hoarsely): "There are no students at this school named Charlotte."

Me: "Oh no?"

DE: "No, or faculty either. Or faculty wives - or <u>any</u> wives for that matter. (Drearily): Any <u>other</u> wives, I should say".

Me: "Your knowledge certainly seems to exceed mine!."

DE: "So what conclusion am I supposed to draw from all this?"

Me: "I don't know - what sorts of conclusions <u>can</u> be drawn?"

DE: "Well, there is the obvious one..."

Me: "And which one would that be?"

DE: "I don't think I have to spell it out for you."

Me: "Sometimes spelling things out can clear the air in a remarkable way."

DE: "Sometimes. But at other times, it can muddy the waters in a dangerous way."

Me: "So, for which result might you be persuaded to spell things out?"

DE: "Neither necessarily. Sometimes things can be spelled out in a more discrete way - *obliquely*, as it were."

Me: "Could you give me a sample of this sort of obliquity?"

DE: "Well, if a certain faculty member were to be asked by a certain administrator about a possible or impossible relationship said faculty member may or may not be having with said administrator's wife..."

Me: "Why, I thought that was the reason you called me in here."

DE: "Reason? No. I - I thought you were, well, with a student..."

Me (indignant): "A student! Excuse me, but what do you take me for? I happen to know that there is a rule here that expressly prohibits faculty from dating students. Do you think I am crazy, to jeopardize my job for such a frivolous reason?"

DE (confused, shakes head): "I really don't know."

Me: "Well then, allow me to spell it out for you: I would only date grown women - mature, blond, *zaftig*..."

DE (hands over ears): "Stop!"

Me: "As you wish."

DE (crushed): "I don't know what else to say."

Me: "I'm not sure there's any more that needs to be said. May I go?"

DE (head in hands): "I really wish you would!"

Me (Arises, glances out the window, says brightly): "Well, it looks like the sun may be trying to peek through the clouds out there."

DE (bleakly): "Not in my house it won't!"

The Encyclopedia of Spurious Etymologies

Introduction:

For several years now, one of my many crackpot ideas was to create a book under the above name. Each of the many entries would be concocted as follows: first, I would choose something common and banal (and preferably with a name to match, such as the "Hoover Vacuum" below.) Second, I would provide the definition, genesis, and uses of that thing in all its crushingly truthful banality (definition 3a.) And finally, I would make up out of whole cloth a brand new etymology for it – one interesting, exotic – and funny. This last I would list right after the actual one (definition 3s.)

Unfortunately (or is it fortunately?), I have only been able to come up with five pairings. And so my idea for such an enterprise languished for lack of sufficient number of entries. (Any encyclopedia worth its salt needs more than five entries – doesn't it?) So I put up an invitation for people to submit their own entries on my weblog. That invitation is still open, though no one has taken the "bait" as yet.

Below are two of my own entries.

Venetian Blinds

5a. Venetian Blinds – A blind, made of thin horizontal slats or louvers, so connected as to overlap one another when closed, and to show a series of open spaces for the admission of light and air when open; they can also be pulled up so that the entire window is clear. In particular, a hanging blind of which the slats are held together by strips of webbing or other flexible material.

The blinds can be tilted by rotating a small knob that is attached to the strings, twisting a long wand, or by pulling a cord; the raising and lowering of the blinds is achieved by pulling a different string.

Venetian blinds were introduced around 1770, possibly in Venice, Italy. Slat width can be between 16-120 mm, however most common are 50 mm (2 in.)

[Sources: Wikipedia etc.]

5a'. Venetian Blinds - Any of a multitude of hunter blinds found in or near the Venetian lagoon.

[Note: I had come up with this under the assumption that it would fall in the 'Spurious' category. Imagine my surprise when I found out that there really is hunting in Venice!]

5s. Venetian Blind – a class of sightless beggars commonly encountered in and around St. Mark's Square in Venice.

These blind beggars are different from almost every other blind person in the civilized world in this respect: they proudly and disdainfully eschew any device – whether cane, guide dog or even another person - which might aid them in finding their way around.

Instead, they orient themselves by means of a unique and elegant acoustical radar: the antiphonal music wafting from St. Mark's Basilica. (I did not use the term "radar" lightly here. The term "antiphonal" refers to music, such as the brass music of the Gabrielis, wherein two or more groups of musicians are spaced significantly apart in the space and "answer" one another. Thus the beggars have at least two different sound sources to use in pinpointing their position at any given time.)

Unfortunately, this ingenious system is not foolproof: once in a while some poor hapless blind beggar strays and winds up falling into the canal. (Whether the radar had failed or the victim, forgetting the thoroughfares were waterways, had been attempting to jaywalk, is often hard to determine.) Usually they are fished out by some enterprising gondolier.

Of course there have always been some persons in Venice (beneath our contempt of course) who were discomforted by the very sight of those blind beggars. When such people lived on or near the Square, they sought to shield themselves from such unseemly beggarly vistas. Thus was commissioned a special kind of window shade - the sort with horizontal slats which could be turned upward (by means of a clever system of strings) just enough to block the view below whilst still affording the viewer both light and the sight of other building facades in the square.

Contrary to popular usage, however, those slated shades should not be referred to as "Venetian blinds". Rather, the proper and correct term is "Venetian blind blinds".

Hoover Vacuum Cleaner

3a. Hoover Vacuum Cleaner – A particular make of vacuum cleaner (a device that uses an air pump to create a partial vacuum to suck up dust and dirt, usually from carpeted floors. The dirt is collected by a filtering system for later disposal.)

The first manually-powered cleaner using vacuum principles was the "Whirlwind", invented in Chicago in 1868 by Ives W. McGaffey. The machine was lightweight and compact, but was difficult to operate because of the need to turn a hand crank at the same time as pushing it across the floor.

The first powered cleaner employing a vacuum was patented and produced by Hubert Cecil Booth in 1901. He noticed a device used in trains that blew dust off the chairs, and thought it would be much more useful to have one that sucked dust. He tested the idea by laying a handkerchief on the seat of a dinner chair, putting his mouth to the handkerchief, and then trying to suck up as much dust as he could onto the handkerchief. Upon seeing the dust and dirt collected on the underside of the handkerchief he realized the idea could work. Booth created a large device, known as Puffing Billy, driven first by an oil engine, and later by an electric motor. It was drawn by horses and parked outside the building to be cleaned. Booth never achieved great success with his invention.

In 1904, James Murray Spangler, a janitor in Canton, Ohio

invented an electric vacuum cleaner from a fan, a box, and a pillowcase. In addition to suction, Spangler's design incorporated a rotating brush to loosen debris. Spangler patented his rotating-brush design in 1908, and eventually sold the idea to his cousin's husband's "Hoover Harness and Leather Goods Factory." In the United States, Hoover remains one of the leading manufacturers of household goods, including cleaners; and Hoover became very wealthy from the invention.

Hoover is also notable for an extremely unusual vacuum cleaner, the Hoover Constellation, which was a canister type but lacked wheels. Instead, the vacuum cleaner was supposed to float on its exhaust, operating as a hovercraft. Introduced in 1952, it tended to be loud, had relatively poor cleaning power, and could not float over carpets.

In Britain Hoover has become so associated with vacuum cleaners as to become a genericized trademark. The word "hoover" (without initial capitalization) is often used as a generic term for "vacuum cleaner". Hoover is also used as a verb, as in "I've just hoovered the carpet".

[Source: Wikipedia]

3s. Hoover Vacuum Cleaner – A fanciful term applied to Franklin Delano Roosevelt – possibly by himself.

As is well known, the administration of Herbert Hoover (1929–33) was helpless to deal with the Great Depression following the stock market crash of 1929. This dearth of leadership resulted in a vacuum – the "Hoover Vacuum", as it came to be called. A good part of this had to do with the Republican Party itself: its corrupting alliances with Big Business against the Working Class.

On the campaign trail in 1932, Democratic candidate Roosevelt made reference to "those corrupt entanglements", and pledged to "clean them all up". Hence his self-description as "a Hoover Vacuum Cleaner."

The machine called the Hoover Vacuum Cleaner was developed in 1933, after Roosevelt's election, as a cynical attempt to cash in on the president's popularity. It became a best seller.

By the way, apparently FDR was responsible for being the first to utter a vulgarism now used by most teens. This also occurred during the 1932 campaign. Letting down his guard on his patrician bearing for a moment, Roosevelt was overheard to remark to an aide, "You know, that Hoover really sucks!"

3s'. Hoover Vacuum Cleaner – A fleeting reference to J. Edgar Hoover by President Eisenhower in his farewell address.

In that speech, as is famously known, Eisenhower warned about the encroaching corrosive influence by what he called "the military-industrial complex." One indication of the threat of such a "complex" (if indeed it was such a threat – perhaps Eisenhower had a military-industrial-complex complex…) was the obvious fact that he waited until his presidency was over to warn us about it (so: Eisenhower the war-hero as peace-chicken?)

But the General gave another warning in that infamous address. This concerned something so dangerous that not only did he issue it as he was saying goodbye, but he delivered it soto voce – that is, in an undertone which virtually no one could hear. And he tacked it onto the other provocative admonition, thus further blunting its message: "We must guard against the acquisition of unwarranted influence, whether sought or unsought, by the military-industrial complex, (as well as by the hideous Hoover vacuum cleaner.")

Well! Only an elect few heard this, but they knew exactly what Ike was talking about. Over the decades, the FBI Director had amassed more and more power for himself. This included illegal surveillance of the private lives of people he felt were a threat, whose politics he didn't agree with, or whom he just didn't like. Like a giant vacuum cleaner, he sucked up all the "dirt" around him, to be used to blackmail or imprison or even have murdered his hapless victims. This is what Eisenhower meant by his metaphor. (At the same time, the president was relatively safe because there really was a Hoover Vacuum Cleaner, and the more naïve might think he was attacking the monopolistic tendencies of that machine's maker.)

But Eisenhower went further than that. Brilliantly, he was also making a literal allusion to Hoover's own hypocritical private life – a life which included cross-dressing.

For example, Hoover would dress up in the uniform of a typical house maid, including a frilly-lacy apron (sometimes he would only wear the apron – wrap your mind around that!), and then he would do the house cleaning. Part of this had to do with prancing about with a vacuum cleaner. And as I said, all this was known to only a few select cognoscenti.

But it was known to Eisenhower. And no doubt he felt that something had to be done about Hoover's evil and hypocrisy, once and for all.

So do you see what Ike was doing? He was outing Hoover to the nation.

As I said, almost no one picked up on this. But the FBI Director did, and reportedly he was livid with rage.

A few short years later, Eisenhower died of a strange, wasting disease no one could explain.

Fiction

The Strange Disappearance of Al Fine

The case of the disappearing cocktail pianist, known professionally as Al Fine, from the Old Refrain Lounge, caused a brief stir at the time because it completely baffled investigators unable to turn up a single clue as to motive or act, nevertheless locate the man, dead or alive. At first, of course, it was assumed that, like most performers in clubs and bars, Fine had connections with The Mob, and that they, for whatever reason, had "done him in". Careful investigation proved otherwise: Al Fine had gotten the job, incredible as it may seem, purely on the basis of merit, of talent. One night he filled in for a regular who decided not to return, and his ability to play virtually every song that has ever been written, from cabaret to obscure movie title songs of the 40's, made it convenient for the manager to retain him. At the time of his disappearance, he was in his seventh year at the Lounge. Fine's private life, his habits, provided no clues whatever, being if anything singularly dull and uneventful. A bachelor, he lived in a single room in one of those seedy hotels whose obscure winding corridors, lined with dull gilded mirrors and musty faded rugs, tiredly whispered of opulent days long gone. He had no family or friends (at least no evidence of such was ever turned up); he spent his days for the most part in the cinema, taking advantage of the so-called Continuous Showing to no doubt garner more tunes for his already vast repertoire. For the rest, his life was a model of routine, of repetition; he played at the Lounge every night of the week.

The circumstances of Al Fine's disappearance, well known to newspaper readers at the time, can be briefly recounted. He vanished sometime during the course of an evening of playing. Certain witnesses, whose perceptions of the exact circumstances were certainly clouded by alcohol, dim lights, and the usual low-key excitement which continuously pervades night clubs, went so far as to suggest that, as it seemed to them, he had vanished during the course of a piece he was playing. None of these had actually seen him disappear or leave; one moment he was there, playing, while the next moment some people realized that he was no longer there, "even while (to quote a paradoxical statement by one) it seemed as though the music continued". Naturally, the authorities discounted such "observations" as "useless". The only other thing concerning that moment-which-no-one-saw worth noting here is the fact, significant because exceptional, that Fine, contrary to his usual custom of drawing from his prodigious memory, used sheet music for the rendition of the particular piece he was playing. Some witnesses recall someone requesting a piece which no one else in the Lounge had ever heard of -- an ignorance which Fine, with genuine incredulity, admitted he shared; that Person (who was never identified or located) then produced -- conveniently -- the sheet music and placed it on the piano stand. Al Fine read the piece expertly (so say the connoisseurs who heard it). Otherwise, testimonies are consistent in their descriptions of the piece (or song) as "longish". Some called it "intoxicating" in its obligato-like repetition. At any rate, the song continued past the point where everyone lost interest -- enough so, that no one could tell at what moment the pianist disappeared: they only realized he had when only an empty piano stool mutely greeted their next request.

The name of that song (as anyone familiar with this case recalls) was, "I Keep Coming Back to You". I have searched the catalogues of all publishers (even the most obscure fly-by-night ones) dating from five years before Al Fine's disappearance up to the present. I was unable to locate a song of that title. The actual sheet of music from which Al Fine played that evening has since been lost -- it was not at the time seized as evidence because investigators did not consider it as "having relevant bearing on the case at hand". Yet, in thinking about this strange case (and, indeed, I have been nearly obsessed by it) I would like to propose that, not only does that song -- or that sheet of music -- have "relevance" to Al Fine's disappearance, but, far more, it must provide (if we could see and peruse it, which obviously we can't) the key and the solution to the whole mystery.

Here is my conjecture: Al Fine was presented on that fateful night with a so-called "typical" piece of popular music. Such pieces have several verses, and a chorus, together with the usual da capos, al signes, codas, and so forth, which make it possible for any hack to write a longish song with a minimum of different notes. Yet this particular piece of music, whether by insidious design or the accident of a printing error, did not allow the hapless musician to ever reach the coda; or, if it did, another direction awaited him by the end to proceed back to an earlier portion of the piece. Forced, contrary to his usual habit, to read the music -- a slave, as it were, of the score -- Al Fine found himself led into a simple-but-effective circular labyrinth from which he could not extricate himself. He played, turned the page, played on, turned back, played again -- on, on, and on -- until the piece swallowed him up.

Embezzlement

It was my first summer job, and I was damn lucky to get it - with a little pull. This friend who got me in -- he worked there too -- his father was the real estate agent who sold Wetson's the land on Route 46. You may have heard of it -- "Wetson's 15¢ Hamburgers" -- it's gone now. They worked our tails off for a buck fifteen an hour, but we weren't about to complain - we were the highest paid, except for the manager. He was a slave driver, but he gave us two guys longer hours so that we could make extra dough. There was an old Greek guy there who shoveled French fries into bags fifteen hours a day, seven days a week, for 75 cents an hour. He didn't complain either, since he was in the Country illegally; and he got a break every couple of hours for a Pall Mall in the back room. I learned how to count up to forty-nine and say "Thank you, Call Again" in Greek -- a sort of free classical education.

I learned a lot that summer besides that -- how to cook thirty hamburgers at a time, clean out sink traps (and practically get sick doing it), make French fries from raw potatoes, and a lot of other things. That fresh French fry process was Wetson's specialty - now all the hamburger places use frozen preprocessed ones.

Wetson's was very tight on money and food. True -- they let

you have free food for lunch; but leave a spare piece of meat laying around and they were on your back. They made you work all the time too -- every moment; if there weren't any customers, you had to shine the creamer or mop the floor. Of course they watched you like a hawk when you were working the register; whenever we rang up anything, we had to yell out the price loud enough for the manager to hear it in the back. They had little tricks to get people to order more than they might want. When someone asked for a Coke, we were to say, "Large size, sir?". That was one of the rules posted on the wall -- no kidding. Cokes were their largest profit item.

My friend there was always looking for ways to cheat Wetson's a little bit. He claimed the pay was lousy and that we should "supplement our income" however we could. I don't know that he ever stole anything, though -- the security was too tight. The manager checked the cash register slips against the money received very carefully every night -- any discrepancy, you had to make up the difference. One guy told us about a drug store he had worked in the summer before. He had made a lot of money on the side by what he called "under-ringing" -- ringing up less than the cost of the article and pocketing the difference. The drug store finally went broke, and had to have a fire to get the insurance. This guy thought that was very funny. Me -- I was happy enough to have that job without pulling any of that stuff. Handling money makes me nervous anyway.

It was the business with the cash register that almost got me in hot water. It was a close call -- I knew important things were on the line and I had to play it cool. What happened was this. A guy came to the window and ordered a burger and a chocolate shake. I gave him the order and called out "Thirty-five cents, sir" just like I was supposed to. I changed the Five I thought he had given me and he started walking back to his car. Suddenly I realized that he had not given me a Five at all but a One. I sort of yelled to him out the window, but he kept walking as if he hadn't heard me (I guess I didn't yell very loud -- I hate to attract attention). For a while I was mad as hell at that crook, but when I started to cool down I realized what I was up against. My register was now short by four dollars! I almost panicked and ran back to tell the manager; I knew he'd make me make good on it. But that didn't worry me so much, as the fact that he would know I was stupid twice over. Yeah -- a dumb jerk who not only gave some wise guy three-plus hours wages but let him walk away with it in the bargain. I couldn't take that, I knew right away. But I knew that, if I didn't do something about it, he'd find out that evening and then I'd be up a creek for not reporting it. I began to consider seriously the possibility of under-ringing for the rest of the day -- I had maybe two hours left to work. But -- no - what the manager didn't see, some customer would -- and then I'd be really up the creek without a paddle -- in jail, probably.

It finally hit me what I had to do. It wasn't easy, I knew, with someone around me all the time, and Big Brother back there knowing when I burped. But I had no other choice. <u>I had to get four dollars into that cash register, by hook or by crook</u>. As soon as there was a lull, I checked the ol' wallet -- thank goodness I had four ones! Now all I had to do was get them in the cash tray. Simple? Not quite. How do you suppose it looks, for a guy to be seen hovering over an open cash register with his wallet in his hand? Right -- I risked being accused of the very opposite of what I was trying to do. I finally decided to use my head and do the thing in two operations: first, I surreptitiously removed the four bills from my wallet when no one was looking, and hid them, crumpled up, in my hand; then, when I waited on the very next customer and rang up his order, I expertly slipped the four dollar bills into the drawer with no one the wiser. Phew, but that was a close call!

No one ever found out about it and you can bet I'll be the last to tell them! Since then I've gone on to bigger and better things -- separating perforated computer sheets in a payroll office at two sixty-five an hour. The job beats Wetson's: I only dread it whenever I have to work with the printed checks. That makes me very nervous. I just hope I don't screw up somewhere - I'd hate to have people think I'm stupid or something.

To Build a Fire

Life intersects with Art

When T. awoke, he realized that he'd been having a recurring obsessive dream. In this dream he had been walking, even running, frantically about looking for the classroom he was scheduled to teach in. First he couldn't find the building. Then he couldn't find the entrance, or the correct floor or room. And then, once all those things were located, he would find no students waiting for him - or hundreds in an all-but-impossible teaching situation.

The interesting thing about those sorts of dreams was T.'s consciousness in the dream that, with all this walking and running about, he was doing something that for him was amazing and unusual.

Lying there in bed, he noticed (through barely opened eyelids) that there was light coming through the window. So it was morning, but at what hour exactly? To find that out he would have to look at his watch. But that arm (as well as the other useless one) was still under the sheet. And he decided that at this point it was too much trouble to look.

He cocked one eye toward the window. It looked to be another dreary day outside, without sun, and cold, dank, perhaps even rainy - though it was well along into April already. But he wouldn't be going outside today anyway.

It felt good, luxurious even, to lie there. He knew that he could continue lying there, luxuriating, all day if he chose to.

But he knew better than to heed that siren call - that it was something akin to giving in to death to continue lying there. (At the same time, he realized that he was being a bit melodramatic; but he knew that the gist of it was true.) Indeed, he knew that he could not lie there for even another hour before he would begin to seethe with impatience to be up.

The problem was that he was helpless to get himself up. Except for his head and left arm (and a bit of his right one), he could not move any part of his body. So he was utterly dependent on someone else for this.

Over the course of the last two years (nearly) that he has been here, he has trained the staff to get him up early. "It is necessary for my mental and physical well being!" he would exclaim. Most of the aides understood this; but there was that stubborn minority that didn't.

After awhile of mounting impatience, he decided to look at his watch. To do this he had to push the sheet back with his left arm, and then lift the arm up close to his face. It was painful to bend; and it felt like it had a ten-pound weight attached to it. Seven-forty: it was already getting into what he termed "the danger zone" since he liked to be up by eight. But, almost immediately, he heard someone come into the room and turn on the water; then he knew he was saved again.

The aide washed him all over and dressed him. Then she placed a nylon sling under him, attached it to a lift on the ceiling, and transferred him ("like cargo out of the hold of a ship", he thought) right into his wheelchair.

As soon as he was in the wheelchair, T. had the freedom to move himself anywhere in the Institution. This afforded him a tremendous psychological boost.

This morning, as first thing every morning, he went over into the corner to write on his computer. Writing had become of great importance to him; in fact, it had very nearly become his *raison d'etre*.

His typing skills were gradually ebbing away. When he had first come to the Institution, he had been typing with the index finger on each hand. But, over the course of that first year, his right hand began to curl up. First the middle finger started to bend, so that when he tried to type he'd hit double letters with his right hand. An occupational therapist tried various splints on the middle finger, but they only made matters worse. It finally reached the point where his right hand was so curled he couldn't use it at all; and even if he could, he couldn't any longer raise his arm to reach the keyboard. (He was fortunate in that his roommate, a computer specialist, had helped him engage the "sticky keys" so that he could make use of the shift with one hand.) So that now he was reduced to writing with the forefinger of his left hand (and the thumb for spacing.)

The loss of his right arm was typical for all his other losses, but it seemed to have come more terrifyingly quickly. He could feel the palpable essence of the disease [dis-ease: a loss of comfort?] gradually creeping up his arm and taking it over. Sometimes he could notice a change from one day to the next.

Now it was beginning to seize control of his left arm as well.

At this time of day he was at his strongest. Nonetheless, this morning he began typing double letters immediately. This was not a good sign - it meant that the middle finger of his left hand was bending. Not very much, but just enough to wreak havoc.

He shrugged inwardly and patiently went back to delete each extra letter or numeral. At this rate he would end up with pitifully little text today. And then the miracle happened: suddenly he was typing well with virtually no extra letters appearing. Somehow the offending finger had straightened out; or else his hand had adjusted to its being bent.

So now he typed quite a bit - even as he felt his hand growing numb and heavy. Finally, due to exhaustion, he began typing double letters, and at that point he knew it was time to quit.

The room was warm, as it usually was. And the corner where his computer resided was the warmest in the room, due to the presence of two baseboard vents.

He knew that he was affected adversely by heat. So that if he sat and worked at his computer for any length of time, he would grow far weaker than if he sat out in the cooler hall. Unfortunately, the temperature in the room was not really negotiable; for his roommate needed it to be warm (he wore a sweater everywhere - even in the summer) and he (the roommate) had been in the room first. So T. would sit out in the cooler hall at regular intervals in order to regain his strength.

(There was a notable exception to this heat-as-debilitator notion: his twice-weekly early morning showers. Those soakings with warm, even hot water made him stronger - at least for awhile. At those times, he found that he could practically type his daily "allotment" of 300 words in one sitting.)

And yet, there were other times - infrequent to be sure - when the air conditioning kicked on and thus lying out in the hall would give him a stiff, even painful neck. At those times the room became a refuge of warmth. (This made him acutely aware of how narrow the "acceptable" range of temperatures really were for him.)

An interesting thing had happened with him and cold. Back when he was healthy, he got cold very easily. So from October to April he would dress ultra-warmly: he'd wear several layers, including a wool "dicky" to prevent the chill from getting down inside his clothes, and a fleece vest which zipped up to his neck. (His many layers became the object of gentle ridicule from family and friends.)

But something changed fundamentally when he got sick. His whole body seemed to grow numb, desensitized. So, gone were the multiple layers. Now the only difference between summer and winter in his *habiliment* was a short sleeve or a long sleeve shirt.

At length, the aide brought in his breakfast. So he left the computer to eat at the table. The breakfast usually consisted of eggs, a muffin, cereal, and juice. But as it got harder to eat various of these (they would slip off his fork or spoon and wind up in his lap), he finally switched to yogurt alone. Not only was this a refreshing way to start the day, but it stayed on the spoon even when the utensil inadvertently turned sideways or even upside down in his palsied hand on occasion.

After breakfast he would rinse his mouth. To do this he had to grasp the plastic cup and hold it under the faucet. Anticipation of the process filled him with dread, for it had become physically trying.

The first task was taking hold of the cup. But due to the numbness of his hand, he could not tell for sure when he had grasped it. And then, once it was grasped, when he reached out he could scarcely get the cup under the water. Was his wheelchair as close to the sink as usual? Yes. So then was his arm shorter? In a sense; for, like the middle finger, his whole left arm was now bent a bit. Could he straighten it out all the way? Not really. And when he tried, it felt like his arm was being constrained by a powerful spring. ("My grasp exceeds my reach," he said to himself sadly.) Finally, it was hard to lift his arm and tip the cup into his mouth (the cup seemed very heavy); and, once lifted and tipped, could he hold onto the cup long enough to rinse?

The irony was that, once he had finished rinsing, his fingers had grown so curled that it was difficult to release his grasp on the cup.

He left his room to go down to the physical therapy room and exercise his arms on the bike. He had been doing this since he had come to the Institution. But it had not been very good for his morale; for, despite his most valiant efforts, his arms had kept getting weaker and weaker. (At this point, he suspected that using the bike may have even contributed to his weakness by putting stress on his system. So he made a resolution not to use it the following week to see what happened.)

Lunch was at noon. T. fed himself with great difficulty, as he could hardly raise the fork of food to his mouth. As a result, he only ate a fraction of what he was given. (Residents often complained about the food. One, however, told T. that he ate for enjoyment. T. replied that he himself ate to survive.) He would drink two cups of juice; but the cups were almost too heavy to hold up for any length of time. (Of course, as he drank, the cup of liquid grew lighter. But did it grow lighter fast enough to compensate for his increasing weakness? He couldn't tell.) The sandwiches came covered on the plate with a veil of plastic wrap. (T. had a morbid joke which stated that the latter was there so that, in case any residents were sufficiently repelled by the food, they always had the option to smother themselves.)

The most ludicrous time at lunch came when he sought to eat a Dixie cup of ice cream by himself. Of course it is virtually impossible to eat one of these with one hand (especially if it is frozen hard, as this was) - unless one does it as T. did. First, he managed to get his teeth on the little tab to pry off the top. Then, also with his teeth, he tore off chunks of the Styrofoam container - half of the sides as well as the bottom. At that point he was able to hold it by what remained of the container and eat the ice cream as some sort of strange cone.

The dubious entertainment value of such actions aside, T. realized that he was balanced on the knife edge of dependency. He decided to speak that day with the charge nurse about getting help to feed himself.

At 1:15 he went down to Reading with Paul. This was a man whose sister had been there in the Institution (she had died during the past year). He still came each week to read. By some coincidence, Paul taught in the same school at which T. had last taught. So each week Paul brought him anecdotes about his former colleagues.

Today Paul announced that he was going to read Jack London's "To Build A Fire". T. knew this story pretty well: he had read it in high school, of course; and then many years later when he was in his socialist "phase". But he hadn't read it recently - certainly not during the dozen or so years he had been sick.

Paul began to read:

> *"Day had broken cold and grey, exceedingly cold and grey, when the man turned aside from the main Yukon trail and climbed the high earth-bank, where a dim and little-traveled trail led eastward through the fat spruce timberland. It was nine o'clock. There was no sun nor hint of sun, though there was not a cloud in the sky. It was a clear day, and yet there seemed an intangible pall over the face of things, a subtle gloom that made the day dark, and that was due to the absence of sun." [...]*

> *"But all this--the mysterious, far-reaching hairline trail, the absence of sun from the sky, the tremendous cold, and the strangeness and weirdness of it all--made no impression on the man. It was not because he was long used to it. He was a new-comer in the land, a chechaquo, and this was his first winter. The trouble with him was that he was without imagination. He was quick and alert in the things of life, but only in the things, and not in the significances. Fifty degrees below zero meant eighty odd degrees of frost. Such fact impressed him as being cold and uncomfortable, and that was all. It did not lead him to meditate upon his frailty as a creature of temperature, and upon man's frailty in general, able only to live within certain*

narrow limits of heat and cold; and from there on it did not lead him to the conjectural field of immortality and man's place in the universe." [...]

"As he turned to go on, he spat speculatively. There was a sharp, explosive crackle that startled him. He spat again. And again, in the air, before it could fall to the snow, the spittle crackled. He knew that at fifty below spittle crackled on the snow, but this spittle had crackled in the air. Undoubtedly it was colder than fifty below--how much colder he did not know. But the temperature did not matter. He was bound for the old claim on the left fork of Henderson Creek, where the boys were already." [...]

"At the man's heels trotted a dog, a big native husky, the proper wolf-dog, grey-coated and without any visible or temperamental difference from its brother, the wild wolf. The animal was depressed by the tremendous cold. It knew that it was no time for traveling. Its instinct told it a truer tale than was told to the man by the man's judgment. In reality, it was not merely colder than fifty below zero; it was colder than sixty below, than seventy below. It was seventy-five below zero."

Here, for emphasis, Paul slowly stressed those last six words and punched at the air with the index finger of his free hand. (Interestingly, T. had remembered that number.)

"Since the freezing-point is thirty-two above zero, it meant that one hundred and seven degrees of frost obtained. The dog did not know anything about thermometers. Possibly in its brain there was no sharp consciousness of a condition of very cold such as was in the man's brain. But the brute had its instinct." [...]

"[The man] unbuttoned his jacket and shirt and drew forth his lunch. He smiled agreeably to himself as he thought of those biscuits, each cut open and sopped in bacon grease, and each enclosing a generous slice of fried bacon. [Paul: 'Not something recommended by the American Heart Association, I imagine!'] The action consumed no more than a quarter of a minute, yet in that brief moment the numbness laid hold of the exposed fingers. He did not put the mitten on, but, instead, struck the fingers a dozen sharp smashes against his leg. Then he sat down on a snow-covered log to eat. The sting that followed upon the striking of his fingers against his leg ceased so quickly that he was startled, he had had no chance to take a bite of biscuit. He struck the fingers repeatedly and returned them to the mitten, baring the other hand for the purpose of eating. He tried to take

*a mouthful, but the ice-muzzle prevented. He had forgotten to
build a fire and thaw out." [...]*

Paul would sometimes pause and emphasize something he had just
read by repeating a few select words. T. liked this way of reading.
Here Paul said, "So you see he wants to eat his lunch, but he realizes
he needs to warm himself up first."

*"There was no mistake about it, it was cold. He strode up and
down, stamping his feet and threshing his arms, until reassured
by the returning warmth. Then he got out matches and proceeded
to make a fire. From the undergrowth, where high water of the
previous spring had lodged a supply of seasoned twigs, he got
his firewood. Working carefully from a small beginning, he soon
had a roaring fire, over which he thawed the ice from his face
and in the protection of which he ate his biscuits." [...]*

Paul was good at summing things up in the story: "So everything
seems to be fine for this man. It's very cold, but he is able to warm
himself up with a fire and eat his lunch."

*"The creek he knew was frozen clear to the bottom--no creek
could contain water in that arctic winter--but he knew also that
there were springs that bubbled out from the hillsides and ran
along under the snow and on top the ice of the creek. He knew
that the coldest snaps never froze these springs, and he knew
likewise their danger. They were traps." [...]*

Paul also liked to presage the future: "And we'll see how he gets
into trouble with one of those springs."

*"There did not seem to be so many springs on the left fork of the
Henderson, and for half an hour the man saw no signs of any.
And then it happened. At a place where there were no signs,
where the soft, unbroken snow seemed to advertise solidity
beneath, the man broke through. It was not deep. He wetted
himself half-way to the knees before he floundered out to the
firm crust.*

*"He was angry, and cursed his luck aloud. He had hoped to get
into camp with the boys at six o'clock, and this would delay him
an hour, for he would have to build a fire and dry out his foot-
gear. This was imperative at that low temperature--he knew
that much; and he turned aside to the bank, which he climbed."
[...]*

"But it was surprising, the rapidity with which his cheeks and

> *nose were freezing. And he had not thought his fingers could go lifeless in so short a time. Lifeless they were, for he could scarcely make them move together to grip a twig, and they seemed remote from his body and from him. When he touched a twig, he had to look and see whether or not he had hold of it. The wires were pretty well down between him and his finger-ends." [...]*

Suddenly T. found himself struck by a resonance with those last few sentences - something he had never felt when he had read the story before. <u>Then</u>, those images attached literally to the tale and had no extra connotation. Now, however, they formed an exact description of something with which he was very familiar. It was uncanny.

Meanwhile, Paul read on (the man is trying to build another fire.) T. forced his attention to the new text, all of which seemed to confirm and intensify the initial resonance.

> *"He made a new foundation for a fire, this time in the open; where no treacherous tree could blot it out. Next, he gathered dry grasses and tiny twigs from the high-water flotsam. He could not bring his fingers together to pull them out, but he was able to gather them by the handful. In this way he got many rotten twigs and bits of green moss that were undesirable, but it was the best he could do. He worked methodically, even collecting an armful of the larger branches to be used later when the fire gathered strength." [...]*

> *"When all was ready, the man reached in his pocket for a second piece of birch-bark [which he needs to start the fire with.] He knew the bark was there, and, though he could not feel it with his fingers, he could hear its crisp rustling as he fumbled for it. Try as he would, he could not clutch hold of it. And all the time, in his consciousness, was the knowledge that each instant his feet were freezing."*

There was no doubt about it for T. - it was an amazing coincidence (the attempt to grasp the birch-bark was particularly telling.) He looked about to see whether any other resident had made the connection - none seemed to have.

> *"Next he brought out his bunch of sulphur matches. But the tremendous cold had already driven the life out of his fingers. In his effort to separate one match from the others, the whole bunch fell in the snow. He tried to pick it out of the snow, but failed. The dead fingers could neither touch nor clutch. He*

> *was very careful. He drove the thought of his freezing feet, and nose, and cheeks, out of his mind, devoting his whole soul to the matches. He watched, using the sense of vision in place of that of touch, and when he saw his fingers on each side the bunch, he closed them--that is, he willed to close them, for the wires were drawn, and the fingers did not obey. He pulled the mitten on the right hand, and beat it fiercely against his knee. Then, with both mittened hands, he scooped the bunch of matches, along with much snow, into his lap. Yet he was no better off."*

> *"After some manipulation he managed to get the bunch between the heels of his mittened hands. In this fashion he carried it to his mouth. The ice crackled and snapped when by a violent effort he opened his mouth. He drew the lower jaw in, curled the upper lip out of the way, and scraped the bunch with his upper teeth in order to separate a match. He succeeded in getting one, which he dropped on his lap. He was no better off. He could not pick it up. Then he devised a way. He picked it up in his teeth and scratched it on his leg. Twenty times he scratched before he succeeded in lighting it. As it flamed he held it with his teeth to the birch-bark. But the burning brimstone went up his nostrils and into his lungs, causing him to cough spasmodically. The match fell into the snow and went out." [...]*

Now T. remembered what would happen with the man: he did not have the manual dexterity to make another fire.

> *"A large piece of green moss fell squarely on the little fire. He tried to poke it out with his fingers, but his shivering frame made him poke too far, and he disrupted the nucleus of the little fire, the burning grasses and tiny twigs separating and scattering. He tried to poke them together again, but in spite of the tenseness of the effort, his shivering got away with him, and the twigs were hopelessly scattered. Each twig gushed a puff of smoke and went out. The fire-provider had failed." [...]*

The story continued on for awhile longer, until it reached its grim, inevitable conclusion. When Paul had finished reading the story, T. asked him whether he was aware of the connection which he (T.) had made. At first it seemed as though Paul thought T. was accusing him of something - perhaps an insensitivity. But T. hastened to assure him that he was not offended; that, as a matter of fact, he was grateful to Paul for the story he chose, which allowed him (T.) to see an old familiar tale in a new light.

After he left Paul, T. went directly to the charge nurse about getting help at meals. As he made his case for being fed, he felt that there might be an unnatural tone to his voice (he was not totally free of guilt) which she would be able to detect. But she assured him that he would receive the help he needed. (Just like that, he thought, I have given in...)

> "As he looked apathetically about him, [the man's] eyes chanced on the dog, sitting across the ruins of the fire from him, in the snow, making restless, hunching movements, slightly lifting one forefoot and then the other, shifting its weight back and forth on them with wistful eagerness. The sight of the dog put a wild idea into his head. He remembered the tale of the man, caught in a blizzard, who killed a steer and crawled inside the carcass, and so was saved. He would kill the dog and bury his hands in the warm body until the numbness went out of them. Then he could build another fire. He spoke to the dog, calling it to him; but in his voice was a strange note of fear that frightened the animal, who had never known the man to speak in such way before."

In the later afternoon, as was his wont every day, T. read some leftist political weblogs on his computer. But he could only do that for an hour or so, because his lower back began to hurt from sitting up so long. (At that point he would go out into the hall and recline his chair and rest his back.) Then there was supper (of Texas-style French toast and bacon) - and someone was there to aid him. (Funny, he thought, how quickly the feeling of guilt goes away when it is supplanted by a genuine feeling of relief at finally having help.) At six o'clock he went down for jokes with the boys (and girls). After that, he called his wife.

And so the rest of his day passed and on came the evening.

The aide came in around eight-forty to get T. ready for bed. When he had first come here to the Institution, such a time had seemed ridiculously early. But now, nearly two years later, he was apt to look forward to bed by this time with eager anticipation.

The process that had been used to get him up this morning was now reversed.

When he was ready, the sheet was pulled all the way up to his chin and over his shoulders, this to "protect" him from the blowing fan - which in turn relieved the feeling of stagnant warmth in the room. And, in this precariously balanced ecosystem, he was perfectly and utterly comfortable.

This feeling of desire for bed was the opposite of the one in the morning. Then he had been impatient to get up, fearing being left abed too long. But now he relished the chance to lie there, utterly immobile, for at least ten hours in guilt-free comfort.

> *"A certain fear of death, dull and oppressive, came to [the man.] This fear quickly became poignant as he realized that it was no longer a mere matter of freezing his fingers and toes, or of losing his hands and feet, but that it was a matter of life and death with the chances against him. This threw him into a panic, and he turned and ran up the creek-bed along the old, dim trail. The dog joined in behind and kept up with him. He ran blindly, without intention, in fear such as he had never known in his life. [...]*
>
> *"The warmth and security of the animal angered him, and he cursed it till it flattened down its ears appeasingly. This time the shivering came more quickly upon the man. He was losing in his battle with the frost. It was creeping into his body from all sides. The thought of it drove him on, but he ran no more than a hundred feet, when he staggered and pitched headlong. It was his last panic."*

As always at this time of night, there was a soft comforting light behind his roommate's curtain. T. would often use this time before he fell asleep to exercise his mind: he would plan out his next day's writing, or solve a mental math problem. Tonight, however, he began to focus on his possible future with this disorder.

Early in the course of the disease, T. had gotten a book about multiple sclerosis and looked up the Chronic Progressive type (his diagnosis.) The prognosis read in part: "*In ten years, the loss of all meaningful motor function.*" In the face of such dire predictions, he tried to maintain his sense of humor: (What did that word "meaningful" mean? Would he at least still keep the meaningless functions? That didn't follow logically, he decided.) True, it did not say the disease was fatal; nor did it say it would take his mind (such as it was). But did that matter with such a prognosis? When he asked his MS specialist about this, she said not a word; in fact, she gave only the barest hint of a reaction: the almost imperceptible shrug of a shoulder. At the time, he had taken this to mean that he should take the prognosis with a grain of salt. Or rather, this was how he had wanted, even needed to understand it. Now, after more than ten years, he understood why she didn't say anything: she didn't dare, because the sentence was so terrifyingly true.

He would lose the use of his left arm - and sooner rather than later. And that meant the loss of his independence in three crucial ways: his mobility, his ability to feed himself (already essentially gone), and his ability to type. True, there were solutions for the first and last here at the Institution: an addition to his wheelchair which would allow him to direct it with his head alone; and voice recognition software for writing. But then, assumedly (see "*all* meaningful motor function") won't he eventually ("*ten* years": was he not already functioning on borrowed time?) lose his head movements as well? And what about his speech (which was already more labored) - was that a motor function? He imagined it might be, at least in part...

(His fears began to tumble out, though he couldn't help adding humorous interjections. [Did humor, he wondered, retard or advance the disease? Did it depend on the humor?]: What about (gulp) swallowing? Or (gasp!) breathing?)

And then what? Then, speechless and helpless, he would be totally dependent on other people (as he was utterly dependent now for being put into and out of bed.) He would not be able to go anywhere without someone taking him. He would not be able to communicate with others in speech or in writing. He would not even be able to ask others to so much as scratch his nose, nevertheless be able to do it for himself. He would be totally subject to the whims of his caregivers.

A friend had recently confessed that the mere thought of being in such a state struck him with "terror". T. had a brother-in-law who all but stated that he would commit suicide in such a situation. (How? wondered T.) His own father would probably tell him to "face things like a man" - that is, stoically; bite the bullet and all that.

"When [the man] had recovered his breath and control, he

> *sat up and entertained in his mind the conception of meeting death with dignity. However, the conception did not come to him in such terms. His idea of it was that he had been making a fool of himself, running around like a chicken with its head cut off—such was the simile that occurred to him. Well, he was bound to freeze anyway, and he might as well take it decently. With this new-found peace of mind came the first glimmerings of drowsiness. A good idea, he thought, to sleep off to death. It was like taking an anesthetic. Freezing was not so bad as people thought. There were lots worse ways to die." [...]*

Of course, no one had told T, in voice or in print, what it was like to live in a state of helpless silence - for reasons that are obvious.

T, however, decided to deal with such a thing in the same way he had faced all his other losses such as walking, playing the piano, and so on - by immediately cutting those losses and cultivating the skills he had left. (Once when he told a psychologist that he was a "glass-is-half-full kinda guy", she had replied, "Maybe the glass is too large.") He would do it calmly, dispassionately.

In truth, he found the contemplation of this possible state of affairs to be rather intriguing.

Would he become a purely sensate being? Well, hopefully he would still have his mental faculties at that point. (If he didn't, then nothing much would matter, would it.) He would be able to understand things happening around him. He hoped that people would come and speak and read to him and play music for him, even if he couldn't answer back, nevertheless have a discussion.

Other than those one-way interactions, though, he would become an utter solipsist. (Poetic justice, he thought wryly, for one who was always an egoist anyway! [Ambrose Bierce: "One who cares more for himself than he does for me."]) And thus, in order to continue to have a life at once meaningful and enjoyable, he would have to cultivate, in some extreme form, a purely inner life of the mind.

If he retained his long-term memory (a significant "if", but still), he could retrieve wonderful things from his past: exquisite times with his wife and daughters; sublime pieces of music he had learned to play; music and prose he had composed; and so forth. Each of these he could turn over and over in his mind, until gradually he would recreate every nuance. Here he would be conjuring up things from the well of his past.

The only problem with that is precisely that it would all be of the past, hence mere recreations of things and events which already existed. So:

If he retained his short-term memory (another big "if"), he could gradually compose things literary and musical in his mind. To be sure, nothing very lengthy or arduous like an opera. But things he could recall from one day to the next and then elaborate upon: short literary vignettes, or musical bagatelles. Here he would be plucking things out of the future, albeit the future of his own mind.

He would be not merely recreative, but creative as well.

Then he suddenly realized what might constitute a sort of potential private hell for him in this sort of situation: the better his mental compositions, the more he would want to share them with someone else. But he wouldn't be able to do that.

Of course (he thought), such a problem would be effectively solved if he were simply to embrace Sartre's dictum - that Hell is Other People. (He called this "the Gordian knot solution.") He could even alienate everyone before he lost his speech, so that there would be no one left to remind him of the loss of his communication skills. Could he do all that?

He smiled. That wasn't very likely, he decided - he liked other people too much.

In fact, he had another "solution": that, in the same mind which imagined his creative flights of fancy, he would imagine as well the intelligent responses of those whom he knew well and loved. He could concoct meta-dialogues, themselves comic, creative fantasies, about his compositions, using the personality traits of friends and family as his "themes".

In short, he would become the literal embodiment of that old cliché-parody, "A legend in his own mind."

And with that amusingly lingering thought, T. fell asleep.

"*Then the man drowsed off into what seemed to him the most comfortable and satisfying sleep he had ever known. The dog sat facing him and waiting. The brief day drew to a close in a long, slow twilight. There were no signs of a fire to be made, and, besides, never in the dog's experience had it known a man to sit like that in the snow and make no fire. [...] Later, the dog whined loudly. And still later it crept close to the man and caught the scent of death. This made the animal bristle and back away. A little longer it delayed, howling under the stars that leaped and danced and shone brightly in the cold sky. Then it turned and trotted up the trail in the direction of the camp it knew, where were the other food-providers and fire-providers.*

(9 May 2007)

About the Author

Theo (Theodore, Ted, Teddikins) May grew up (if in fact he did grow up) in Verona, New Jersey. He was psychologically formed by the age of five. One day in his first grade classroom he began to spontaneously laugh out loud for no discernible reason. The teacher placed him in the cloakroom for a half hour as punishment. Ever since that seminal moment, he has worked diligently and tirelessly to make laughter socially acceptable. "But once in a while there have been occasions when I've been "cloakroomed" again!" he said with a laugh.

Mr. May taught mathematics for many years, and he called this "the ideal field to be in: no matter how many times I was fired, no matter how many interviews I botched, there was always a new interview, a new job available for me." He was also a professional organist in a career which spanned five decades: "For a shy guy like me who couldn't snag dates in high school, the organ works of J. S. Bach were the only other avenue to ecstasy open to me." But shortly after he began teaching, he married the singer and teacher, Dorothy, the girl of his dreams. "Then I had the best of both worlds!" he remarked with a gleam in his eye. They gave many concerts together while living in Medford, Massachusetts, and raising their two daughters, Gretchen and Heidi.

Mr. May's dual careers ended shortly after he was diagnosed with multiple sclerosis in the 1990s. He now lives in The Boston Home (a skilled facility to help people with MS and other diseases), a place he describes as "the Magic Mountain with a perpetually ongoing writers' colony." He writes using voice recognition software on his computer. As for this book, he has this to say: "My voice itself may be soft and weak, but the writing is strong and sure, thanks to one of the oldest of media wed to one of the newest."

As always, he wants to assure us that his personal motto remains, "the situation is hopeless, but not serious."